Microsoft®

Inside
Microsoft Windows®
Communication Foundation

Justin Smith

PUBLISHED BY
Microsoft Press
A Division of Microsoft Corporation
One Microsoft Way
Redmond, Washington 98052-6399

Library of Congress Control Number: 2007920381

Printed and bound in the United States of America.

1 2 3 4 5 6 7 8 9   QWE   2 1 0 9 8 7

Distributed in Canada by H.B. Fenn and Company Ltd.

A CIP catalogue record for this book is available from the British Library.

Microsoft Press books are available through booksellers and distributors worldwide. For further information about international editions, contact your local Microsoft Corporation office or contact Microsoft
Press International directly at fax (425) 936-7329. Visit our Web site at www.microsoft.com/mspress.
Send   comments   to   [For   Resource   Kits: rkinput@microsoft.com.;   For   Training   Kits:
tkinput@microsoft.com.; For all other titles: mspinput@microsoft.com.]

Acquisitions Editor: Ben Ryan
Project Editor: Kathleen Atkins
Editorial and Production Services: Waypoint Press
Technical Review: CM Group, Ltd.
Copy Editor: Jennifer Harris
Proofreader: Shawn Peck
Indexer: Seth Maislin

Body Part No. X13-23790

To my parents,
Mike and Nancy Smith

Contents at a Glance

Table of Contents

What do you think of this book? We want to hear from you!

Microsoft is interested in hearing your feedback so we can continually improve our books and learning resources for you. To participate in a brief online survey, please visit:

www.microsoft.com/learning/booksurvey/

Acknowledgments

Dozens of people helped me write this book. Their dedication of time and energy has helped ensure that this book is well organized and factually correct. They deserve credit for everything that is correct, and none of the blame for any of the mistakes. Blame rests with me.

Although many have helped with this book, Jeffrey Richter has gone above and beyond. His input has helped me become a better developer, presenter, and author. His reputation in the Microsoft Windows development community is well deserved. I will never be able to repay him for his investment in me.

My Review Crew diligently reviewed my chapters and were very open with feedback. This book is much better as a direct result of their input: Arun Chandrasekhar, Doug Holland, George Ivanov, Guy Burstein, Jalil Vaidya, Jason Davis, David Jensen, Krishnan R., Marcelo Lopez, Martin Kulov, Mitch Harpur, Paul Ballard, Rick Casey, and Rob Hindman.

My long-suffering editors also deserve special mention: Kathleen Atkins, Scott Seely, Jennifer Harris, and Ben Ryan. Your patience has been epic.

One of the benefits of working for Wintellect is the high caliber of the staff. Though they may not have helped with the book directly, many Wintellectuals have helped me both professionally and personally: Jeff Prosise, John Robbins, Paula Daniels, Cara Allison, Brendon Schwartz, Sara Faatz, Jim Bail, Sam Easterby, Lewis Frazer, and Todd Fine.

Introduction

Services are a major part of modern software architecture, and Microsoft Windows Communication Foundation (WCF) is the platform for building services for Microsoft Windows. Services written in WCF are able to interoperate with services from other vendors (for example, IBM, BEA, and Novell), and WCF is extensible enough to keep pace with the inevitable evolution of industry standards. Regarding transports, WCF supports TCP/IP, HTTP, Microsoft Message Queuing (MSMQ), and named pipes. WCF also supports a full array of WS-* (pronounced "WS-star") protocols like WS-Addressing, WS-ReliableMessaging (WS-RM), WS-AtomicTransaction (WS-AT), WS-Security, WS-SecureConversation, WS-Trust, and WS-Federation. Applications that use WCF can send and receive SOAP messages and Plain Old XML (POX) messages. In the future, Microsoft will undoubtedly broaden the capabilities of WCF to include new transports, protocols, and message structures. Microsoft views WCF as the I/O system for services. Although the future is never certain, it is safe to say that Microsoft is not going to replace WCF with another product in the foreseeable future. Consider as evidence the fact that many products like Microsoft BizTalk Server and Microsoft Windows Live Server are fully embracing WCF.

The goal of this book is to equip the reader with the information necessary to design, develop, and maintain services using WCF. In my opinion, these tasks require more than just having a working knowledge of the WCF programming model. Success with WCF requires an understanding of the principles behind services, the WCF programming model, and the WCF infrastructure.

This sort of coupling is not a new idea; it comes from past experience. When object orientation was gaining popularity, developers and architects making the transition from procedural programming to an object-oriented language needed to know more than just the new syntax of the language. If procedural programmers began using a more modern language without understanding how to design objects, they simply created procedural applications in the new language. Although these applications could be compiled and run, they did not take advantage of the functionality offered through object orientation. It is my view that the same will be true of developers who start to use WCF without a clear picture of how to leverage the power of service-oriented application designs.

Some think that this approach is a waste of time. In their opinion, the WCF team has successfully abstracted the messaging infrastructure away from the normal programming model, and as such, there is no need to address the underlying service-oriented paradigms or how the WCF infrastructure implements these paradigms. I completely disagree with this viewpoint. The level of abstraction attained by the WCF team allows applications to be developed more quickly. It does not, however, completely release the developer or architect from the responsibility of making the shift to service orientation or understanding how a WCF application works internally. In much the same way that successful adoption of an object-oriented language like C++ or Java required developers to shift their thinking from procedural programming to object orientation, successful adoption of WCF requires developers to evolve from a component-oriented mindset to a service-oriented mindset. If we fail to make this shift, we run the risk of missing out on many of the features offered through service orientation. Simply writing a WCF application and getting it to compile and run is only part of the battle. Understanding what's inside as well as understanding the new programming paradigm are equally (if not more) important in the long run.

Even if we do not care about the features offered by service-oriented architectures, we should understand the WCF infrastructure. In other words, we should know our platform. The common language runtime (CLR) offers supporting evidence for this stance. The CLR team did a great job abstracting the garbage collector and the JIT compiler away from the developer. As a result, it is technically possible for us to write Microsoft .NET Framework applications with little or no knowledge of how these subsystems work. Failing to understand these concepts, however, increases the risk that we will write inefficient applications. For example, a C++ developer moving to C# without any knowledge of the garbage collector will instinctively add a finalizer to all type declarations. Unknowingly, this developer will have increased the time required to allocate these objects and increased the lifetime of these objects. For most C++ developers, simply saying "don't do it" isn't enough. They want to know why. Technically, adding a finalizer to a type is not a bug, but it is certainly an inefficiency that could have been averted through a couple of hours spent with a book or in a good training course.

In a similar vein, understanding the WCF infrastructure can avert unnecessary inefficiencies in WCF applications and allows developers to tailor their application functionality to business requirements. For example, changing the reliable messaging parameter in the constructor of a binding has a dramatic impact on the messaging choreography between endpoints. The WCF team has rightfully abstracted the nuts and bolts of this choreography away from the developer and partially exposed it via compatible bindings. This messaging choreography is sometimes necessary, and it is only through an understanding of this choreography that a developer can make the decision whether to use this feature. Furthermore, anyone trying to debug an application that is using reliable messaging must have a grasp of the reliable messaging choreography.

It is my hope that this book strikes the right balance between critical service-oriented concepts, the WCF programming model, and the WCF infrastructure. This book gives you a serious look at WCF from the inside so that you will be able to design, build, debug, and maintain scalable and reliable distributed applications.

Who This Book Is For

This book is for architects, developers, and testers who want to learn how to design, write, or test distributed applications with WCF. The first few chapters of this book will also prove helpful to business decision makers who want to learn more about WCF or evaluate it for use in a project. This book is not for beginning developers or developers who are new to .NET Framework programming. If you find yourself in either category, I recommend reading Jeffrey Richter's *CLR via C#* (Microsoft Press, 2006) or Jeff Prosise's *Programming Microsoft .NET* (Microsoft Press, 2002) before reading this book. It is helpful, but not necessary, for the reader to also have some familiarity with distributed application development.

How This Book Is Organized

This book is organized in three parts. Part I, "Introduction to WCF," describes the principles behind service-oriented applications, introduces the major WCF subsystems, and describes how these subsystems interact with one another. Part I includes a chapter on service orientation, another on messaging concepts, and one on WCF architecture. At a high level, WCF is comprised of two principle layers: the Channel layer and the ServiceModel layer. The Part II, "WCF in the Channel Layer," and Part III, "WCF in the Service Model Layer," describe the channel layer and the service model layer, respectively. Part II begins with a chapter that describes the *Message* type and continues with chapters on channels and channel managers. Part III includes chapters that cover bindings, contracts, and dispatchers and clients. Each chapter in Parts II and III dissects the important types in their respective topics and offers code samples to illustrate the core concepts. On the whole, the flow of this book takes the reader from the conceptual, to WCF core internals, to the WCF main developer-facing application programming interface (API). In other words, this book offers an inside-out view of WCF.

Code Samples and System Requirements

All of the code samples discussed in this book can be downloaded from the book's companion content page at the following address:

> *http://www.microsoft.com/mspress/companion/9780735623064*

Microsoft Press provides support for books and companion content at the following Web site:

> *http://www.microsoft.com/learning/support/books/*

The code samples shown in this book are written for the .NET Framework 3.0. The redistributable for the .NET Framework 3.0 and the requirements to install it are at the following Web site:

> *http://www.microsoft.com/downloads/details.aspx?displaylang=en&FamilyID=10CC340B-F857-4A14-83F5-25634C3BF043*

Questions and Comments

If you have comments, questions, or ideas regarding this book or the companion content or questions that are not answered by visiting the preceding sites, please send them to Microsoft Press via e-mail to

mspinput@microsoft.com

Or via postal mail to

Microsoft Press
Attn: Inside Microsoft Windows Communication Foundation Editor
One Microsoft Way
Redmond, WA 98052-6399

Please note that Microsoft software product support is not offered through the preceding addresses.

Part I
Introduction to WCF

In this part:

Chapter 1
The Moon Is Blue

Businesses and markets appear to have an insatiable appetite for new application functionality. I have yet to hear a product manager say after a product release, "This product does everything our customers want; there is nothing we need to plan for the next release. Let's all go home." Around a release date, you are more likely to hear, "No, this release doesn't do that—we might be able to add that feature in the release after the next one." In the universe of software applications, these functional requirements occasionally align themselves so that they appear, from a distance, as one universal requirement. Sometimes, one of these universal requirements gives birth to a new universal concept that holds the promise of meeting that universal requirement. On occasion, interest in this universal concept fuels the development of a new technology that allows developers to apply that concept to their applications, thereby fulfilling the universal requirement. And every *once in a blue moon*, the universal requirement, universal concept, and subsequent technology are so large and overarching that they force us to reconsider software designs. I'm not sure whether you noticed, but the moon was blue the day Microsoft released Windows Communication Foundation (WCF). It is time to rethink the way we design and build distributed applications.

The Universal Requirement

For the most part, businesses are no longer in search of the "magic" application suite that will solve all of their computing problems. Over time, many software vendors, like the big Enterprise Resource Planning (ERP) and middleware vendors, have sold these sorts of systems with varying degrees of success. Businesses, however, place so many demands on software that no single vendor can deliver a comprehensive product suite that addresses every one of these demands. Furthermore, as businesses grow, they often need to improve their infrastructure and processes to accommodate their growth. Software that worked well when a company had 100 employees doesn't work well when that company grows to 1,000 employees. The problem is even more complex when considering mergers and acquisitions. Migrating an acquired company to the software of the parent company is often a painful, tedious, and expensive undertaking.

As a result, most corporate computing infrastructures contain a mix of applications that meet department-level and enterprise-level needs. This mix is often called an *accidental architecture*. The chances are good that these applications were developed, either internally or by a vendor, to solve a specific set of business problems, and each of these applications often manages isolated sets of information. Occasionally, this accidental architecture is standardized to run on one hardware type, operating system, and platform, but this is hardly ever true. More often than not, the computing systems in an enterprise are composed of independent, stove-piped applications, running on different hardware, operating systems, and platforms, all working for the betterment of the business (we hope). If you look at this image just right, you might be reminded of an M. C. Escher drawing.

From a business perspective, applications are seldom totally independent, as their very existence is tied, in some form or fashion, to helping the business run more efficiently. As a result, someone is bound to demand, in the name of cost reduction, increased sales, or regulatory compliance: "I want to know in Application A something from Application B." The catchy phrase for this sort of a requirement is *connectedness*.

Connectedness typically comes in two flavors: application-to-application, and application-to-enterprise. Simply put, application-to-application connectedness is connecting two applications, such as accounts receivable and shipping. An example of application-to-enterprise connectedness is an airline that wants to publish, to any concerned application, every time an airplane takes off or lands. This information has far-reaching impacts in the enterprise, including maintenance, crew scheduling, and quality assurance. People, markets, and businesses are now demanding both forms of connectedness in their applications to the point that connectedness has truly become a universal requirement. Whether you work for a software vendor or an internal IT department, you have probably seen this demand to connect applications. If this is the first you have heard of it, just read some of the comments made by the heads of major software companies and take note of what they are saying about future product and service releases. Almost without exception, you will hear and see the terms *integrate*, *connect*, and *interoperate* at least once. These all imply connectedness. In short, connectedness is the new universal requirement.

The Universal Concept

Meeting the universal requirement is a somewhat daunting task, especially when the applications we want to connect run on different hardware, different operating systems, and different platforms. After all, each hardware type, operating system, and platform can have its own type system, memory management scheme, transports, and protocols. When viewed in the light of the accidental architecture of most organizations, we need a way to connect applications in a vendor-neutral manner. Over time, the industry has attempted several times to standardize type systems, memory management schemes, transports, and protocols across hardware, operating system, and platform boundaries. These include CORBA, DCE / RPC, RMI, COM+ and DCOM. For the most part, each of these efforts has failed to gain industry-wide acceptance in the long-term..

However, the industry has universally embraced the Internet and its accompanying standards. Without exception, modern hardware, operating systems, and platforms are able to communicate over the Internet. The acceptance of Internet standards results from the universal nature of HTTP, HTML, and XML. In essence, communicating over the Internet requires the ability to send or receive data that adheres to these standards and does not require a proprietary type system, memory management scheme, or internal protocols. To put it simply, Internet communication focuses on *the data that is transmitted* rather than focusing on a particular type system, operating system, or platform.

This underlying principle can be abstracted to provide a conceptual model for application-to-application and application-to-enterprise connectedness. The name for this concept is *service orientation*. The universal concept of service orientation holds the promise of addressing both forms of the universal requirement of connectedness. Applications built with a service-oriented paradigm are concerned with sending or receiving messages that adhere to a specific structure, much in the same way that a Web site sends and receives HTTP and HTML. Applications that receive these messages are typically called *services*.

> **Note**   The term *service* is extremely overloaded, and it might conjure up any number of different ideas for the reader. In this book, a service is functionality exposed via a structured messaging scheme. The structure of the messaging scheme can be virtually anything (SOAP, XML, JavaScript Object Notation, and so on), and the transport those messages are sent over can be practically anything (HTTP, TCP/IP, UDP, SMTP, CD/DVD, or even carrier pigeons).

For now, it is permissible to think of a service as being something conceptually similar to the Microsoft Virtual Earth Services.

From a business perspective, the universal concept of service orientation promises to simplify and streamline the work required to connect, version, and replace applications. Internal development work can be reduced through reuse of existing application functionality exposed as a service. Furthermore, the implementation of the service can be versioned (given some constraints) without any consuming application knowing about the change, or having to update itself. For example, if an application is required to plot delivery routes, would it be cheaper to develop a mapping solution internally or to use an existing service like Virtual Earth? Certainly the specific situation dictates the answer, but for most business applications, I assert that using a service like Virtual Earth would be a cheaper, more functional, and reliable alternative. Conceptually, it is easier, cheaper, and more reliable to reuse services that someone else has developed, tested, and exposed rather than redevelop and test the same set of functionality internally. In addition, as long as the messages and contracts remain compatible, the service can be versioned without coordinating the changes with applications that consume the service. These benefits, however, are paired with a new dependence on that service. A service consumer becomes beholden to the service provider for functionality. If the service provider goes out of business or their service is interrupted, that functionality will no longer be available to the service consumer. Furthermore, some service providers limit the ways in which their service can be consumed.

To be fair, this story is similar to the one told when components first arrived on the scene. Components offer a tremendous leap forward when compared to their predecessors, but component architectures have limitations, especially when viewed in the light of the universal requirement of connectedness. For example, component architectures need a common platform and operating system, and distributed applications built with component architectures usually have to version simultaneously. The tight coupling found in distributed component architectures makes versioning components and their underlying platforms extremely difficult. While this model might work for application-to-application connectedness, it does not work at all for application-to-enterprise connectedness. As you'll see later in this book, service-oriented applications are able to version in a more flexible manner and are good candidates for meeting both forms of the universal requirement of connectedness.

From the perspective of the developer, the concept of service orientation focuses on the message rather than the implementation, platform, or runtime of the service itself. Sending a message from one application to another might not seem like a big deal and, at first glance, might not seem to be the answer to the universal requirement of connectedness. After all, applications of all shapes and sizes have sent messages to other like-minded applications since the reign of the mainframe. The barrier to the widespread adoption of this concept has traditionally been a lack of agreement on a message structure. Software vendors have traditionally developed their own proprietary message structure for use within a vendor toolset, but these message structures were never universally adopted. As a result, interoperability was practically unattainable. But what if a messaging structure could be agreed upon to the extent that it is considered a universal structure? If a message structure is globally adopted, any application that adopts that message structure can communicate with any other application that also adopts it. The key to the universal requirement of connectedness is the development of a standard message structure and the widespread adoption of that structure.

How then can there ever be agreement on a message structure? Well, one possibility is for software vendors like Microsoft, IBM, BEA, Sun Microsystems, and others to work together to create an interoperable message structure. Given the complexity of the task at hand, they would probably have to conduct years of research, several meetings and, my personal favorite, meetings about meetings. After enough research, meetings (and of course, meetings about meetings), a standard message structure should emerge, or a fight should break out. Either way, it would be interesting to watch.

You might have heard the term WS-* (pronounced "W-S-star") recently. WS-* is a family of specifications that define, among other things, universal message structures and messaging choreographies. This family of specifications includes WS-Addressing, WS-Security, WS-Trust, WS-SecureConversation, WS-Federation, WS-ReliableMessaging, WS-AtomicTransaction, WS-Coordination, WS-MetadataExchange, WS-Policy, and WS-PolicyAttachment. Together, these specifications represent a vendor-agnostic way for applications to communicate reliably, securely, and in a transacted manner. These specifications use message structures based on XML and SOAP; they were written by representatives from most major software vendors and are the product of years of open consultations and meetings. These specifications are gaining widespread adoption because many of the major software vendors have participated in the creation of these specifications. Practically speaking, the major software vendors have agreed upon a de facto standard message format.

Before the ink dried on these SOAP-based specifications, other message structures appeared on the horizon. JavaScript Object Notation (JSON) is the most notable example. JSON is heavily used by Asynchronous JavaScript and XML (AJAX) Web applications as a means for a Web browser to send messages back to the Web server without forcing a page refresh. JSON completely diverges from XML-based message formats. It is based on JavaScript Eval function calls and does not fit the same mold as the WS-* specifications. In the purest sense, however, JSON interactions between the browser and the Web server are still service-oriented interactions. The important point here is that a service must have an agreed upon message format. Over time, the message formats used in applications will undoubtedly evolve to meet the requirements of the day.

The Business Example

All of this talk about industry initiatives and blue moons might leave you wanting a real-world example of exactly what a service-oriented application, and subsequently a WCF application, can do. For that, let's look at the application requirements facing Contoso, Ltd. (a fictitious company). In our example, Contoso is the world's leading boomerang manufacturer. Currently, orders for Contoso's boomerangs can be made by calling a sales representative in a field office or at a call center at corporate headquarters or by ordering online via the Contoso Web site. The field offices, call centers, and Web site all contain their own ordering logic. Changing the ordering logic requires upgrading each of these applications. Figure 1-1 illustrates the current application topology.

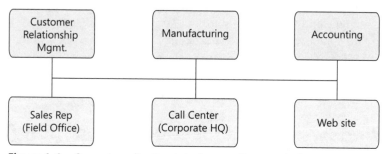

Figure 1-1   Current application topology at Contoso, Ltd.

For the sake of the example, assume that all applications wanting to place orders have their own implementation of the ordering business logic. If the business process for ordering products changes (maybe for regulatory compliance), all applications must be changed, and the versioning must be carefully orchestrated. This has proven to be an expensive and tedious process.

In the next six months, Contoso wants sales representatives in the field to be able to place orders using their handheld devices. Also, upper management has been pushing for years to allow external trading partners to place orders from their applications. With the current architecture, each new application would be required to implement its own version of the order processing business logic. While this might be possible with the handheld devices scenario, it is impossible in the trading partner scenario. As a result of the cost associated with versioning the current system and the new requirements, Contoso's small but competent development staff has been planning a new, consolidated order processing system.

A service-oriented alternative to the current architecture, like the one shown in Figure 1-2, holds the promise of solving both the versioning and the extension problems.

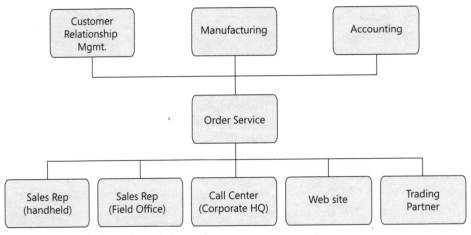

Figure 1-2   A service-oriented alternative

In fairness, this example is a bit contrived, but the principle is sound. Walk up to any medium or large IT infrastructure, and you will likely see the same business logic embedded in multiple applications. This simple fact of IT life dramatically increases the cost of changing that logic and is a barrier to adding new applications to the enterprise. In a nutshell, WCF is a technology that allows us to design, build, and manage applications like the one illustrated in Figure 1-2, ultimately allowing us to better respond to business needs.

Introducing Windows Communication Foundation (WCF)

Microsoft and others saw the universal requirement of connectedness and the universal concept of service orientation in the 1990s. At the time, there were no widely accepted messaging standards, and as a result, there was no platform, application programming interface (API), or runtime that allowed developers to easily write service-oriented applications. Technically, it was possible to author service-oriented applications, but the capability of the developer tools and application runtimes made that a daunting undertaking. Luckily, Microsoft and others began defining an infrastructure that would ultimately result in a universal message structure.

The end result of these efforts is the WS-* family of specifications. In parallel with these efforts, Microsoft also planned a technology roadmap that would ultimately give developers the tools and the runtime they needed to build and deploy service-oriented applications that leveraged WS-* specifications. The waypoints on this roadmap include the Microsoft .NET Framework, ASP.NET Web Services (ASMX), Web Services Enhancements (WSE), Windows Vista, and of course, WCF.

Not Just Another API

Over time, the developer community has seen many new APIs, each promising all sorts of new and wonderful functionality. Often, these new APIs were wrappers around other functionality. As a result, you might instinctively treat WCF as just another API. Resist this temptation. Jackie Gleason says it best in *Smokey and the Bandit* (one of my all-time favorite movies): "Boy, ... don't do it... You can think about it, but don't do it." WCF is not just a wrapper around existing functionality or just another whiz-bang API. WCF is the evidence that a tectonic shift has occurred in distributed software development. Microsoft made huge investments in this technology because it enables true service-oriented application development and, as a result, provides greater reach for applications built on the Microsoft platform. IBM, BEA, SAP, and others have made similar moves, each fueled by the drive to connect applications residing on different platforms.

WCF from 10,000 Feet

WCF is a set of types built on the Microsoft .NET Framework, and ultimately on the Microsoft Windows operating system, that act as a bridge between the service-oriented world and the object-oriented world. In general, working with objects is more productive and less error prone than working directly in the service-oriented world, even when those objects might ultimately send, receive, and process service-oriented messages. WCF gives us the ability to work in either world, but it is geared toward allowing us to program in the object-oriented world with which many developers are familiar.

Beneath It All: Windows

Distributed applications need to communicate most commonly across process boundaries. Distributed applications also need to be hosted, and as a result, they depend on services like Windows Activation Services (WAS), Internet Information Services (IIS), and Microsoft Windows NT services. Operating systems like Windows XP with Service Pack 2, Windows Server 2003, and of course Windows Vista are part of the roadmap that enables connected applications. These operating systems have built-in support for services, and as such, they are an important part of distributed computing.

At the lowest level, WCF applications send and receive messages through the operating system I/O mechanisms (sockets, named pipes, and so on). WCF developers, however, are shielded from many of the gory details by common layers of abstraction.

Helpful Products: The Windows Server System

Microsoft has many products that automate and simplify the tasks associated with distributed computing:

- BizTalk Server
- Commerce Server
- Application Center
- Internet Security and Acceleration Server
- SQL Server
- Exchange Server
- Host Integration Server

Over time, I expect that these products will communicate, in some form or fashion, via WCF.

In the future, expect to see support that allows WCF applications to interact directly with some of these servers. For example, there will be support for leveraging the Transaction Broker in SQL Server 2005 directly from WCF applications.

The Development Platform: The Microsoft .NET Framework

Since 2002, the Microsoft .NET Framework has been the platform of choice for Windows development. It is built on four pillars: automatic memory management, JIT compilation, metadata, and code access security. These pillars support a platform that enables rapid component development, a type-safe execution environment, language choices, simplified deployment scenarios, and component security. (I could go on.) WCF is built entirely on the .NET Framework and was written entirely in C#.

The .NET Framework abstracts operating system I/O mechanisms through types like *System.Net.Sockets.Socket* and *System.Messaging.MessageQueue* (to name a few). These types are used by the WCF infrastructure to send and receive messages. As you will see later in this book, it is also possible to interact with these types directly through WCF extensibility points.

The Distributed Platform: WCF

WCF is Microsoft's API for creating independently versionable, secure, reliable, and transacted service-oriented applications. It fully embraces the concepts of service orientation, and it can create messages that comply with many WS-* specifications, but it can also be used in the Representational State Transfer (REST) architecture and other distributed architectures that use Plain Old XML (POX) messages. In essence, WCF is the developer's bridge to the service-oriented world. Before WCF, it was possible to write service-oriented applications by using technologies like WSE and ASMX, but WCF provides more security, reliability, flexibility, and performance options than any previous service-oriented technology from Microsoft.

In other words, WCF answers the universal requirement of connectedness, and as such, *the moon is blue.*

Putting It All Together

Figure 1-3 illustrates how Windows, the .NET Framework, WCF, and WCF applications fit together conceptually.

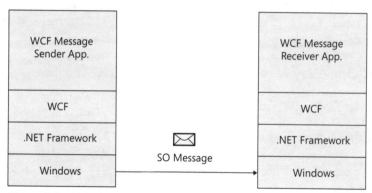

Figure 1-3   WCF in context

Conceptually and logically, WCF is a set of assemblies that allow developers to quickly write service-oriented applications. Applications that use WCF can communicate using message schemas and choreographies defined in the WS-* specifications, with REST architectures, or POX messages. WCF shields developers from many of the nuances of both the raw communication stacks and the WS-* specifications. Physically, WCF is a set of assemblies that expose a set of types. These WCF types comprise a developer-facing API and an inward-facing set of types. As you might imagine, the developer-facing API is intended to be used in applications written by non-WCF team members, and the internal-facing types interact with the .NET Framework and ultimately the operating system for the purpose of sending, receiving, or otherwise processing messages. WCF was built with its own extensible architecture, so developers can change the out-of-the-box WCF functionality to fit the requirements of a specific application.

WCF Features

Designing, building, maintaining, and versioning distributed applications is a complex undertaking. Factor in the typical requirements of security, reliability, transactional support, and scalability, and the task becomes even more complex. As a result of the complex problems WCF is designed to solve, WCF is a fairly complex technology. In an attempt to provide a clear view of WCF's features, I have split the major functionality into 10 categories: independent versioning, asynchronous forward-only messaging, platform consolidation, security, reliability, transactional support, interoperability, performance, extensibility, and configurability.

Independent Versioning

Versioning of applications has always been a difficult problem. As I mentioned earlier, component-oriented designs simply didn't address this problem well in distributed systems. Any technology that hopes to gain acceptance in the distributed applications space must allow independent versioning of the different parts of the distributed application. Adherence to the WS-* specifications, and the focus that WS-* puts on messages, allow WCF services to develop at a different rate from that of service consumers. While this feature is not so much a part of WCF as it is part of the underlying principles that are used to create the WCF applications, I see this as one of the most important byproducts of using WCF.

Asynchronous One-Way Messaging

Many of our applications are written using request-reply calls to functions. Typically, we call a function, wait for it to return, and act based on the return value. This paradigm is reinforced every time we use the Internet. Every time we make a request for a Web page, we have to wait for a reply from that Web page. As a result of our conditioning, the request-reply model is the default way most of us write distributed applications. Even though it might seem uncomfortable at first, asynchronous forward-only messaging is far more efficient for the I/O bound tasks required of a distributed application. WCF is built from the ground up to support asynchronous forward-only messaging. I see this feature as another major benefit to using WCF. Asynchronous forward-only messaging allows for the efficient use of available processing power and facilitates more advanced functionality, reliability, and responsiveness in our applications.

Platform Consolidation

Microsoft has shipped many distributed technologies over the years; some have been part of the roadmap that eventually leads to WCF, and many others are holdovers from previous initiatives. For example, before the WCF release, Microsoft supported five major technology stacks for distributed computing: RPC, WSE, ASMX, Remoting, COM+, and MSMQ. In the past, the best technology choice for a distributed application depended on the requirements for that application. For example, if all nodes in a distributed application were .NET Framework applications, one might choose to use .NET Remoting since it is an efficient means of communication between .NET Framework applications. If, however, an application required guaranteed message delivery and durability, MSMQ was the best choice. Both of these technologies have very different APIs, programming paradigms, operational demands, and configuration requirements. As a result, application code has been tightly bound to the technology, and the technology has been tightly bound to a particular set of functionality. A few technologies allowed us to combine features. The prototypical example is the transactional and queued capability of COM+. As long as requirements don't change or combine in a way that won't work for the technology, this model is workable.

What if your application requires efficient communication with other .NET Framework applications *and* non–.NET Framework applications *and* support for transactional processing? Before WCF, there were no good options. Essentially, this combination of requirements forced developers to either ignore one of the requirements or write their own distributed technology. In contrast with the old technologies, WCF combines features from different technologies and unifies them under one programming model, as shown in Table 1-1.

Table 1-1   WCF Feature Comparison

Feature	WSE	ASMX	Remoting	COM+	MSMQ	WCF
WS-* support	X			X		X
Basic Web service interoperability		X		X		X
.NET -to-.NET communication			X			X
Distributed transactions				X	X	X
Queued messaging					X	X

In fairness, WCF does not provide us with unlimited combinations of features, but it does provide many more feature combinations than we had before.

Security

No one sets out to build an application full of security holes. Quite the contrary, we typically go to great lengths to ensure that our applications are secure. If we don't do this, we certainly should. In the past, it has been up to us, the developer, the architect, or the tester, to know how to configure our application in such a way that it is secure. When we see the myriad of available technologies that provide security in our applications, it is often difficult to know which technology or combination of technologies is right for securing our application.

Out of the box, WCF supports many different security models, and makes it easy to implement widely accepted security measures. Since WCF has an extensible architecture, it is also relatively easy to extend WCF security to meet the needs of a particular application. The default security options range from the traditional transport-centric security to the more modern, message-based security, as dictated in WS-Security and related specifications. It's also very important to note that WCF is secure by default in many scenarios.

Reliability

Distributed applications often require reliable messaging. In distributed computing, reliable messaging is often described in terms of *assurances*. An assurance is like a guarantee. There are four assurances that apply to distributed computing scenarios:

- **At Most Once**   A message is guaranteed to arrive at the destination no more than one time. If a message arrives at a destination more than once, it is ignored or considered an error.

- **At Least Once**   A message is guaranteed to arrive at the destination at least one time. If a message does not arrive at a destination at least once, it is considered an error.

- **Exactly Once**   The combination of At Most Once and At Least Once, this is a guarantee that a message will arrive at a location one time.

- **In Order**   One logical set of information can be physically distributed in many messages. As these messages are sent, they are sent in a particular order. The In Order assurance guarantees that the messages will be processed in the same order they were sent.

Experience has taught us that networks and applications that generate network traffic are unreliable. In general, if an application sends two messages through the network to another application, assurances that the messages arrived at their destination have traditionally come from the transport. It is certainly possible that one or both of the messages were lost in transmission. It is also possible that the arrival order of the messages is different from the sending order, and even that messages arrive more times than they were sent. Many factors contribute to this unreliability, including excessive network traffic, network connectivity loss, application bugs, and environmental changes.

An unreliable network is annoying when you're trying to check e-mail or surf the Web, but it is particularly troublesome when factored into distributed computing scenarios. For example, if an order processing application loses messages during transmission between processing nodes, the problem can materialize as missed ship dates and angry customers. If, however, an application can learn when a failure has occurred, the application can take some remedial action.

In the past, an application's reliability requirements dictated the technology used in the application. For example, MSMQ provides, among other things, reliable delivery. If an application required reliable message delivery, MSMQ was the logical technology choice. Implementing MSMQ, while fairly straightforward, required MSMQ-specific knowledge and MSMQ-specific code. Writing this code and setting up the correct environments required MSMQ-specific knowledge that was unique and nontransferable to other technologies. In essence, the decision to send a message reliably from one application to another application has had, in the past, a dramatic impact on the code in the applications and the knowledge required to write it.

WCF contains mechanisms that provide At Most Once, At Least Once, Exactly Once, and In Order delivery assurances. WCF can provide these assurances with little or no modification to the application. Even better, the delivery assurance mechanisms are decoupled from the transport, thereby opening the door for delivery assurances even when messages are sent over traditionally unreliable transports.

> **Note**   Do not confuse *reliable messaging* with *durable messaging*. At a high level, durable messages persist in a nonvolatile store as they are being processed. If the application exits unexpectedly and volatile memory is cleared, the messages are still available in the persistent store.

Transactional Support

In the connected world, the work performed upon receipt of a message involves subsequent message sends to other applications. Sometimes this work needs to be performed in the scope of a transaction. Simply stated, a *transaction* is a way to ensure that all or none of the work is done. WCF allows transactional scopes to flow across multiple applications.

Interoperability

WCF is designed from the ground up to interoperate with other systems. This includes applications that run on different operating systems and platforms. It is WCF's inherent ability to focus on the message that makes this capability possible. Out of the box, applications built on WCF can communicate with other applications that understand WS-*, Basic Profile (BP), and XML messages over TCP, HTTP, Named Pipes, and MSMQ. Developers are free to write components that extend the default WCF capabilities, and this includes writing custom extensions that allow WCF to communicate with applications that require proprietary binary message encodings (like legacy mainframe applications).

Traditionally, the requirements to interoperate with another platform (like Java) have dictated much of our application design. In the past, if we wanted to communicate with another platform, we would either use ASMX or write our own interoperability layer. WCF is much different. From an interoperability perspective, WCF is a single technology that has interoperability features previously spread across several different technologies. WCF achieves the promise of true interoperability by embracing WS-* and also by supporting REST architectures and POX messaging styles.

Performance

Distributed technologies usually have a fixed performance cost; this cost is usually balanced with the features that technology provides. For example, .NET Remoting is a relatively efficient way for two .NET Framework applications to communicate, but it cannot easily interoperate with non–.NET Framework applications. ASMX, on the other hand, is not as highly performing as Remoting, but it can interoperate with non–.NET Framework applications. MSMQ is not highly performing from an end-to-end perspective, but the very nature of queuing helps the efficiency of the sending application. To put it another way, the total time required to generate, send, deliver, and receive an MSMQ message is not trivial, but the durability and reliability of MSMQ gives the sending application the assurance that it can generate and send the message and not wait for delivery or receipt of the message. The net effect in the sending application is an overall increase in throughput. The downside to this technology is that it does not, by default, interoperate with other queuing systems. (There is, however, a bridge between MSMQ and IBM's MQSeries.) When viewed as a whole, the distributed technology used by a distributed application has traditionally impacted the performance of that application.

In contrast, WCF applications can provide different levels of interoperability and performance. For example, WCF applications can be more efficient when communicating with other WCF applications than they are when communicating with a Java-based Web service.

Extensibility

The common language runtime (CLR) contains magic. For example, the JIT compiler, the verification subsystem, and the garbage collector are nearly impossible to replicate. Microsoft has published partial information about how these subsystems work, but these subsystems cannot be replaced by third parties. For example, all .NET Framework applications are subject to the garbage collector. We can and should be intelligent about how we write our code to take advantage of the features of the garbage collector. However, no one outside Microsoft can write a .NET Framework application that uses the CLR, with *his or her* version of the garbage collector *instead* of the CLR's garbage collector.

In contrast, WCF contains no magic. Don't let this detract from your impression of the power of the platform. Quite to the contrary, WCF is extremely powerful, due in large measure to its extensible design. WCF is designed to work with custom transports, channels, bindings, encodings, and architectural paradigms. Chapter 4, "WCF 101," describes many of these WCF extensibility points.

Configurability

One of the touted WCF features is its rich configuration support through XML configuration files. Using this feature, it is possible to configure transports, addresses, behaviors, and bindings in an XML file. When making these configuration changes, it is possible to radically alter the behavior of a WCF application without modifying any source code and without having to recompile the application. This is attractive from an administrative perspective, because it allows nondevelopers to move, maintain, and alter the behavior of the application without the involvement of the development team. I see this as a blessing and a curse. When used wisely, this feature can greatly reduce the pressure and workload on development teams. When abused, it will create unpredictable results.

Summary

WCF provides functional capabilities that are a quantum leap forward for distributed application developers. WCF allows us to design, build, debug, and maintain distributed systems much more quickly than before, and with more features than were possible before. WCF fully embraces SOAP and WS-*, but it is also able to send POX messages and can fit within REST architectures. It consolidates the disparate technology stacks of RPC, COM+, Remoting, ASMX, WSE, and MSMQ. WCF is also highly extensible. This extensibility serves two purposes: First, it gives the WCF team the ability to change the product more easily over time. Second, it provides companies with the flexibility they need to adapt WCF to the requirements of their applications. As a result of this flexibility, the WCF API is fairly complex but powerful. Because describing all the different ways that WCF can be used would be virtually impossible, this book focuses on the WCF internals. In my view, this approach helps both the application developer and the framework developer leverage WCF for their distributed computing tasks.

Chapter 2
Service Orientation

The Internet is awash with talk of service orientation (SO), and most of that discussion addresses service orientation in the abstract. We are going to take a slightly different approach in this chapter. In the next few pages, we'll look at service orientation from a requirements perspective. More specifically, we're going to look at a generic messaging application and expose what is required to make it tick. Through this process, we'll unearth some of the concepts that are essential to comprehending service orientation. The last sections of this chapter are devoted to a more formal definition of service orientation and a discussion of why service orientation makes sense in today's world of distributed computing.

If you ask 10 "SO-savvy" people to define service orientation, you'll probably get 10 different answers. If you ask them again in a couple of years, you'll probably get a different set of answers. This phenomenon is not new. When object orientation (OO) and component-driven development arrived in the mainstream, many developers were confused as to how they should adapt or reconceive their procedural designs given these new architectural models. Understanding OO and component architectures required a fundamental shift in thinking about application designs. The process was at times painful, but the payoffs are more robust designs, greater code reuse, advanced application functionality, easier debugging, and shorter time to market. In my opinion, moving to SO designs from component-driven designs will require a fundamental shift in thinking of the same magnitude as the move from procedural architectures to OO. The good news is that SO designs offer tremendous benefits in the form of richer communication patterns, loosely coupled applications, improved application functionality, and fulfilling the promise of true application interoperability. Because the term *interoperability* is heavily overloaded, some specificity is needed to avoid confusion. In this context, interoperability refers to the ability for a system to change hardware, operating system, or platform without affecting the other participants in the distributed scenario.

Service orientation, despite the current confusion associated with its definition, is not a new concept. It has been around since the reign of the mainframe and has been more recently adopted as a paradigm in middleware. Recent initiatives toward interoperability and richer communication patterns have reignited interest in service orientation and are moving SO into the mainstream. It's reasonable to assume that the definition of service orientation will evolve as it becomes more widely implemented.

A Quick Definition of Service Orientation

In a nutshell, service orientation is an architectural style in which distributed application components are loosely coupled through the use of messages and contracts. Service-oriented applications describe the messages they interact with through contracts. These contracts must be expressed in a language and format easily understood by other applications, thereby reducing the number of dependencies on component implementation.

Notice that I am not mentioning vendors or technologies when describing service orientation. SO is a concept that transcends vendor and technology boundaries, much in the way that object orientation also transcends these boundaries. OO can be a confusing concept, both initially and when taken to extremes, and I expect the same to be true of SO. For this reason, I will first illustrate SO with a series of examples, and I'll avoid defining abstract concepts with other abstract concepts.

Getting the Message

Messages are the fundamental unit of communication in service-oriented applications. For this reason, service-oriented applications are often called *messaging applications*. At some point, every SO application will send or receive a message. It is helpful to think of a service-oriented message as similar to a letter you receive in the mail. In the postal system, a letter is an abstract entity: it can contain almost any type of information, can exist in many different shapes and sizes, and can relate to almost anything. Likewise, a service-oriented message is an abstract entity: it can contain almost any data, can be encoded in many different ways, and can relate to virtually anything, even other messages. Some properties of a postal letter are widely accepted to be true. For example, a letter is always sent by someone, sent to someone, and might be delivered by someone (more on that "might be" in a moment). Likewise, a service-oriented message is sent by a computer, sent to a computer, and might be delivered by computer. To satisfy the theory wonks, I must say that in the purest sense, entities that interact with service-oriented messages do not have to be computers. Theoretically, they could be carrier pigeons, Labradors, or maybe even ligers. Regardless, the entities that interact with service-oriented messages are called *messaging participants*, and in this book, a messaging participant will be a process on a computer.

Messaging Participants

Let's imagine that I need to send a thank-you letter to my friend Rusty for giving me tickets to a football game last week. Let's also assume that I will send the letter to Rusty's office. In real life, it's probably easier and cheaper to send an e-mail message to Rusty, but that makes for a more complicated example, and sometimes a written letter is simply more appropriate. What sort of steps would I follow to send Rusty the thank-you letter?

As we all know, the order of these steps is open to several variations, but at some point before I send the letter, I have to write the letter. As I am writing the letter, I'll probably want to reference the football game, as it would be unusual to send a thank-you letter expressing thanks for nothing in particular. Next I would put the letter in an envelope. Then I would write the delivery address on the envelope and place the necessary postage on the envelope. The last step is to drop the letter in any mailbox and let the postal service deliver the letter to Rusty. I am assuming that Rusty will know the letter is from me and that he will know that I appreciated the football tickets.

When we describe messaging participants, it's often helpful to label them according to the role they play in the message delivery. In general, there are three types of messaging participants: the *initial sender*, the *ultimate receiver*, and the *intermediaries*. In our thank-you letter scenario, I am the initial sender, Rusty is the ultimate receiver, and the mail system and Rusty's office staff are intermediaries.

Let's imagine a more real-world business scenario—the order processing system at Contoso Boomerang Corporation. Basically, customers place boomerang orders on the Web site, and the Web site generates an order message and sends it to other internal systems for processing and fulfillment, as shown in Figure 2-1.

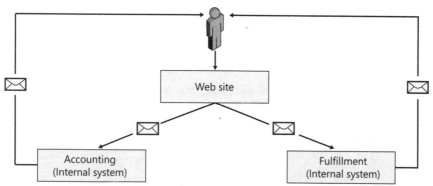

Figure 2-1   Message flow at Contoso Boomerang Corporation

Several facts are implied in this scenario:

- The Web site and the other internal systems have previously agreed upon the format of the message.

- The Web site can create the message in the previously agreed upon format.

- The Web site knows how to send the message to other internal systems.

- The internal systems can use data in the received message to fill the order, send a confirmation message, and ship the order.

Contoso's order processing system has at least two messaging participants. The Web site is the initial sender, and the internal systems are the ultimate receivers. It might be the case that we also have a load-balancing messaging router that routes Web site orders to the proper internal system. As shown in Figure 2-2, we can consider this router an intermediary.

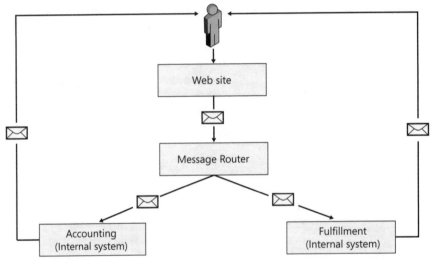

Figure 2-2   Message flow at Contoso Boomerang Corporation with a messaging router

The Initial Sender

Identifying the initial sender can be harder than it looks. In our thank-you letter example, I might appear to be the initial sender. It is plausible, however, to look at my letter as a response to Rusty's action of sending me the tickets. If we follow this train of thought, Rusty is the initial sender, and I am sending him a thank-you letter as a response to his generosity. Along those same lines, it is also possible that I sent Rusty a letter two months ago asking him for the tickets. In this case, I am the initial sender. Rusty was responding to me when he sent the tickets, and my thank-you message is a response to Rusty's response. It is also possible that one of our common friends suggested to Rusty that he should send me the tickets. In this case, our common friend is the initial sender.

Our order processing system can display the same ambiguity. At first glance, the Web site might appear to be the initial sender. It might not look that way, however, from the perspective of the internal systems. From that point of view, the initial sender might appear to be either the Web site or another internal system (remember the message router). We could go on an on, but the reality is that the initial sender is *relative*. By relative, I mean that the initial sender of a message might change based on the context assigned to the message. In both of our examples, we can draw an arbitrary boundary around two or more participants and change the initial sender of the message.

If we drop the *initial* in initial sender, we have a much more concrete vision of a messaging participant. If we revisit the thank-you letter example, Rusty probably doesn't care who the initial sender is; he simply needs to know who sent the thank-you letter. In practice, the distinction between the initial sender and just a sender is often not worth determining. For this reason, I will use the term *sender* instead. If you see the term *initial sender* in any World Wide Web Consortium (W3C) documents or specifications, be aware of the subtlety embodied in the definition. Given these parameters, the following is how I describe a sender:

A sender is an entity that initiates communication.

Intermediaries

Several people have handled the thank-you letter as it was being delivered to Rusty. To name a few:

- The postal worker who picked up the letter from the mailbox
- The postal workers at the sorting facility
- The postal worker who delivered the mail to Rusty's office building
- The mailroom workers at Rusty's office building who delivered the letter to his office

Through experience, we have come to understand that we don't know how many people will handle a letter as we send it through the mail. We do expect certain behaviors, however, from those handling our mail. For example, we expect them to not open the mail or materially alter its contents. We also expect that each mail handler will move the letter closer, either in process or in location, to our intended recipient. These message waypoints are called intermediaries. Given these parameters, I define an intermediary as follows:

An intermediary is invisible to the sender and is positioned between the sender and the ultimate recipient.

Identifying intermediaries is also harder than it looks at first glance. In our postal example, isn't a mail carrier simply picking up a message and sending it forward to another mail carrier? Isn't the next mail carrier simply picking up a message delivered from another mail carrier and forwarding the message on? Wouldn't a mail carrier be an initial sender if he or she sends the message forward? It is physically true that each mail carrier handling the letter is sending the letter forward in the process. It is also true that each mail carrier handling the letter receives the letter from either another mail carrier or the sender. Logically, however, the mail carrier might be invisible to the sender and therefore not specifically addressed by the sender. It is also true that mail carriers do not create the message; they are simply handling and delivering the message.

It is also possible, however, that the message envelope will be altered at some point during handling. Think of a postmark. Postmarks do not materially change the contents of the message, but they do provide some information that describes when and where the letter was received into the postal system. The postal service may also add a "Return to Sender" mark on the envelope if the delivery address is not valid. At a high level, these are the types of operations that can be performed by an intermediary. An intermediary should not, however, change the contents of the message.

Let's reexamine Contoso's order processing system for a more computer-based example of an intermediary. As it turns out, Contoso sells custom boomerangs and standard boomerangs. Orders for standard boomerangs are processed through Contoso's inventory system, while custom boomerangs must be sent to the manufacturing system. The system architects at Contoso might have decided to put this logic in a routing system, further encapsulating business logic away from the Web site. The effect of this design is that the Web site sends messages to message routing servers. This routing system might not materially change the contents of the message, but it does route the order to either system. At a high level, the routing system is acting as an intermediary between the initial sender (the Web site) and the ultimate receiver (the inventory or manufacturing systems).

A Few Words About Business Logic

This additional layer in the architecture can be very useful in capturing a business process. In the past, applications "hard-coded" business processes in their applications. For example, business requirements or regulations might require the Contoso accounting system to receive payment for boomerangs before orders are fulfilled. The traditional distributed system paradigm spreads the logic of this business process between the Web site, the accounting system, and the fulfillment system. This design has a major drawback: when business requirements or regulations evolve, each part of the system requires modification.

In recent years, companies have spent fortunes trying to develop their own internal mechanism for dealing with this problem. Often these efforts involved defining a proprietary XML grammar for expressing business processes and building a custom runtime engine for interpreting these rules. It is my guess that, more often than not, these efforts ended badly.

As mentioned in Chapter 1, "The Moon Is Blue," Microsoft Windows Communication Foundation (WCF) ships with a product called Windows Workflow Foundation (WF). Among other things, WF is designed to capture these sorts of business processes. WF does much of the heavy lifting previously required to build this sort of business process engine. In the next few years, expect workflow to be more a part of business application development.

The Ultimate Receiver

My thank-you letter was intended to go to my friend Rusty. When I sent the letter, I had no idea how many people were going to handle it, but I hoped that each handler would work toward delivering the letter to Rusty. As a result, I define the ultimate receiver as follows:

The ultimate receiver is the intended, addressable target of a message.

A single message can have only one logical ultimate receiver. For example, it is not possible to address a postal letter to more than one address. Physically, however, one address could reference multiple entities. For example, if Rusty's department is responsible for sending the football tickets, I could address the thank-you message to the entire department. My intention in this case is that everyone in the department will receive the message. It is also possible that my message is posted on a bulletin board, sent around to each individual in the department, or announced in a department meeting. In the end, however, the message is intended for one logical entity, the ultimate receiver.

The Anatomy of a Message

Early in life, we learn that a postal stamp belongs in the upper-right corner of an envelope and that the address goes somewhere in the center. If we want, we can also add a return address in the upper-left corner of the envelope. All mail handled by the postal service must adhere to this basic structure. If mail is not metered, a delivery address is not present, or the delivery address is illegible, the postal service considers the mail invalid and will not deliver the letter. If we're lucky, invalid mail will be delivered to the return address (if one is specified). Imagine the chaos that would follow if such a structure did not exist. If senders were allowed to place postage or delivery addresses anywhere on the parcel, the postal service would have to scan the entire parcel for postage and delivery addresses. More than likely, the added infrastructure required to complete these tasks would add more than a couple of cents to the next postage rate hike! In practice, the parcel structure as defined by the postal service improves mail handling efficiency and consistency without sacrificing much usability from the sender's perspective.

In contrast to the postal example, SO messages do not have to follow structural pattern. Like the postal example, however, a predefined message structure does improve the processing efficiency, reliability, and functionality of the system. Remember that messaging applications are not conceptually new. Messages originating from a variety of application vendors have been passed between applications for decades. Without a standardized structure, each vendor is free to develop its own structure, and the result is a disparate set of message structures that do not interoperate well with one another.

If we look at companies like FedEx, UPS, and DHL, we see a similar paradigm. Each of these organizations has defined its own addressing format and packaging. It is atypical for an overnight package in a UPS box with a UPS label to be sent via FedEx. Technically it is possible, but business pressures and efficiency preclude these companies from interacting with another type of address and parcel format.

It's not a huge leap to examine purchasable enterprise computing systems with the same concept. On the whole, vendors have not wanted their applications to interoperate with other systems. Vendors had a hard enough time getting their systems to communicate within a single product suite, let alone interoperate with other systems. In the past, customers were willing, to some extent, to stick within one particular application vendor's toolset to meet all of their enterprise needs. The choice customers faced was one of "Who can sell me the complete package?" rather than "What products are the best for each of my needs?" Over time, the one-stop-shopping paradigm has resonated less and less with would-be customers. As a result, software vendors have had to come to the table to produce a series of common messaging specifications and standards and make their applications produce messages that adhere to these standards. It has taken many years for these standards to be created and agreed upon, but they are finally here, and we can expect more over time.

There are literally dozens of these messaging standards available, and we will examine many of these specifications as you move through this book. Many of these specifications are based, in one form or another, on SOAP, and each serves a specific purpose. For the intellectually curious, the full SOAP specification is available at *http://www.w3.org/TR/soap12-part1/*. As a result of SOAP's flexibility, modern SO messages are usually SOAP messages.[1] At its core, SOAP is a messaging structure built on XML. SOAP defines three major XML elements that can be used to define any XML message you want to send: the envelope, the body, and the header. Here is an example of the key parts of a raw SOAP message:

```
<?xml version='1.0' ?>
<env:Envelope xmlns:env="http://www.w3.org/2003/05/soap-envelope">
<env:Header>
    ...
    </env:Header>
  <env:Body>
    ...
  </env:Body>
</env:Envelope>
```

Because WCF is an SO platform intended for, among other things, interoperability with other systems, it sends, receives, and processes SOAP messages. As you'll see in Chapter 4, "WCF 101," we can think of WCF as a toolkit for creating, sending, and parsing SOAP messages with a myriad of different behaviors. For now, let's take a closer look at what all SOAP messages have in common.

---

1   WCF supports SOAP, REST, and POX. Most of the current WCF application programming interface (API), however, is dedicated to the SOAP message structure. This will undoubtedly expand in the future to include other message structures, like JSON.

Envelope

As its name implies, the envelope wraps both the body and the header. All SOAP messages have an envelope as a root element. The envelope element is often used to define the different namespaces (and prefixes) that will be used throughout the message. There is not much else that's terribly exciting about SOAP envelopes.

Header

A SOAP header is optional and, if present, it must be the first element after the envelope start tag. A SOAP header is composed of zero or more SOAP header blocks. SOAP header blocks contain information that can be used by the ultimate receiver or by an intermediary. Typically these header blocks contain data that is orthogonal to the message body's data. To put it another way, security information, correlation, or message context can be placed in a header part. Header blocks are mandatory if certain messaging behaviors are expected. Once again, this idea can be illustrated through the postal system. If I want to send a piece of mail through the postal system and receive a return receipt when the parcel is delivered, I have to fill out a special return receipt label and affix it to the envelope. Adding a return receipt to the parcel does not materially change the contents of the parcel. It can, however, change the behavior of messaging participants: I have to fill out and affix the return receipt request, the postal carrier must ask for a signature, the ultimate receiver must sign the receipt, and the postal carrier must deliver the receipt to me (or at least my mailbox).

SO messages can contain similar information in the header. For example, in our order processing scenario, the Web site might want to receive a confirmation that the order message was received by an entity other than the message router. In this case, the Web site could assign a unique identifier to the message and add a special header to the message requesting an acknowledgment. Upon receipt, the message router forwards the message on to the appropriate system and demands that the system produce an acknowledgment. That acknowledgment could then be returned to the Web site directly or through the message router.

It is also possible that an intermediary might modify an existing SOAP header block or even add a brand new SOAP header block to a message. In practice, however, an intermediary should never change or delete a header block unless it is intended for them. Using this model, it would be fairly easy to create a message that contains auditable records of its path. Each intermediary can add its own SOAP header, so by the time the message arrives at the ultimate receiver, the message contains a list of all intermediaries that have touched the message. As described earlier, this behavior is modeled in the real world in the postal system with postmarks or as described in our message router example.

Body

The body element is mandatory and typically contains the payload of the message. By convention, data found in the body is intended for the ultimate receiver only. This is true regardless of how many firewalls, routers, or other intermediaries process the SOAP message. This is only an informal agreement. Just as there is no guarantee that the postal service will not open our mail, there is no guarantee that an intermediary will not open or change the SOAP body. It is possible, however, to use digital signatures and encryption to digitally ensure the integrity of a message as it passes from initial sender to ultimate receiver.

Message Transports

SOAP messages are transport agnostic. In other words, there is no need to place transport-specific information into a message. This simple feature is one of the key features that make SOAP such a powerful messaging structure. Once again, our postal service example can provide an illustration. If a postal message was sent with a dependency on the transport, it would be equivalent to telling your postal carrier where you want the message to be delivered and not including that information on the envelope of the message. If we follow this train of thought, the message is tightly bound to the postal carrier. This tight coupling is bad for several reasons:

- The message can be delivered only to places the postal carrier can go.
- No other postal worker can interact with the message (unless the previous postal carrier communicates it).
- Batch sorting and delivering of messages is difficult.
- Because there is no return address on the message, the sender cannot be notified if something goes wrong while the message is processed.

From a service-oriented perspective, this is a terrible scenario. A much better plan would be to include all relevant addressing information in the message itself, thereby preventing a strong tie to the transport layer. When messages include this information, a myriad of SOAP behaviors (including the aforementioned behaviors) are possible. For example, we all know that mail is picked up by a postal carrier, delivered to a sorting facility, and then sent on to other sorting facilities and postal carriers via planes, trains, boats, or trucks. In our everyday mail example, we see that the transport can change during the delivery of the message (carrier, sorting facility, plane, and so on), and this improves efficiency. None of that is possible if each message does not contain an address.

Message Encodings

Over time, many of us have been conditioned to think of XML (and therefore SOAP) as structured text. After all, text is human readable, and every computing system can process text. The universal nature of text-based XML resonates with our desire to interoperate with connected systems. Text-encoded XML, while being easy to interpret, is inherently bulky. It is reasonable to expect some performance penalty when using XML. Just as it takes some effort to place a thank-you letter in an envelope, it takes some processing time to interact with XML. In some cases, however, the sheer size of text-encoded XML restricts its use, especially when we want to send an XML message over the wire.

Furthermore, if we restrict ourselves to text-encoded XML, how can we send binary data (like music or video) in an XML document? If you've read up on your standard XML Schema data types, you will know that two binary data types exist: *xs:base64Binary* and *xs:hexBinary*. Essentially, both of these data types represent data as an ordered set of octets. Using these XML data types might have solved the problem of embedding binary data in a document, but they have actually made the performance problem worse. It is a well-known fact that base64-encoded data inflates data size by roughly 30%. The story is worse for *xs:hexBinary*, since it inflates the resultant data by a factor of 2. Both of these factors assume an underlying text encoding of UTF-8. These factors double if UTF-16 is the underlying text encoding.

The XML Infoset

To find the answer to our performance dilemma, let's take a closer look at exactly what makes up an XML document. If we look at the specifications, XML is a precise syntax for writing structured data (as defined at *http://www.w3.org/TR/REC-xml/*). It demands that well-formed XML documents have start and end elements, a root node, and so on. Oddly enough, after the XML specification was released, a need arose to abstractly define XML documents. The XML Infoset (as defined at *http://www.w3.org/TR/xml-infoset/*) provides this abstract definition.

In practice, the XML Infoset defines the relationship between items, without defining any specific syntax. This lack of a specific syntax in the XML Infoset leaves the door open for new, more efficient encodings. If our parser adheres to the XML Infoset, as opposed to the XML syntax, we can interpret a variety of different message encodings, including ones more efficient than text, without materially altering our application.

SOAP and the XML Infoset

Remember that SOAP is built on XML. This raises a question: Are SOAP messages built on the earlier XML syntax or on the XML Infoset? The answer is both. Two SOAP specifications exist: SOAP 1.1 and SOAP 1.2. SOAP 1.1 is built on the older XML syntax, while SOAP 1.2 is built on the XML Infoset. Given this fact, it is reasonable to assume that a SOAP 1.2 message might not be readable by a SOAP 1.1 parser. WCF is built on the XML Infoset, but it has the capability to process both SOAP 1.1 and SOAP 1.2 messages.

WCF can be adapted and customized to work with virtually any message encoding, as long as the message is SOAP 1.1 or 1.2 compliant (it can also work with messages that are not SOAP messages). As you will see in subsequent chapters, WCF has a very pluggable and composable architecture, so custom encoders can be easily added to the WCF message pipeline. As new encodings are developed and implemented, either Microsoft or third parties can create these new encoders and plug them into the appropriate messaging stack. I will describe message encoders in greater detail in Chapter 6, "Channels." For now, let's take a look at the encoders included in WCF. At the time of this writing, WCF ships with three encoders: text, binary, and Message Transmission Optimization Mechanism (MTOM).

The Text Encoder

As you can guess from its name, the output of the text encoder is text-encoded messages. Every system that understands Unicode text will be able to read and process messages that have been passed through this encoder, making it a great choice when interoperating with non-WCF systems. Binary data can be included in text-encoded messages via the *xs:base64Binary* Extensible Schema Definition (XSD) data type. Here is a message that has been encoded by using the WCF text encoder (with some elements removed for clarity):

```
<s:Envelope xmlns:s="http://www.w3.org/2003/05/soap-envelope">
  <s:Header>...</s:Header>
  <s:Body>
    <SubmitOrder xmlns="http://wintellect.com/OrderProcess">
      <Order xmlns:i="http://www.w3.org/2001/XMLSchema-instance">
      <OrderByte xmlns="http://wintellect.com/Order">
mktjxwyxKr/9oW/jO48IhUwrZvNOdyuuquZEAIcyO8aa+HXkT3dNmvE/
+zI96Q91a9Zb17HtrCIgtBwmbSk4ys2pSEMaIzXV3cwCD3z4ccDWzpWx1/
wUrEtSxJtaJi3HBzBlk6DMWOeghvnl6521KEJcUJ6Uh/LR1Zz3x1+aereeOgdLkt4gCnNOEFECL8CtrJtY/taPM4A+k/
4E1JPnBgtCRrGWWpVkOOUqRXahz2XbShrDQnzgDwaHDf/
fHDXfZgpFwOgPF1IG88KQZOOJncSYKIp5I8OPYTeqDOyVhB8QSt9sWw59yzLHvU65UKoYfXA7RvOqZkJGtV6wZAgGcA=
=
      </OrderByte>
      <OrderNumber xmlns="http://wintellect.com/Order">
        12345
      </OrderNumber>
    </Order>
  </SubmitOrder>
  </s:Body>
</s:Envelope>
```

The Binary Encoder

The binary encoder is the most highly performing message encoder and is intended for WCF-to-WCF communication only. Of all the encoders in WCF, the binary encoder produces the smallest messages. Keep in mind that this encoder produces a serialized Infoset, even though it is in a binary format. It is likely that in the future, a standard binary encoding will be universally adopted, as these types of encodings can dramatically improve the efficiency of a messaging application.

The MTOM Encoder

The MTOM encoder creates messages that are encoded according to the rules stated in the MTOM specification. (The MTOM specification is available at *http://www.w3.org/TR/soap12-mtom/*.) Because the MTOM encoding is governed by a specification, other vendors are free to create infrastructures that send and receive MTOM messages. As a result, WCF messages that pass through the MTOM encoder can be sent to non-WCF applications (as long as those applications understand MTOM). In general, MTOM is intended to allow efficient transmission of messages that contain binary data, while also providing a mechanism for applying digital signatures. The MTOM message encoding enables these features through the use of Multipurpose Internet Mail Extensions (MIME) message parts and inline base64 encoding. The content of the MTOM message is defined by the Xml-binary Optimized Packaging recommendation. For more information, see *http://www.w3.org/TR/xop10/*.

At run time, the MTOM encoder creates an inline base64-encoded representation of the binary data for digital signature computation and makes the raw binary data available for packaging alongside the SOAP message. An MTOM encoded message looks as follows:

```
// start of a boundary in the multipart message
--uuid:7477fff7-61e6-4cd9-a8a5-e38f47fb042e+id=1
Content-ID: <http://wintellect.com/0>
Content-Transfer-Encoding: 8bit

// set the content type to xop+xml
Content-Type: application/xop+xml;charset=utf8; type="application/soap+xml"
<s:Envelope xmlns:s="http://www.w3.org/2003/05/soap-envelope">
  <s:Header>...</s:Header>
  <s:Body>
    <SubmitOrder xmlns="http://wintellect.com/OrderProcess">
      <order xmlns:i="http://www.w3.org/2001/XMLSchema-instance">
        <OrderByte xmlns="http://wintellect.com/Order">
          // add a reference to another message part
          <xop:Include href=cid:http://wintellect.com/1/12345
            xmlns:xop="http://www.w3.org/2004/08/xop/include"/>
        </OrderByte>
        <OrderNumber xmlns="http://wintellect.com/Order">
          12345
        </OrderNumber>
      </order>
    </SubmitOrder>
  </s:Body>
</s:Envelope>

// end of the boundary in the first message part
--uuid:7477fff7-61e6-4cd9-a8a5-e38f47fb042e+id=1

// add the binary data as an octect stream
Content-ID: <http://wintellect.com/1/12345>
Content-Transfer-Encoding: binary
Content-Type: application/octet-stream

// raw binary data here
```

Notice that the binary data is kept in its raw format in another part of the message and referenced from the SOAP body. Since the binary data is packaged in a message part that is external to the SOAP message, how can one apply a digital signature to the SOAP message? If we use an XML-based security mechanism, like those stated in XML Encryption and XML Digital Signature, we cannot reference external binary streams. These encryption and signing mechanisms demand that the protected data be wrapped in a SOAP message. At first glance, it appears that there is no way around this problem with multipart messages. In fact, this was the Achilles' heel of Direct Internet Message Encapsulation (DIME) and SOAP with Attachments. MTOM provides an interesting way around this problem.

The MTOM encoding specification states that an MTOM message can contain inline binary data in the form of base64-encoded strings or as binary streams in additional message parts. It also states that a base64-encoded representation of any binary data must be available during processing. In other words, additional binary message parts can be created for message transmission, but inline base64 data must be temporarily available for operations like applying digital signatures. While the message is in this temporary inline base64-encoded state, an XML-based security mechanism can be applied to the SOAP message. After the security mechanism has been applied, the message can then be serialized as a multipart message. When the receiver receives the message, the message can be validated according to the rules set forth by the specific XML security mechanism.

It is also interesting to note that the WCF MTOM encoder reserves the right to serialize the binary chunks of a message as either inline base64-encoded strings or as binary streams in additional message parts. The WCF encoder uses the size of the binary data as a key determining factor. In our previous message, the *OrderBytes* element was about 800 KB. If we reduce the size of the *OrderBytes* element to 128 bytes and check the message format, we see the following:

```
// start of a boundary in the multipart message
--uuid:14ce8c5f-7a95-48d3-a4de-a7042f864fbc+id=1
Content-ID: <http://wintellect.com/0>
Content-Transfer-Encoding: 8bit

// set the content type to xop+xml
Content-Type: application/xop+xml;charset=utf8; type="application/soap+xml"

<s:Envelope xmlns:s="http://www.w3.org/2003/05/soap-envelope">
  <s:Header>...</s:Header>
  <s:Body>
    <SubmitOrder xmlns="http://wintellect.com/OrderProcess">
      <order xmlns:i="http://www.w3.org/2001/XMLSchema-instance">
        <OrderByte xmlns="http://wintellect.com/Order">
kF+k2CQd/1CitSYvXnLhuOtaMCk/tZaFZIWeW7keC3YvgstAWoht/wiOiR5+HZPo+TzYoH+qE9vJHnSefqKXg6mw/
9ymoV1i7TEhsCt3BkfytmF9Rmv3hW7wdjsUzoB19gZ1zR62QVjedbJNiWKvUhgtq8hAGjw+uX1ttSohTh6xu7kkAjgoO
3QJntG4qfwMQCQj5iO4JdzJNhSkSYwtvCaTnM2oi0/fBHBUN3trhRB9YXQG/mj7+ZbdWsskg/
Lo2+GrJAwuY7XUROKyY+5hXrAEJ+cXJr6+mKM3yzCDu4B9bFuZv2ADTv6/MbmFSJWnfPwbH1wKOLQi7Ixo95iF
        </OrderByte>
```

```
    <OrderNumber xmlns="http://wintellect.com/Order">
      12345
    </OrderNumber>
    </order>
  </SubmitOrder>
  </s:Body>
</s:Envelope>
--uuid:14ce8c5f-7a95-48d3-a4de-a7042f864fbc+id=1-
```

In this case, the WCF encoder opted to serialize the binary element as an inline base64-encoded string. This optimization is perfectly legal according to the MTOM specification.

Choosing the Right Encoding

Choosing the correct message encoding forces one to consider current and future uses of the message. For the most part, application interoperability and the type of data in the message will dictate your choice of message encodings. Performance, however, can also play a role in determining which encoding is best suited to your system. Table 2-1 ranks encodings based on what type of message is being sent and what sorts of systems can receive the message.

Table 2-1   Message Encodings by Rank and Scenario

Type of Message	Binary	Text	MTOM
Text payload, Interop with other WCF systems only	1	2	3
Text payload, Interop with modern non-WCF systems	N/A	1	2
Text payload, Interop with older non-WCF systems	N/A	1	N/A
Large binary payload, Interop with other WCF systems only	1	3	2
Large binary payload, Interop with modern non-WCF systems	N/A	2	1
Large binary payload, Interop with older non-WCF systems	N/A	1	N/A
Small binary payload, Interop with other WCF systems only	1	2	3
Small binary payload, Interop with modern non-WCF systems	N/A	1	2
Small binary payload, Interop with older non-WCF systems	N/A	1	N/A

It shouldn't be surprising that the binary encoding is the most efficient means to send messages to other WCF systems. What may come as a surprise, however, is the fact that MTOM messages can be less efficient, in an end-to-end sense, than text messages. Interoperability and the size of the binary data being sent are the two factors that should help you decide between MTOM and text encodings in your application. For the most part, one can send MTOM only messages to systems that implement an MTOM encoder. At the time of this writing, MTOM is a fairly new specification, so only modern systems can effectively process MTOM messages. From a performance perspective, the MTOM encoder makes sense only when the binary data being wrapped in a message is fairly large. MTOM should never be used with messages that do not contain binary data because MTOM's performance will always be worse than the regular text encoding. It is important, however, to run independent tests using messages that accurately represent those in production.

Luckily, as we'll see in Chapter 4, "WCF 101," WCF is designed in such a way that these encoding choices do not require a major change in the application. In fact, it is possible to have one service that can interact with different message encodings. For example, one service can interact with both binary-encoded and text-encoded messages. The benefit in this scenario is that the service can be very highly performing when communicating with other WCF participants and still interoperate with other platforms, like Java.

Addressing the Message

Now that you have seen the entities that can interact with a message, taken a close look at message anatomy, and seen the different message encoders that ship with WCF, let's examine how we can express where we want a message to be sent. After all, messages aren't terribly useful unless we can send them to a receiver. Just as the postal service requires a well-defined addressing structure, service-oriented messages also require a well-defined addressing structure. In this section, we will build our own addressing scheme, see whether it is broadly applicable to messaging applications, and then relate it to the addressing scheme that is typically used with WCF messages.

In-Transport Addressing vs. In-Message Addressing

Service-oriented messages specify the ultimate receiver directly in the message. This is a subtle but important point. If the target of the message is specified in the message itself, a whole set of messaging patterns becomes possible. You will learn more about messaging patterns in Chapter 3, "Message Exchange Patterns, Topologies, and Choreographies".

When we insert an address directly into a message, we pave the way for more efficient message processing. Efficiency can mean many things, and in this sense, I am talking about the ease of implementing more advanced messaging behaviors, as opposed to the speed with which a message can be created. Just as writing an address on an envelope takes time, serializing an address into a message takes time. However, just as writing an address on an envelope improves postal efficiency, serializing an address into a message improves processing efficiency, especially when more advanced messaging behaviors are implemented (like message routers and intermediaries).

Specifying the Ultimate Receiver

So what sorts of items should we place in an address? For starters, an address should identify the ultimate receiver we want to send a message to. Since the ultimate receiver might be hosting multiple services, we should also have a way to uniquely identify the specific service on the ultimate receiver. It's possible that one address element might be able to describe both the ultimate receiver hosting the service and the service itself. Take the following example:

```
http://wintellect.com/OrderService
```

In the age of the Internet, we have come to understand that this address includes both the location of the ultimate receiver and a protocol that we can use to access it. Since most SO messages are SOAP messages, we need some SOAP construct that will convey the same information.

We have learned already that SOAP messages can contain three types of elements: an envelope, one header with multiple header blocks, and a body. The envelope isn't a good choice, since the envelope can occur only once. That leaves the header blocks and the body as the only two remaining candidates. So what about the body? From our earlier discussion, we know that the body is intended for use only by the ultimate receiver. By process of elimination, we see that the only logical place for us to put an address is in the header of a message. So what should this header block look like? How about:

```
<Envelope>
  <Header>
    <To>http://wintellect.com/OrderService</To>
  </Header>
  <Body> …</Body>
</Envelope>
```

At a high level, this simple XML structure accomplishes our goal of identifying the ultimate receiver and service we would like to send a message to.

Specifying the Initial Sender

It might also be useful to add sender information to the message, sort of like a return address on a letter. Adding sender information to the message serves two purposes: to indicate the sender to the ultimate receiver, and to indicate the sender to any intermediaries. We have already seen that a URL can be used to identify the target of a message. So maybe we can in fact use the same construct to identify the sender. Take the following example:

```
<Envelope>
  <Header>
    <To>http://wintellect.com/ReceiveService</To>
    <From>http://wintellect.com/SendService</From>
  </Header>
  <Body> …</Body>
</Envelope>
```

Adding this simple element to the SOAP message indicates where the message came from, and it can be used either by an intermediary or by the ultimate receiver.

Specifying Where to Send an Error

What if there's a problem processing the message? Every modern computing platform has some way to indicate errors or exceptions. These error handling mechanisms make our applications more robust, predictable, and easier to debug. It is natural to want the same mechanism in our messaging applications. Given that we already have a *<To>* and a *<From>* in our message, we could send all of our error notifications to the address specified in the *<From>* element. What if we want error notifications to go to a location specifically reserved for handling errors? In this case, we have to create yet another element:

```
<Envelope>
  <Header>
    <To>http://wintellect.com/OrderService</To>
    <From>http://wintellect.com/SendService</From>
    <Error>http://wintellect.com/ErrorService</Error>
  </Header>
  <Body> …</Body>
</Envelope>
```

Adding the *<Error>* element to the header clearly indicates where the sender would like error messages to be sent. Because this URL is in the header, it can be used by either the ultimate recipient or an intermediary.

Identifying a Message

Our simple addressing scheme requires the sender to add our *To*, *From*, and *Error* information as header blocks in the message and then send the message to the ultimate receiver. As processing occurs at an intermediary or the ultimate receiver, an error might occur. Given that we now have the error element in our message, the intermediary or ultimate receiver should be able to send us an error message. This error message will be an entirely different message from the one originally sent. From the initial sender's perspective, receiving error messages is troubling in and of itself, but it is especially troubling if we don't know the message send that caused the error. It would be great for debugging, troubleshooting, and auditing if there were a way for us to correlate the original message with the error message. To do this, we need two separate elements in our message: a message identifier element, and a message correlation element. Let's look at the message identifier first:

```
<Envelope>
  <Header>
    <MessageID>15d03fa4-1b99-4110-a5e2-5e99887dea23</MessageID>
    <To>http://wintellect.com/OrderService</To>
    <From>http://wintellect.com/SendService</From>
    <Error>http://wintellect.com/ErrorService</Error>
  </Header>
  <Body>...</Body>
</Envelope>
```

In this example, we have called our message identifier element <MessageID>. For now, we can think of *MessageID*'s value as a globally unique number. Upon generation, this number does not mean anything to other participants. If the initial sender generates a message as described earlier, all intermediaries and the ultimate receiver know where to send an error message, but they can also use *MessageID* to reference the particular message that caused the error. If the ultimate receiver for error messages and the sender are different, these processes must exchange information between themselves to fully understand the message send that caused the error.

Relating Messages to Other Messages

If we assume that either an intermediary or the ultimate receiver has encountered a problem processing a message, it follows that a new message should be sent to the address specified in the error element. If an intermediary or an ultimate receiver sends an entirely new message, the intermediary or the ultimate receiver becomes the sender of the new message. Likewise, the address specified in the original *Error* header block now becomes the ultimate receiver of the new message. We just established that the initial message that caused the error will contain a *MessageID* element. Somehow, the error message needs to contain a reference to this *MessageID* element. The correlation between the original message and the error message can be described by using a *RelatesTo* element:

```
<Envelope>
  <Header>
    <MessageID>66bc85ab-9799-433c-b338-3d718e491dc2</MessageID>
    <RelatesTo>15d03fa4-1b99-4110-a5e2-5e99887dea23</RelatesTo>
    <To>http://www.wintelelct.com/ErrorService</To>
    <From>http://wintellect.com/OrderService</From>
    <Error>http://wintellect.com/ErrorService</Error>
  </Header>
  <Body> …</Body>
</Envelope>
```

The error service at *http://wintellect.com/ErrorService* is the ultimate recipient of this message. When this error service reads the message, information about the message that caused the error is available in the *RelatesTo* element. Although the error service might not do anything with the *RelatesTo* information, it can be used for debugging, troubleshooting, and auditing. Notice also in this example that the *To*, *From*, and *Error* elements have all changed to reflect the new context of the message.

Who Is Listening for a Response?

Let's step away from error messages for a bit and go back to the initial message. As you've seen, we have a way to specify the ultimate receiver, the address of the initial sender, a unique identifier for the message, and where error notifications should be sent. It is possible that we want a way to specify a reply address while still specifying the address of the initial sender. Examples of this behavior abound in the real world. For example, invoices commonly have a "Send further correspondence here" address that is different from the initial sending address. Our SO messages need a similar construct. We can once again use the notion of an address combined with a new element to describe this information. We will call this new element *ReplyTo* in the following example:

```
<Envelope>
  <Header>
    <MessageID>e563751c-3ed0-40b9-a6da-0cc9d3b34396</MessageID>
    <To>http://wintellect.com/OrderService</To>
    <ReplyTo>http://wintellect.com/OrderReplyService</ReplyTo>
    <From>http://wintellect.com/SendService</From>
    <Error>http://wintellect.com/ErrorService</Error>
  </Header>
  <Body> …</Body>
</Envelope>
```

It might seem repetitive to have both a *From* and a *ReplyTo* element in the same message. It's important to remember, however, that *From* and *ReplyTo* might be describing exactly the same service, but they can also describe two different services. Adding a *ReplyTo* element simply adds more flexibility and functionality to the set of header blocks we are creating.

Specifying an Operation

This next header block will require a little context, especially if you don't have much experience dealing with Web services. Once again, I would like to step into a real-world example first. We all know that postal addresses can contain an ATTN line. Typically, this line is used to route the parcel to a particular person, department, or operation. Take a look at the following postal address:

Contoso Boomerang Corporation ATTN: New Customer Subscriptions 2611 Boomerang Way Atlanta, GA 30309

From experience, we know that this address refers to Contoso Boomerang Corporation. More precisely, we know that the address specifically refers to the New Customer Subscriptions group within Contoso Boomerang Corporation.

If you expect to send mail to a large company, you may not have to specifically address a particular department. You could send mail to Contoso Boomerang Corporation and expect someone to ultimately open the mail, make a decision about who should receive the mail, and route the mail to the inferred recipient. Clearly this process will take longer than if we specifically addressed the message to the correct department or group.

Contoso Boomerang Corporation might have several groups that can receive mail. Each group might have its own set of actions to perform. For example, Contoso might have one group responsible for signing up new customers, another group responsible for customer support, and yet another group for new product development. At an abstract level, addresses can specify different levels of granularity for the destination, and each destination might have its own set of tasks or actions to perform.

So far, we have created elements that define the ultimate receiver, a reply-to receiver, an error notification receiver, a message identifier, a message correlation mechanism, and the initial sender. We have not, however, defined a way to indicate an action or operation for the message. Let's assume, for now, that we can use another header element containing a URL as a way to identify an action or operation. The following example illustrates this assumption with the addition of a new header:

```
<Envelope>
  <Header>
    <MessageID>ca9b172b-9f67-49af-9abd-7fa4b3a63c10</MessageID>
    <To>http://wintellect.com/OrderService</To>
    <Action>urn:ProcessOrder/Action></Action>
    <ReplyTo>http://wintellect.com/OrderReplyService</ReplyTo>
    <From>http://wintellect.com/SendService</From>
    <Error>http://wintellect.com/ErrorService</Error>
  </Header>
  <Body> …</Body>
</Envelope>
```

In this example, the *Action* element states that the *ProcessMsg* operation should be performed on this message. It is possible that *OrderService* defines additional operations. For example, we can send another message to the archive message operation by using the following *Action* element:

```
<Envelope>
  <Header>
    <MessageID>6d73f358-cf18-4e3b-8b28-9871c8a21cda</MessageID>
    <To>http://wintellect.com/OrderService</To>
    <Action>urn:ArchiveMessage</Action>
    <ReplyTo>http://someotherurl.com/OrderReplyService</ReplyTo>
    <From>http://wintellect.com/SendService</From>
    <Error>http://wintellect.com/ErrorService</Error>
  </Header>
  <Body> ... </Body>
</Envelope>
```

The Need for Standard Header Blocks

We have just arbitrarily defined seven elements that help us address messages. By no means can we assume that our element names will be universally adopted. We could, however, build our own infrastructure that understands these elements and use this infrastructure in each of our messaging participants. In other words, we can't send these messages to an application that does not understand what our seven message headers mean. Likewise, our application could not receive messages that contained different addressing headers. For example, another application vendor could have defined message headers like the following:

```
<Envelope>
  <Header>
    <MessageIdentifier>1</MessageIdentifier>
    <SendTo>http://wintellect.com/OrderService</SendTo>
```

```
      <Op>http://wintellect.com/OrderService/ArchiveMessage</Op>
      <Reply>http://someotherurl.com/OrderReplyService</Reply>
      <SentFrom>http://wintellect.com/SendService</SentFrom>
      <OnError>http://wintellect.com/ErrorService</OnError>
    </Header>
    <Body>...</Body>
  </Envelope>
```

Applications that contain our infrastructure cannot process this message.

If we were to take a survey of most enterprise applications, we would see that software vendors have followed this exact model in defining their own messages. For several years, SOAP has been the agreed-upon message format, but there was no agreement on the header blocks that could appear in a message, and as a result, applications could not easily interoperate. True SOAP message interoperability requires a set of header blocks that are common across all software vendors. As mentioned in Chapter 1, the WS-* specifications go a long way toward solving this problem by defining a common set of messaging headers.

WS-Addressing

WS-Addressing is one of the WS-* specifications that has been widely embraced by the software vendor community. It provides a framework for one of the most fundamental tasks of any service-oriented application—indicating the target of a message. To this end, all other WS-* specifications (for example, WS-ReliableMessaging, WS-Security, WS-AtomicTransaction, and so on) build on WS-Addressing. The full WS-Addressing specification is available at *http://www.w3.org/TR/ws-addr-core/*.

This specification defines two constructs that are normally found in the transport layer. The purpose of these constructs is to convey addressing information in a transport-neutral manner. These two constructs are *endpoint references* and *message addressing properties*.

Endpoint References

So far, we have used the terms *initial sender*, *intermediary*, and *ultimate receiver* to describe the entities participating in a message exchange. These participants can also be considered *service endpoints*. Simply defined, a service endpoint is a resource that can be the target of a message. Endpoint references, as defined in the WS-Addressing specification, are a way to refer to a service endpoint.

Can't we just use a URL to identify the target of a message? URLs will work in some cases, but not all. URLs are not well suited for expressing certain types of references. For example, many services will create multiple server object instances, and we might want to send a message to a particular instance of the server object. In this case, a simple URL just won't do. Based on our experience with the Internet, we might assume that we could add parameters to the address, thereby associating our message with a specific set of server objects. This introduces a few problems. For example, adding parameters to a URL will tightly bind our message to a transport, and we might not know the specific parameters until after we have initiated contact with the server (as is the case with Amazon's session IDs).

A Legitimate Debate

It's reasonable to ask the question "Why do we need more than a URL to refer to a service endpoint?" In fact, this is a really good question, and one that is actively debated in distributed architecture communities today. On one side of the discussion is a community that says a service should be referenceable via a URL. Furthermore, it is even possible to reference a specific instance of a service through a URL, as this is commonly done on the Internet today. All you have to do to prove this point is take a look at the URL generated as you purchase something at Amazon.com. You'll notice that after you sign in, your URL changes to contain a unique session ID. That session ID is tracked on the Amazon server and associated with you and your shopping cart. The people on this side of the debate see no reason to ever venture outside of describing a service with the URL, and they use the global adoption of the Internet as evidence of the viability of their position. Representational State Transfer (REST) is an architectural style that embraces this mode of thought. WCF can be used in the REST architectures.

On the other side of the debate is a group that says that HTTP URLs and the PUT/DELETE/GET/POST HTTP commands are not sufficient for all services. If we take another look at the Amazon example, several things are implicit. For example:

- HTTP is always the right transport.
- Security is provided via the transport (HTTPS).
- We need to secure only the message transmission (from client to Web server).
- It is OK to make a request for session-specific parameters.

The people on this side of the debate claim that these limitations are not acceptable for all services and distributed applications. In their opinion, service orientation demands transport independence and security outside the transport. Those who agree with SOAP and the WS-* specifications embrace this side of the debate.

In my view, there is room for both architectural styles, and each has its place. There is no question that the architecture of Amazon.com is wildly successful for publicly available services, but for back-end processing, I do not think that the implicit limitations in a REST architecture will work in all circumstances. The big limitations I see with the REST architectural style are dependence on a single transport, a lack of message-based security, and a lack of transactional support.

Clearly, WCF can be used in SOAP/WS-* implementations, and most of this book is dedicated to describing these concepts. In future releases of WCF, there will be more support for REST architectures.

URI, URL, and URN

The terms URI, URL, and URN (Uniform Resource Indicator, Uniform Resource Locator, and Uniform Resource Name) are used frequently in the WS-* specifications. To comprehend the full impact of what the WS-* specifications reference, we must understand the subtle differences between these three terms. In general, URI, URL, and URN are ways to name and/or locate a resource. If we were to think of the information world as an information space, a URI is a string that one can use to locate or name a point in that space. A URL, as opposed to a URI, is strictly intended to locate a resource. A URN, as opposed to a URL, is strictly intended to name a resource. From a set perspective, the URL and URN sets are members of the greater URI set.

These logical properties are physically implemented as XML Infoset element information items. Some properties, like *Reference Properties*, *Reference Parameters*, and *Policy*, can wrap other XML element information items. Here's how these properties can be represented in XML:

```
<wsa:EndpointReference xmlns:wsa="http://schemas.xmlSOAP...">
  <wsa:Address> ... </wsa:Address>
  <wsa:ReferenceProperties> ... </wsa:ReferenceProperties>
  <wsa:ReferenceParameters> ... </wsa:ReferenceParameters>
  <wsa:PortType> ... </wsa:PortType>
  <wsa:ServiceName> ... </wsa:ServiceName>
  <wsp:Policy> ... </wsp:Policy>
</wsa:EndpointReference>
```

Message Information Headers

WS-Addressing also defines a set of standard SOAP headers that can be used to fully address a message. As you might expect, these headers are actually XML Infoset element information items that represent the same functionality we derived in the section "Addressing the Message" earlier in this chapter. The real benefit seen here is a standard set of headers whose function can be commonly agreed upon between application vendors.

The following code snippet contains message information headers and their data types as defined in the WS-Addressing specification. These headers should look quite familiar:

```
<wsa:MessageID> xs:anyURI </wsa:MessageID>
<wsa:RelatesTo RelationshipType="…"?> xs:anyURI </wsa:RelatesTo>
<wsa:To> xs:anyURI </wsa:To>
<wsa:Action> xs:anyURI </wsa:Action>
<wsa:From> endpoint-reference </wsa:From>
<wsa:ReplyTo> endpoint-reference </wsa:ReplyTo>
<wsa:FaultTo> endpoint-reference </wsa:FaultTo>
```

Notice that the *MessageID*, *RelatesTo*, *To*, and *Action* elements are of type *xs:anyURI*. Why is *To* of type *xs:anyURI* instead of an endpoint reference? After all, we just went through great pains describing the reasons a simple URI is not enough to address a message. The answer lies in how additional properties that would normally be in an endpoint reference are serialized into a message header. WS-Addressing defines a default way to represent an endpoint reference that happens to be the target of a message as follows.

If a message is going to be sent to the endpoint reference as described here:

```
<wsa:EndpointReference xmlns:wsa="..." xmlns:wnt="...">
  <wsa:Address>http://wintellect.com/OrderService</wsa:Address>
  <wsa:ReferenceProperties>
    <wnt:OrderID>9876543</wnt:OrderID>
  </wsa:ReferenceProperties>
  <wsa:ReferenceParameters>
    <wnt:ShoppingCart>123456</wnt:ShoppingCart>
  </wsa:ReferenceParameters>
</wsa:EndpointReference>
```

That endpoint reference can be serialized in a message as follows:

```
<S:Envelope xmlns:S="..." xmlns:wsa="..." xmlns:wnt="... ">
  <S:Header>
    ...
    <wsa:To>http://wintellect.com/RcvService</wsa:To>
    <wnt:OrderID>9876543</wnt:OrderID>
    <wnt:ShoppingCart>123456</wnt:ShoppingCart>
    ...
  </S:Header>
  <S:Body>
    ...
  </S:Body>
</S:Envelope>
```

Notice that the *ReferenceProperty* and *ReferenceParameter* elements for *To* were promoted to full-fledged headers, no longer subordinate to the *EndpointReference* element. This happens only for the *To* element, as the *From*, *FaultTo*, and *ReplyTo* elements are endpoint references.

Message Information Header Block Dependencies

As you might expect, certain message information header blocks depend on other message information header blocks. For example, if a *ReplyTo* header block is present, it would stand to reason that a *MessageID* header must also be present. Table 2-2 describes the dependencies of the standard message information headers.

Table 2-2   Message Information Header Dependencies

Header #	Header Name	Min Occurs	Max Occurs	Depends On
1	wsa:MessageID	0	1	N/A
2	wsa:RelatesTo	0	Unbounded	N/A
3	wsa:ReplyTo	0	1	1
4	wsa:From	0	1	N/A
5	wsa:FaultTo	0	1	1
6	wsa:To	1	1	N/A
7	wsa:Action	1	1	N/A

The Four Tenets of Service Orientation

So far, we have explored the concept of service orientation, looked at the structure of service-oriented messages, examined the requirements for message addresses, and discussed the industry standard for message addressing. If you understand the motivation for a standard addressing structure in an SO message, then it is not much of a stretch to understand the principles of service orientation. Every service-oriented design adheres to the following four principles (often called the four tenets).

Explicit Boundaries

In service orientation, services can interact with each other by using messages. To put it another way, services can send messages across their service boundary to other services. Services can send and receive messages, and the shapes of the messages that can be sent or received define the service boundaries. These boundaries are well defined, clearly stated, and the only accessible point for the service's functionality. More practically, if Service1 wants to interact with Service2, Service1 must send a message to Service2. In contrast, an object-oriented or component-oriented world would demand that Service1 should create an instance of Service2 (or a proxy referring to Service2). In this case, the boundary between these services is blurred, since Service1 is, for all intents and purposes, in control of Service2.

If Service1 sends a message to Service2, does it matter where Service2 is located? The answer is no, as long as Service1 is allowed to send the message to Service2. One must assume, however, that sending a message across a boundary comes with a cost. This cost must be taken into consideration when building services. Specifically, our services should cross service boundaries as few times as possible. The antithesis of an efficient service design is one that is "chatty."

Service Autonomy (Sort Of)

In my opinion, service-oriented systems should strive to be sort of autonomous, because pure autonomy is impossible. True service autonomy means that a service has no dependencies on anything outside itself. In the physical world, these types of entities are nonexistent, and I doubt we will see many pure autonomous services in the distributed computing world. A truly autonomous service is one that will dynamically build communication channels, dynamically negotiate security policy, dynamically interrogate message schemas, and dynamically exchange messages with other services. A purely autonomous service reeks of an overly late-bound architecture. We have all seen these sorts of systems, whether in the excessive use of *IUnknown* or the compulsive use of reflection. The bottom line is that developers and architects have proven time after time that these types of architectures just do not work (even though they look great on paper). I must temper these comments by admitting that movement in the area of service orientation is picking up at a blinding pace. Just five years ago, service-oriented applications were few and far between, and now they are commonplace. This momentum may take us to a place where purely autonomous services are the way to go, but for now, I think it is reasonable to settle for a diluted view of autonomy.

So what does autonomy mean in a practical sense? From a practical perspective, it means that no service has control of the lifetime, availability, or boundaries of another service. The opposite of this behavior is exhibited with the SQL 2000 database and agent services. Both of these services are hosted as separate Microsoft Windows services, but the agent service has a built-in dependency on the database service. Stopping the database service means that the agent service will be stopped as well. The tight coupling between these two services means that they can never be considered as separate, or versioned independently of each other. This tight coupling reduces the flexibility of each service, and thereby their use in the enterprise.

Contract Sharing

Since service orientation focuses on the messages that are passed between participants, there must be a way to describe those messages and what is required for a successful message exchange. In a broad sense, these descriptions are called *contracts*. Contracts are not a new programming paradigm. On the Windows platform, contracts came into their own with COM and DCOM. A COM component can be accessed only through a published and shared contract. Physically, a COM contract is an interface, expressed in Interface Definition Language (IDL). This contract shields the consumer from knowing implementation details. As long as the contract doesn't break, the consumer can theoretically tolerate COM component software upgrades and updates.

Service-oriented systems conceptually extend the notion of COM IDL contracts. Service-oriented systems express contracts in the widely understood languages of XSD and WSDL. More specifically, schemas are used to describe message structures, and WSDL is used to describe message endpoints. Together, these XML-based contracts express the shape of the messages that can be sent and received, endpoint addresses, network protocols, security requirements, and so on. The universal nature of XML allows senders and ultimate recipients to run on any platform more easily than with a technology like COM. Among other things, a sender must know the message structure and format of the receiving application, and this is answered by the contract. In essence, a message sender requires a dependency on the contract, rather than the service itself.

Compatibility Based on Policy

Services must be able to describe the circumstances under which other services can interact with it. For example, some services might require that any initial sender possess a valid Active Directory directory service account or an X509 certificate. In this case, the service should express these requirements in an XML-based policy. At the time of this writing, WS-Policy is the standard grammar for expressing these types of requirements. In a fanatically devoted service-oriented world, message senders would interrogate this metadata prior to sending a message, further decoupling a message sender from a message receiver. For the same reasons stated earlier, it is more probable that service policy will be interrogated at design time more than at run time.

Putting It All Together

I hope that by this point in the chapter you have a clear conceptual view of service orientation. For the next few pages, let's look at how this concept can physically take shape in WCF applications. In our example, we will be building a simple order processing service that receives customer orders. To keep things simple, there are two message participants, as shown in Figure 2-3.

Figure 2-3   A simple message exchange

The purpose of these code samples is to solidify your vision of service orientation and provide an introduction to WCF, not to detail every aspect of WCF or to build a fully functional order processing system. The types and mechanisms introduced in these examples will be detailed throughout this book.

The Contract

Typically, the place to start in a service-oriented application is to create the contract. To keep our example simple, an order will contain a product ID, a quantity, and a status message. Given these three fields, an order could be represented with the following pseudo-schema:

```
<Order>
  <ProdID>xs:integer</ProdID>
  <Qty>xs:integer</Qty>
  <Status>xs:string</Status>
</Order>
```

From our message anatomy and addressing discussions, we know that messages need more addressing structure if they are going to use WS-Addressing. In our order processing service, both the sender and the receiver agree to use SOAP messages that adhere to the WS-Addressing specification to dictate the structure of the message. Given these rules, the following is an example of a properly structured message:

```
<s:Envelope xmlns:s="http://www.w3.org/2003/05/soap-envelope" xmlns:wsa="http://
schemas.xmlsoap.org/ws/2004/08/addressing">
  <s:Header>
    <wsa:Action s:mustUnderstand="1">urn:SubmitOrder</wsa:Action>
    <wsa:MessageID>4</wsa:MessageID>
    <wsa:ReplyTo>
      <wsa:Address> http://schemas.xmlsoap.org/ws/2004/08/addressing/role/anonymous
      </wsa:Address>
    </wsa:ReplyTo>
    <wsa:To s:mustUnderstand="1">http://localhost:8000/Order</wsa:To>
  </s:Header>
  <s:Body>
    <Order>
      <ProdID>6</ProdID>
      <Qty>6</Qty>
      <Status>order placed</Status>
    </Order>
  </s:Body>
</s:Envelope>
```

After we have created the schemas that describe our messages, our next step is to define the endpoint that will receive those messages. For this, we can turn to WSDL. You might be thinking to yourself: "I am not really in the mood to deal with raw schemas or WSDL." Well, you are not alone. The WCF team has provided a way for us to express a contract (both the schema and the WSDL) in the Microsoft .NET Framework language of our choosing (in this book, it will be C#). Basically, the expression of a contract in C# can be turned into XSD-based and WSDL-based contracts on demand.

When choosing to express our contracts in C#, we can choose to define a class or an interface. An example of a contract defined as an interface in C# is shown here:

```
// file: Contracts.cs
using System;
using System.ServiceModel;
using System.ServiceModel.Channels;

// define the contract for the service
[ServiceContract(Namespace = "http://wintellect.com/ProcessOrder")]
public interface IProcessOrder {
    [OperationContract(Action="urn:SubmitOrder")]
    void SubmitOrder(Message order);
}
```

Notice the *ServiceContractAttribute* and *OperationContractAttribute* annotations. We will talk more about these attributes in Chapter 9, "Contracts." For now, it is enough to know that this interface is distinguished from other .NET Framework interfaces through the addition of these custom attributes. Also notice the signature of the *SubmitOrder* interface method. The only parameter in this method is of type *System.ServiceModel.Message*. This parameter represents any message that can be sent to a service from an initial sender or intermediary. The *Message* type is a very interesting and somewhat complex type that will be discussed thoroughly in Chapter 5, "Messages," but for now, assume that the message sent by the initial sender can be represented by the *System.ServiceModel.Message* type.

Regardless of the way we choose to express our contracts, it should be agreed upon and shared before further work is done on either the sender or the receiver applications. In practice, the receiver defines the required message structure contract, and the sender normally attempts to build and send messages that adhere to this contract.

There is nothing preventing the sender from sending messages that do not adhere to the contract defined by the receiver. For this reason, the receiver's first task should be to validate received messages against the contract. This approach helps ensure that the receiver's data structures do not become corrupted. These points are frequently debated in distributed development communities, so there are other opinions on this matter.

This contract can now be compiled into an assembly. Once the compilation is complete, the assembly can be distributed to the sender and the receiver. This assembly represents the contract between the sender and the receiver. While there will certainly be times when the contract will change, we should consider the contract immutable after it has been shared. We will discuss contract versioning in Chapter 9.

Now that we have our contract in place, let's build the receiver application. The first order of business is to build a class that implements the interface defined in our contract:

```
// File: Receiver.cs

// Implement the interface defined in the contract assembly
public sealed class MyService : IProcessOrder {

  public void SubmitOrder(Message order) {
    // Do work here
  }
}
```

Because this is a simple application, we are content to print text to the console and write the inbound message to a file:

```
// File: Receiver.cs
using System;
using System.Xml;
using System.IO;
using System.ServiceModel;
using System.ServiceModel.Channels;


// Implement the interface defined in the contract assembly
public sealed class MyService : IProcessOrder {

  public void SubmitOrder(Message order) {
    // Create a file name from the MessageID
    String fileName = "Order" + order.Headers.MessageId.ToString() + ".xml";

    // Signal that a message has arrived
    Console.WriteLine("Message ID {0} received",
      order.Headers.MessageId.ToString());

    // create an XmlDictionaryWriter to write to a file
    XmlDictionaryWriter writer = XmlDictionaryWriter.CreateTextWriter(
      new FileStream(fileName, FileMode.Create));

    // write the message to a file
    order.WriteMessage(writer);

    writer.Close();
  }
}
```

Our next task is to allow the *MyService* type to receive inbound messages. To receive a message:

- *MyService* must be loaded into an AppDomain.

- *MyService* (or another type) must be listening for inbound messages.

- An instance of this type must be created at the appropriate time and referenced as long as it is needed (to prevent the garbage collector from releasing the object's memory).

- When a message arrives, it must be dispatched to a *MyService* instance and the *SubmitOrder* method invoked.

These tasks are commonly performed via a *host*. We will talk more about hosts in Chapter 10, but for now, assume that our AppDomain is hosted in a console application and the type responsible for managing the lifetime of and dispatching messages to *MyService* objects is the *System.ServiceModel.ServiceHost* type. Our console application is shown here:

```
// File: ReceiverHost.cs

using System;
using System.Xml;
using System.ServiceModel;

internal static class ReceiverHost {
  public static void Main() {
    // Define the binding for the service
    WSHttpBinding binding = new WSHttpBinding(SecurityMode.None);
    // Use the text encoder
    binding.MessageEncoding = WSMessageEncoding.Text;

    // Define the address for the service
    Uri addressURI = new Uri(@"http://localhost:4000/Order");

    // Instantiate a Service host using the MyService type
    ServiceHost svc = new ServiceHost(typeof(MyService));

    // Add an endpoint to the service with the
    // contract, binding, and address
    svc.AddServiceEndpoint(typeof(IProcessOrder),
                           binding,
                           addressURI);

    // Open the service host to start listening
    svc.Open();

    Console.WriteLine("The receiver is ready");
    Console.ReadLine();

    svc.Close();
  }
}
```

In our console application, we must set some properties of the service before we can host it. As you will see in subsequent chapters, every service contains an *address*, a *binding*, and a *contract*. These mechanisms are often called the ABCs of WCF. For now, assume the following:

- An address describes where the service will be listening for inbound messages.

- A binding describes how the service will be listening for messages.

- A contract describes what sorts of messages the service will receive.

In our example, we are using the *WSHttpBinding* binding to define how the service will listen for inbound messages. We'll talk more about bindings in Chapter 8. Our service also uses the *Uri* type to define the address our service will be listening on. Our service then instantiates a *ServiceHost* object that uses our *MyService* class to provide shape to the *ServiceHost*. *ServiceHost*s do not have default endpoints, so we must add our own by calling the *AddServiceEndpoint* instance method. It is at this point that our console application is ready to start listening at the address *http://localhost:8000/Order* for inbound messages. A call to the *Open* instance method begins the listening loop (among other things).

You might be wondering what happens when a message arrives at *http://localhost:8000/ Order*. The answer depends on what sort of message arrives at the endpoint. For that, let's switch gears and build our simple message sending console application. At a high level, our message sender is going to have to know the following:

- Where the service is located (the address)
- How the service expects messages to be sent (the service binding)
- What types of messages the service expects (the contract)

Assuming that these facts are known, the following is a reasonable message sending application:

```
// File: Sender.cs

using System;
using System.Text;
using System.Xml;
using System.ServiceModel;
using System.Runtime.Serialization;
using System.IO;
using System.ServiceModel.Channels;

public static class Sender {

  public static void Main(){
    Console.WriteLine("Press ENTER when the receiver is ready");
    Console.ReadLine();

    // address of the receiving application
    EndpointAddress address =
      new EndpointAddress(@"http://localhost:4000/Order");

    // Define how we will communicate with the service
    // In this case, use the WS-* compliant HTTP binding
    WSHttpBinding binding = new WSHttpBinding(SecurityMode.None);
    binding.MessageEncoding = WSMessageEncoding.Text;

    // Create a channel
    ChannelFactory<IProcessOrder> channel =
      new ChannelFactory<IProcessOrder>(binding, address);
```

```
        // Use the channel factory to create a proxy
        IProcessOrder proxy = channel.CreateChannel();

        // Create some messages
        Message msg = null;
        for (Int32 i = 0; i < 10; i++) {
          // Call our helper method to create the message
          // notice the use of the Action defined in
          // the IProcessOrder contract...
          msg = GenerateMessage(i,i);

          // Give the message a MessageID SOAP header
          UniqueId uniqueId = new UniqueId(i.ToString());
          msg.Headers.MessageId = uniqueId;

          Console.WriteLine("Sending Message # {0}", uniqueId.ToString());

          // Give the message an Action SOAP header
          msg.Headers.Action = "urn:SubmitOrder";
          // Send the message
          proxy.SubmitOrder(msg);
        }
      }

    // method for creating a Message
    private static Message GenerateMessage(Int32 productID, Int32 qty) {

      MemoryStream stream = new MemoryStream();

      XmlDictionaryWriter writer = XmlDictionaryWriter.CreateTextWriter(
        stream, Encoding.UTF8, false);

      writer.WriteStartElement("Order");
      writer.WriteElementString("ProdID", productID.ToString());
      writer.WriteElementString("Qty", qty.ToString());
      writer.WriteEndElement();

      writer.Flush();
      stream.Position = 0;

      XmlDictionaryReader reader = XmlDictionaryReader.CreateTextReader(
        stream, XmlDictionaryReaderQuotas.Max);

      // Create the message with the Action and the body
      return Message.CreateMessage(MessageVersion.Soap12WSAddressing10,
                                   String.Empty,
                                   reader);
    }
  }
```

Try not to get too distracted by the *ChannelFactory* type just yet—we will fully explore this type in Chapter 4. For now, notice the code in the *for* loop. The instructions in the loop generate 10 messages and assign each one a pseudo-unique ID and an action.

At this point, we should have two executables (ReceiverHost.exe and Sender.exe) representing an ultimate receiver and an initial sender. If we run both console applications, wait for the receiver to initialize, and press ENTER on the initial sender application, we should see the following on the receiver:

```
The receiver is ready
Message ID 0 received
Message ID 1 received
Message ID 2 received
Message ID 3 received
Message ID 4 received
Message ID 5 received
Message ID 6 received
Message ID 7 received
Message ID 8 received
Message ID 9 received
```

Congratulations! You have just written a service-oriented application with WCF. Remember that the service is writing inbound messages to a file. If we examine one of the files that our service wrote, we see the following:

```
<s:Envelope xmlns:s="http://www.w3.org/2003/05/soap-envelope"
            xmlns:a="http://www.w3.org/2005/08/addressing">
  <s:Header>
    <a:Action s:mustUnderstand="1">urn:SubmitOrder</a:Action>
    <a:MessageID>1</a:MessageID>
    <a:ReplyTo>
      <a:Address>http://www.w3.org/2005/08/addressing/anonymous</a:Address>
    </a:ReplyTo>
    <a:To s:mustUnderstand="1">http://localhost:4000/Order</a:To>
  </s:Header>
  <s:Body>
    <Order>
      <ProdID>1</ProdID>
      <Qty>1</Qty>
    </Order>
  </s:Body>
</s:Envelope>
```

The headers in this message should look eerily similar to the ones we see in the WS-Addressing specification, and their values should look like the properties we set in our message sending application. In fact, the *System.ServiceModel.Message* type exposes a property named *Headers* that is of type *System.ServiceModel.MessageHeaders*. This *MessageHeaders* type exposes other properties that represent the WS-Addressing message headers. The idea here is that we can use the WCF object-oriented programming model to affect a service-oriented SOAP message.

Why SO Makes Sense

Developers and architects often ask me, "Why do I need service orientation?" My response is simple: scalability, maintainability, interoperability, and flexibility. In the past, distributed component technologies like DCOM tightly bound distributed components together. At the bare minimum, these distributed components had to share a common type system and often a common runtime. Given these dependencies, upgrades and software updates can become complex, time-consuming, and expensive endeavors. Service-oriented applications, in contrast, do not engender the same sorts of dependencies and therefore exhibit behaviors that better address enterprise computing needs.

Versioning

Application requirements change over time. It has been this way since the dawn of computing, and there are no signs of this behavior slowing down in the future. Developers, architects, and project managers have gone to great lengths to apply processes to software development in hopes of regulating and controlling the amount and pace of change an application endures. Over the lifetime of an application, however, some of the assumptions made during the development process will certainly turn out to be invalid. In some cases, the resultant application changes will cause a cascading series of changes in other parts of the application. Autonomous, explicitly bounded, contract-based service-oriented applications provide several layers of encapsulation that buffer the effects of versioning one part of a system. In a service-oriented application, the only agreement between the message sender and the receiver is the contract. Both the sender and the receiver are free to change their implementations as they wish, as long as the contract remains intact. While this was also true of component architectures, the universal nature of service-oriented contracts further decouples the sender and receiver from implementation, thereby making the upgrade and version cycle shorter. Service orientation does not, however, remove the need for a good versioning process.

Load Balancing

Every application has bottlenecks, and sometimes these bottlenecks can prevent an application from scaling to evolving throughput demands. Figure 2-4 shows an order processing Web site built with components.

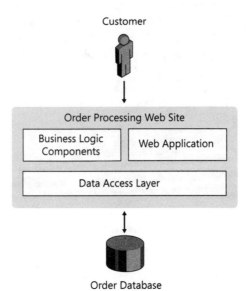

Figure 2-4   A traditional component-oriented application

In this scenario, data retrieval might be the bottleneck. If that is the case, one way to scale the component-driven Web site is shown in Figure 2-5.

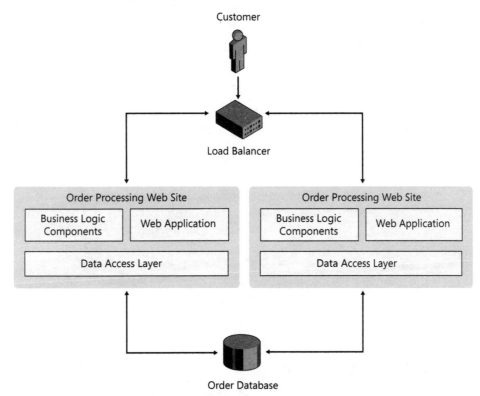

Figure 2-5   Scaling a component-oriented application

Essentially, we re-create the entire Web application on another server and use a load balancer to redirect requests to the least busy Web server. This type of scalability has proven effective in the past, but it is inefficient and costly, and creates configuration problems, especially during versioning time.

A service-oriented way to scale the order processing system in the Figure 2-5 example is shown in Figure 2-6.

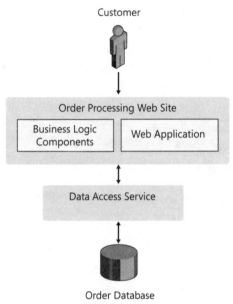

Figure 2-6   Using services

Service-oriented applications can more easily scale the parts of the application that need to be scaled. This reduces total cost of ownership and simplifies configuration management.

Platform Changes over Time

Platforms change, sometimes dramatically, over time. This is true within any platform vendor, as patches and service packs, and ultimately new versions of a platform, are constantly being released. With distributed components, there is often a dependency on a platform component runtime. For example, how does an application architect know that a DCOM component will behave the same on servers running Microsoft Windows Server 2000, Windows Professional 2000, Windows XP, or Windows Server 2003? Since a DCOM component relies on the component runtimes on each of these systems, many testing scenarios appear seemingly out of thin air. When you start to think about testing within each possible configuration, service pack, and hotfix, your nose might bleed from anxiety.

Many of these problems disappear when applications become service oriented. This is largely due to the fact that messaging contracts are expressed in a platform-neutral XML grammar.

This contract language decouples the sender from the receiver. The sender's responsibility is to generate and send a message that adheres to the contract, while the receiver's responsibility is to receive and process these messages. No platform-specific information must be serialized with the message, so endpoints are free to version their platform as they want. Furthermore, testing is much simpler, since each endpoint has to test only to the explicit service boundary.

Content-Based Routing

The nature of service-oriented messages lends itself to routing scenarios that have been very difficult in the past. We can build some business rules around our order processing example for an illustration:

- Orders can be for new items or repairs to existing items.
- Orders for new items should ultimately be sent to the manufacturing system.
- Orders for repairs should be sent to the repair system.
- Both orders, however, must be sent to the accounting and scheduling systems before they are sent to their ultimate destination.

Service-oriented messaging applications are well suited for fulfilling these types of requirements. Essentially, routable information can be placed in SOAP message headers and used by any endpoint to determine a message path.

End-to-End Security

Many distributed systems secure communication at the transport level in a point-to-point manner. While the transmission event might be secure, the data transmitted might not be secure after the transmission. Log files and other auditing mechanisms often contain information that is secured when transmitted, and as a result, they are frequent targets of many security attacks. It is possible, however, using standard XML security mechanisms, to provide end-to-end security with service-oriented messages. Even if the message is persisted into a log file and later compromised, if the message was secured using one of the standard XML security mechanisms, the data in the message can be kept confidential.

Interoperability

When an initial sender sends a message to an ultimate receiver, the initial sender does not need to have a dependency on which platform the ultimate receiver is running. As you've seen with the binary message encoder, this is not *always* the case. Some message formats can introduce platform dependencies, but this is a matter of choice. In the purest sense, service-oriented applications are platform agnostic. This platform independence is a direct result of the universal nature of messaging contracts expressed in XML grammar. It is truly possible (not just theoretically) to send a message to an endpoint and have no idea what platform that endpoint is using. This resonates with businesspeople and managers because systems do not need to be completely replaced with a homogenous set of applications on a single platform.

Summary

This chapter illustrates the motivation for service orientation, and some of the basics of a service-oriented system. Service orientation requires a focus on the messages that an application sends, receives, or processes. Service-oriented systems can take functionality previously reserved for a transport, and place it in the structure of a message (addresses, security information, relational information, etc.). Focusing on the message provides a way to remove dependencies on platforms, hardware, and runtimes. In my view, the version resiliency of a service-oriented application is the biggest win for most IT organizations, because choreographing system-wide upgrades is one of the more expensive parts of maintenance. In the next chapter, we see some of the different ways we introduce the concepts necessary to build advanced messaging applications.

Chapter 3
Message Exchange Patterns, Topologies, and Choreographies

When designing messaging applications, it is necessary to consider how messages flow between the sender, any intermediaries, and the receiver (the previous chapter described these messaging participants). The welter of message exchange possibilities in a system can be described at varying levels of detail. These levels of detail are generally known as Message Exchange Patterns (MEPs), Message Topologies, and Message Choreographies. When viewed as a whole, these three levels of detail allow us to abstractly describe any messaging scenario. This chapter examines message exchange patterns, message topologies, and message choreographies and how they are used to provide advanced functionality in our Microsoft Windows Communication Foundation (WCF) applications.

Message Exchange Patterns

The most granular level of detail we use to describe a message exchange is a *Message Exchange Pattern* (MEP). According to the W3C drafts (*http://www.w3.org/2002/ws/cg/2/07/meps.html*), a MEP is "a template that describes the message exchange between messaging participants." The industry has generally accepted that a MEP is limited to one logical connection between one sender and one receiver. Since MEPs are a somewhat abstract concept, it is helpful to closely look at some real-world examples for clarification. Let's examine the following phone conversation between me and a friend as we discuss a football game:

1. I pick up my phone and dial Rusty's phone number.

2. Rusty picks up his phone.

3. Rusty says, "Hello."

4. I say, "Did you watch the game today?"

5. Rusty says, "Yep—it was awful. I can't believe we didn't win."

6. Rusty says, "They totally choked."

The conversation continues...

Steps 1 through 3 can be thought of as transmission-specific events (I call Rusty, and he acknowledges that he is ready to talk). In step 4, I send Rusty a message in the form of a question, and custom dictates that he should answer. In step 5, Rusty sends me a message in response to my question. Step 6 is an unsolicited message sent to me that may or may not solicit a response. The message correlation is implicit, since it is part of the natural flow of conversation. If this correlation weren't assumed, I would have no idea exactly what he thought was awful; it might have been a sales call or a chess match.

In this scenario, both Rusty and I are free to talk at will (as shown in step 6), and we are even free to talk over one another. As we all know, this is the nature of most phone conversations. Not all phone conversations are two-way; some are one-way. A one-way conversation might happen by design, as in a shareholder conference call, or because one party terminates the call before a response can be sent. Let's look at another phone call to illustrate:

1. Lewis (my boss) picks up his phone and dials my phone number.
2. I pick up my phone and say, "Hello."
3. Lewis says, "You're doing a great job. I'm giving you a 100 percent raise, effective immediately."
4. Lewis then hangs up his phone.
5. I call Lewis back.
6. Lewis answers his phone.
7. I say. "That is too generous; I will accept only a 50 percent raise."
8. I hang up the phone.
9. Lewis calls me back.
10. I answer my phone.
11. Lewis says, "A 100 percent raise is final, and I am throwing in a blue Porsche 911 Turbo to make sure that you can get to engagements faster."
12. Lewis then hangs up his phone.

In the preceding scenario, I can respond, but Lewis is so intent on giving me raises and perks that he isn't listening for my response. I have to call him back to further the discussion. Conceptually speaking, responses in a message exchange require the sender to listen for a response either in an existing connection or in a new connection.

Conversations can even fit a more rigid model. Consider the communications between a commercial airline pilot and a radio tower. If you have ever listened to these communications, the structure is obvious:

1. The control tower calls to the pilot: "Contoso 437, turn to 180 degrees, 300 knots, descend to 10,000 feet."

2. The pilot responds: "Contoso 437, turning to 180 degrees, 300 knots, descending to 10,000 feet."

In this scenario, the heading change request initiated by the tower demands a response. If no response is transmitted from the plane, the now-annoyed air traffic controller will repeat the command until a proper response is transmitted, or some other action is taken. Furthermore, this protocol demands that the pilot not interrupt the tower while the tower is communicating.

These simple analogies go a long way to describing the interactions between messaging participants in a service-oriented application. In general terms, MEPs are classified according to how participants interact with each other and, more specifically, the number of responses that are allowed and whether those responses require new logical connections between the sender and receiver. While there might be a womptillion different ways to talk on the phone or on a radio, there are generally three types of MEPs in the service-oriented world: datagram, request-response, and duplex.

The Datagram MEP

Figure 3-1 illustrates the datagram MEP. Also called *simplex*, this MEP represents a one-way message send, or a fire-and-forget send. Messages sent using this MEP are called datagrams. Conceptually, a datagram is similar to leaving a voice-mail message in the sport of phone tag. While you are leaving the voice-mail message, you probably don't expect a response *during the call*. You might, however, expect a response in the form of a return call. Responses to datagram messages are considered *out of band*. In other words, responses to datagrams require a new connection between a sender and a receiver.

Figure 3-1   The datagram MEP

Datagrams and WSDL

A datagram MEP is expressed in Web Services Description Language (WSDL) as an operation that contains a *wsdl:input* element and no *wsdl:output* elements. For example, the following WSDL snippet describes one operation that accepts input only and is therefore an operation that uses the datagram MEP:

```
...
<wsdl:portType name="ISomeContract" ...>
    <wsdl:operation name="SomeOperation">
      <wsdl:input wsa10:Action="urn:SomeActionInput" ... />
    </wsdl:operation>
</wsdl:portType>
...
```

Datagrams and WCF Contracts

Creating a WCF application that uses the datagram MEP is fairly straightforward. As always, we start with the contract:

```
// File: Contract.cs
using System;
using System.ServiceModel;
using System.ServiceModel.Channels;

[ServiceContract(Namespace="http://wintellect.com/SomeContract",
  Name="ISomeContract")]
public interface ISomeContract {
  [OperationContract(Name="SomeOperation",
                     Action="urn:SomeActionInput",
                     IsOneWay=true)]
  void SomeOperation(Message message);
}
```

There are two important things to notice in this example: the *void* return type on the *SomeOperation* method and the *IsOneWay* instance property on the *OperationContractAttribute* type.

The *void* Return Type   Because we are using a C# interface method to describe a datagram messaging operation, we need to use a return type that reflects this one-way messaging operation. Methods that are used to describe datagram messaging operations *must* have a *void* return type. Specifying some other return type results in an *InvalidOperationException* thrown by the WCF runtime during the verification of the contract.

The *OperationContractAttribute's IsOneWay* Property   Defining an interface method with a *void* return type is not enough when defining a datagram operation. Consider the following contract:

```
// File: Contract.cs
using System;
using System.ServiceModel;
using System.ServiceModel.Channels;

[ServiceContract(Namespace="http://wintellect.com/SomeContract",
  Name="ISomeContract")]
public interface ISomeContract {
  [OperationContract(Name="SomeOperation",
                     Action="urn:SomeActionInput",
                     ReplyAction="urn:SomeActionOutput")]
  void SomeOperation(Message message);
}
```

This contract can ultimately be rendered in WSDL as follows:

```
<wsdl:portType name="ISomeContract" ...>
  <wsdl:operation name="SomeOperation">
    <wsdl:input wsaw:Action="urn:SomeActionInput" .../>
    <wsdl:output wsaw:Action="urn:SomeActionOutput".../>
  </wsdl:operation>
</wsdl:portType>
```

The presence of the *wsdl:output* element indicates to the sender that a reply will follow the message send. Since the return type of our interface method is *void*, the message will have an empty *<Body>* element. Even though there is no data sent in the body, this is still a reply. It is important to note that the WCF runtime must generate this reply and requires processing overhead every time a valid message is received. In WCF, the only way to remove this reply message is to set the *IsOneWay* instance property of the *OperationContractAttribute* to *true*. If this property is set to false by default, the setting makes the operation use the Request/Reply MEP (discussed shortly).

Error Handling Considerations

The datagram MEP introduces an interesting service-oriented twist in the area of error handling. As you'll see in Chapter 4, "WCF 101," errors may be serialized as SOAP faults, and these faults can be sent to the specified endpoint. With the datagram MEP, the sender is not under any obligation to listen for these faults. If the sender wants to receive these fault messages or have them sent to another endpoint, the sender must specify that endpoint in the *<FaultTo>* header block of outbound messages. It is then the receiver's responsibility to make its best effort to send these fault messages to the specified endpoint.

HTTP and the Datagram MEP

All transports support the datagram MEP, but some transports, like HTTP and HTTPS, have response mechanisms built into the transport. When messages are sent over one of these protocols, the sender expects to receive a reply, and the receiver expects to send a reply. For example, when we make an HTTP request for a Web page, we expect one HTML reply. Likewise, the Web server expects to be able to send the HTML reply to the client after it receives a request for a resource. HTTP replies are transmitted via the *transport backchannel*. For the purposes of this discussion, it is permissible to think of this backchannel as a listener that stops listening after the reply has been transmitted.

In WCF, when we send a datagram via HTTP, we are sending data over HTTP, and the reply is an HTTP response code of 202.[1] In general, when a datagram message is sent using a transport that demands these built-in acknowledgment mechanisms, the response contains a transport-specific acknowledgment and no message-specific information. The following is an example of the response to a datagram sent over HTTP:

```
HTTP/1.1 202 Accepted
Content-Length: 0
Server: Microsoft-HTTPAPI/1.0
Date: Sun, 25 Feb 2007 17:01:36 GMT
```

WCF applications that receive datagrams over HTTP send the 202 reply upon receipt of the datagram but before processing the datagram. This optimization means that the client does not wait unnecessarily for the transport reply, and the exchange is as close to one-way as possible.

The Request/Reply MEP

In a broad sense, the Internet is built on the Request/Reply MEP (also referred to as *half-duplex*). We have come to expect that a single Web page request will yield one HTML reply. If we would like to see another Web page, we initiate another Web request. In other words, the reply to our request is *in band*. Figure 3-2 conceptually illustrates the Request/Reply MEP.

---

1 An HTTP status code of 202 is defined as follows: The request has been accepted for processing, but the processing has not been completed. The request might or might not eventually be acted upon, as it might be disallowed when processing actually takes place. There is no facility for resending a status code from an asynchronous operation such as this.

The 202 response is intentionally noncommittal. Its purpose is to allow a server to accept a request for some other process (perhaps a batch-oriented process that is run only once per day) without requiring that the user agent's connection to the server persist until the process is completed. The entity returned with this response should include an indication of the request's current status and either a pointer to a status monitor or some estimate of when the user can expect the request to be fulfilled.

Figure 3-2   The Request/Reply MEP

> **Note**   The request/reply MEP is so pervasive that we hardly notice when we are using it. For the most part, our experience has conditioned us to think in terms of request/reply. For example, most of our component-based frameworks require us to call a method and wait for that method to return. Many distributed component frameworks (like DCOM) reinforced this conditioning, because these frameworks allowed us to call a method and wait for a response. As a result of our conditioning, many of us will default to the request/reply MEP when first working with WCF. I encourage you to "free your mind" from this default MEP by forcing yourself to consider the other MEPs that are possible in WCF. Doing so will open the door for more advanced functionality and higher performance by reducing bandwidth use in your applications.

Request/Reply and WSDL

Request/Reply MEPs are expressed in WSDL as an operation that has *wsdl:input* and *wsdl:output* elements. For example, the following WSDL snippet describes a Request/Reply MEP:

```
...
<wsdl:portType name="ISomeContract" ...>
    <wsdl:operation name="SomeOperation">
        <wsdl:input wsaw:Action="urn:SomeActionInput" ... />
        <wsdl:output wsaw:Action="urn:SomeActionOutput" ... />
    </wsdl:operation>
</wsdl:portType>
...
```

It is important to note the order of the *wsdl:input* and *wsdl:output* elements in this WSDL snippet. The order of these elements dictates that an input message must be received before an output message can be sent.

Request/Reply and WCF Contracts

WCF operation contracts use the Request/Reply MEP by default. Any return type that is considered serializable by WCF can be specified as a return type. (Chapter 9, "Contracts," discusses data and message serialization.) For example, the following contract uses Request/Reply:

```
// File: Contract.cs
using System;
using System.ServiceModel;
using System.ServiceModel.Channels;

[ServiceContract(Namespace="http://wintellect.com/SomeContract",
  Name="ISomeContract")]
public interface ISomeContract2 {
  [OperationContract(Name="SomeOperation",
                     Action="urn:SomeActionInput",
                     ReplyAction="urn:SomeActionOutput")]
  Message SomeOperation(Message message);
}
```

Transport Considerations

Some transports, like User Datagram Protocol (UDP) and MSMQ, are inherently one-way. As of the initial release of WCF, there is no out-of-the-box support for the Request/Reply MEP using MSMQ, and there is no support for UDP. Using the MSMQ transport with a Request/Reply MEP requires a connection between the sender and the receiver as well as a connection between the receiver and the sender. As a result, a custom channel is also required. We will examine how channels work in Chapter 6, "Channels."

As you saw in Chapter 2, "Service Orientation," there are several WS-Addressing header blocks that dictate where a receiving application should send a reply or fault. When using a transport like TCP, HTTP, or Named Pipes, the receiver can "send" the response over the transport backchannel. WS-Addressing states that the *<ReplyTo>* header block may be set to *http://www.w3.org/2005/08/addressing/anonymous* in these scenarios. This results in outbound messages that look like the following:

```
<s:Envelope ... >
  <s:Header>
    <a:Action s:mustUnderstand="1">urn:SomeActionRequest</a:Action>
    <a:MessageID>urn:12345</a:MessageID>
-   <a:ReplyTo>
      <a:Address>http://www.w3.org/2005/08/addressing/anonymous</a:Address>
    </a:ReplyTo>
    <a:To s:mustUnderstand="1">
      net.tcp://localhost:8000/SomeOperation
    </a:To>
    </s:Header>
    <s:Body>...</s:Body>
  </s:Envelope>
```

And reply messages look like the following:

```
<s:Envelope ... >
  <s:Header>
    <a:Action s:mustUnderstand="1">urn:SomeContractReply</a:Action>
    <a:RelatesTo>urn:12345</a:RelatesTo>
    <a:To s:mustUnderstand="1">
      http://www.w3.org/2005/08/addressing/anonymous
    </a:To>
    </s:Header>
    <s:Body>...</s:Body>
  </s:Envelope>
```

The Duplex MEP

Duplexing is the ability to simultaneously transmit and receive messages and is the sort of interaction we have come to expect in a phone conversation. In a messaging application, the duplex MEP defines a set of operations that allow simultaneous message passing from the sender to the receiver and vice versa. Figure 3-3 illustrates the Duplex MEP.

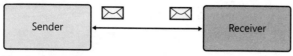

Figure 3-3   The Duplex MEP

The Duplex MEP and WSDL

Because both the sender and the receiver can freely pass messages back and forth in the Duplex MEP, the WSDL associated with this MEP contains two operations. One operation (*SomeOperation*) represents messages inbound to the receiver, and the other (*SomeCallbackOperation*) represents messages traveling from the receiver to the sender.

```
<wsdl:portType name="ISomeContract" ...>
  <wsdl:operation name="SomeOperation">
    <wsdl:input wsa10:Action="urn:SomeActionRequest" ... />
  </wsdl:operation>
  <wsdl:operation name="SomeCallbackOperation">
    <wsdl:output wsa10:Action="urn:SomeCallbackRequest" ... />
  </wsdl:operation>
</wsdl:portType>
```

In one sense, the duplex MEP is a combination of other MEPs. For example, the preceding WSDL snippet describes two datagram operations. In other words, a datagram can be sent from the sender to the receiver or vice versa. It is also possible that the messages sent between these participants rely on the request/reply MEP. Consider the following WSDL snippet:

```
<wsdl:portType name="ISomeContract">
  <wsdl:operation name="SomeOperation">
    <wsdl:input wsaw:Action="urn:SomeActionRequest" ... />
    <wsdl:output wsaw:Action="urn:SomeContractReply" ... />
  </wsdl:operation>
```

```
  <wsdl:operation name="SomeCallbackOperation">
    <wsdl:output wsaw:Action="urn:SomeCallbackContractRequest" ... />
    <wsdl:input wsaw:Action="urn:SomeCallbackContractReply" ... />
  </wsdl:operation>
</wsdl:portType>
```

The *SomeOperation* operation describes the message sent from the sender to the receiver (*urn:SomeActionRequest*) and the message sent back to the sender (*urn:SomeContractReply*). The *SomeCallbackOperation* operation represents the message sent from the receiver to the client (*urn:SomeCallbackContractRequest*) and the message sent back to the receiver (*urn:SomeCallbackContractReply*).

The Duplex MEP and WCF Contracts

The WCF contract semantics for creating a Duplex MEP are a bit odd at first glance. As previously stated, duplex communication requires two contracts. By convention, the contract that describes the messages (and replies, if they are present) inbound to the receiver application are called *service contracts*, and contracts that describe messages sent from the receiver to the sender are called *callback contracts*. These two contracts are linked by the *ServiceContractAttribute.CallbackContract* property of the service contract, as shown here:

```
// File: Contract.cs

using System;
using System.ServiceModel;
using System.ServiceModel.Channels;
using System.Runtime.Serialization;

// the service contract looks the same as before, except
// for the addition of the CallbackContract property
// IsOneWay=true can also be set
[ServiceContract(Namespace="http://wintellect.com/SomeContract",
                 Name="ISomeContract",
                 CallbackContract=typeof(ICallbackContract))]
public interface ISomeContract3 {
  [OperationContract(Name="SomeOperation",
                     Action="urn:SomeActionRequest",
                     ReplyAction="urn:SomeContractReply")]
  void SomeOperation(Message message);
}

// No ServiceContract is necessary on the callback contract
// IsOneWay=true can also be set
public interface ICallbackContract {
  [OperationContract(Name="SomeCallbackOperation",
                     Action="urn:SomeCallbackContractRequest",
                     ReplyAction="urn:SomeCallbackContractReply")]
  void SomeCallbackOperation(Message message);
}
```

Notice that the callback contract is referenced by the *CallbackContract* property of the *ServiceContractAttribute* type.

> **Tip**   When creating a duplex contract, it is typically a good idea to make the operations one-way. If the *OperationContractAttribute*'s *IsOneWay* property is not set, the message exchanges will be request-reply, and both participants will incur the overhead of creating reply messages. Setting the *IsOneWay* property to *true* reduces the overhead required for each messaging interaction.

Message Topologies

Message topologies describe how messages are sent between one or more senders and one or more receivers. Message topologies can describe simple application-to-application connectedness, but they can also describe complex application-to-enterprise connectedness. When looking at the latter, the real power of service-oriented applications is apparent. In a nutshell, the possible topologies are much richer and enable complexity far beyond what is was within reach with component-oriented applications.

On one level, a message topology is composed of one or more MEPs. While there are boundless permutations of possible topologies, there are four generally accepted categories of message topologies: point-to-point, datagram point-to-point, brokered, and peer-to-peer (P2P). It is important to note that unlike MEPs, the names of these various message topologies are not widely agreed upon, so I have taken some liberty with their names. Likewise, it is possible to increase or decrease the number of message topologies, but these four are adequate for the purposes of this discussion.

Point-to-Point

The simplest and most widely used message topology, point-to-point is the fundamental building block for other message topologies. Simply stated, the point-to-point topology is one sender exchanging messages with one receiver. As you saw in the preceding section, this message exchange can be described by a datagram, request-reply, or duplex MEP.

Forward-Only Point-to-Point

In my opinion, datagram point-to-point is the most interesting topology, but it is also the hardest to implement. In essence, the forward-only point-to-point topology is a chain of datagram messages sent to different participants. It is important to note that this topology is composed of datagram MEPs only. It is possible for a message to return to a participant, but this must be explicitly stated in the address of the message, rather than implied, as it often is in the Request-Reply MEP. In general, this topology relies heavily on the *<From>*, *<ReplyTo>*, *<FaultTo>*, *<RelatesTo>*, *<MessageID>*, and *<To>* WS-Addressing header blocks.

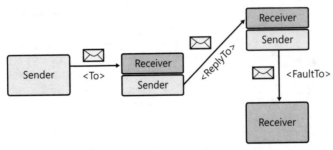

Figure 3-4   Forward-only point-to-point message topology

Brokered

As the development community embraces messaging applications, it will become more and more important to broker the messaging interactions between these applications. A similar need appeared when the Internet and e-commerce started to gain popularity. The prototypical example from this era is a load balancer in a server farm. Among other things, a load balancer directs traffic to available resources. Over time, load balancers have become more and more intelligent, and this trend shows no sign of slowing down. I expect the same sort of evolution to happen in the world of service-oriented applications.

In general terms, a *broker* is a messaging participant that forwards messages to other endpoints. The broker can use a set of processing rules to determine when, where, and how messages are forwarded to other participants. A brokered topology can be further categorized to include distributed brokering, centralized brokering, or hybrid brokering. These brokering topologies are similar to the various e-mail server topologies in use today.

Furthermore, the famous publish-subscribe topology fits within the definition of the brokered topology. In publish-subscribe, participants subscribe to certain messages by registering interest with one or more publishing participants. When a message that subscribers have registered interest in is sent to the publishing participant, the publishing participant distributes that message to all subscribers. In other words, the publisher is the broker. In SOAP speak, a broker is an intermediary, but it can be addressed directly. Figure 3-5 illustrates a basic brokered topology.

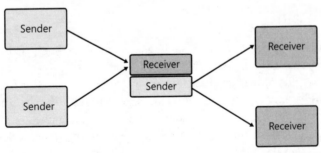

Figure 3-5   Brokered topology

Peer-to-Peer

Peer-to-peer (P2P) applications, like Groove and Microsoft Windows Live messenger, have rapidly gained popularity. Essentially, a true P2P application is one that communicates directly with other P2P applications. P2P applications can communicate with other P2P applications in a one-to-one, one-to-many, and even many-to-many scenario. P2P applications do not have the traditional dependency on a server because they are able to communicate directly with other applications via a *mesh*. A mesh is a named, discoverable, self-maintaining set of nodes. Before participating in a P2P message exchange, an application must first join the mesh. In general, P2P message topologies are highly scalable and resilient while still providing rich interactions between participants. Figure 3-6 shows a P2P topology. As you will see later in this book, WCF provides out-of-the-box support for P2P topologies.

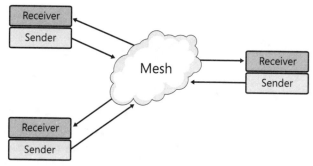

Figure 3-6   Peer-to-peer topology

Message Choreographies

A *message choreography* is an organized set of message exchanges that represents one logical operation. We participate in a type of message choreography when we buy our spouse or significant other a gift using a credit card. The logical operation of making the purchase is composed of several message exchanges that include the following:

1. The store sends information to a merchant service.

2. The merchant service sends data to the bank.

3. The bank sends an approval code.

Each of these data exchanges is not terribly interesting on its own, but when viewed together, they represent one logical operation.

Message choreographies play a key role in service-oriented applications, particularly in the areas of security, reliability, and transactional capability. As you saw in Chapter 1, "The Moon Is Blue," providing these features without dependencies on a particular transport requires us to place more information in messages. It is important to note, however, that we must also define how messages flow between participants. When providing message-centric security, we must consider how the sender and receiver will sign and encrypt data. When providing reliability, we must consider how the receiver will communicate to the sender which messages have arrived. Likewise, with transactional processing, we must consider how participants in the transaction can indicate whether actions have successfully been committed. All of these considerations require a well-defined set of message choreographies.

Among other things, many WS-* specifications define choreographies that are used to provide security, reliability, and transactional capability. WCF contains types that understand these WS-* choreographies, and as a result, it is possible to provide security, reliability, and transaction capability in our WCF applications without a dependency on a particular transport.

We are also free to define our own message choreographies. These choreographies can describe business processes, rules to a game, or particular functionality in a message exchange. While it is technically possible to author WCF components that provide our own custom choreographies, the process is tedious, especially with more complex choreographies. Tools like Microsoft BizTalk Server and WF are typically better suited to the task.

Summary

As we saw in Chapter 2, a messaging application sends and/or receives messages. In this chapter, I introduce a grammar for describing the message exchange between messaging participants. The terms used when describing a message exchange depend on the level of granularity you wish to describe. MEPs are the most granular way to describe the message exchange between two messaging participants. The three most widely known MEPs are datagram, request/reply, and duplex. MEPs may be grouped among messaging participants into message topologies. Furthermore, a set of message exchanges can fit a predefined message choreography. In the next chapter, we will see how the major architectural components of a WCF application fit together.

Chapter 4
WCF 101

The Microsoft Windows Communication Framework (WCF) is a complex framework, and its complexity stems from the fact that WCF is, on an abstract level, a messaging framework that must remain relevant and useful against the backdrop of industry standards that are constantly evolving. During the WCF design phase, SOAP and WS-* were viewed as the dominant messaging structures and protocols of the future. It is doubtful that any of the architects responsible for the complexion of WCF knew that JavaScript Object Notation (JSON) would ascend to become as relevant as it is today. They did however, understand that WCF must easily embrace and adapt to message structures and transports that sprout seemingly overnight. As a result, Microsoft designed WCF to be highly extensible and adaptable to meet the messaging requirements of today as well as those unforeseen in the future. The result of these efforts is a complex platform that is easy to use but, from a holistic perspective, somewhat difficult to understand.

As anyone who has tried to build a broad framework can attest, designing, building, testing, and maintaining it is a daunting task. Having designed, consulted on, and built several frameworks, I understand how difficult this can be. When designing a framework, the adage attributed to Alan Kay "Simple stuff should be simple, complex stuff should be possible" must be a primary design rule. When I look at WCF as it stands today, I think Microsoft successfully implemented this adage, and even took it further by making a lot of complex "stuff" simple. This is not to say that I think WCF is perfect or contains no errors, but rather that the product as a whole is well thought out and well designed.

One of the core requirements of WCF is exposing an object model to the developer that is consistent across all transports and protocols. As a concrete example, the architects on the WCF team wanted the code required to send a message over the TCP/IP transport to look very similar to the code required to send a message over the MSMQ transport. This sort of feature has several benefits. First, it means that the platform does not force developers to learn the eccentricities of the wide array of transport and protocol object models. In effect, developers who understand the WCF object and execution model are able to build support for different transports and protocols into their applications. Second, it means that as the WCF infrastructure matures to include new transports, protocols, and functionality, developers don't necessarily have to learn new ways to incorporate the new features into their applications. Instead, they can rely on the paradigms already implemented in the framework.

As a result of these types of requirements, the WCF architecture is composed of many interwoven layers. Over time, I have found that gaining a full understanding of any particular layer in the WCF infrastructure requires first understanding a little bit about every layer in the WCF infrastructure. The purpose of this chapter is to introduce the major layers in WCF applications and to provide context for the rest of this book, where we will more fully explore many of these layers.

WCF Quick Start

In this section, we pay homage to the computer science gods by building a Hello WCF messaging application. After building the application, we will dissect it to see the moving parts. To keep the example as simple as possible, we will combine the sender and receiver into a single console application. Let's get started by building the infrastructure required in a console application:

```
// File: HelloWCFApp.cs
using System;

sealed class HelloWCF {
  static void Main(){

  }
}
```

Defining the Service Contract

The first WCF-specific step in building our HelloWCF application is creating the service contract. Contracts are covered in detail in Chapter 9, "Contracts", but for now, suffice it to say that contracts are the primary way that we express the shape of our messaging application. By *shape*, I mean the operations our service exposes, the message schemas those operations produce and consume, and the Message Exchange Patterns (MEPs) each operation implements. In short, contracts define what our messaging application produces and consumes. Most contracts are type definitions annotated with attributes defined in the WCF application programming interface (API). In our example, the service contract is an interface annotated with the

System.ServiceModel.ServiceContractAttribute and the
System.ServiceModel.OperationContractAttribute, as shown here:

```
// File: HelloWCFApp.cs
[ServiceContract]
public interface IHelloWCF {
  [OperationContract]
  void Say(String input);
}
```

At a high level, our service contract states that our receiving application contains one operation named *Say* and that operation accepts a parameter of type *String* and has a *void* return type. A sending application can use this service contract as a means to construct and send messages to the receiving application. Now that we have defined the service contract, it's time to add the code that defines where the receiving application will listen for incoming messages and how the application will exchange messages with other messaging participants.

Defining the Address and the Binding

Defining the location *where* our application listens for incoming messages requires us to use the *System.Uri* type, and defining *how* our application exchanges messages with other participants requires us to use the *System.ServiceModel.Channels.Binding* type or one of its derived types. The following code snippet illustrates how to use the *Uri* type and the *Binding* type in our application:

```
// File: HelloWCFApp.cs
static void Main(){
  // define where to listen for messages
  Uri address = new Uri("http://localhost:8000/IHelloWCF");

  // define how to exchange messages
  BasicHttpBinding binding = new BasicHttpBinding();
}
```

Notice that the *address* local variable indicates a Uniform Resource Identifier (URI) that uses the HTTP scheme. Choosing this address forces us to choose a binding that uses the HTTP transport. At a high level, a binding is the primary means we use to indicate the transport, the message choreographies, and the message encoder used in the application. The *binding* local variable is of type *BasicHttpBinding*. As you can tell from the name, *BasicHttpBinding* creates a messaging infrastructure that uses the HTTP transport.

Creating an Endpoint and Starting to Listen

Next we must use the address, the binding, and the contract to build an endpoint and then listen on that endpoint for incoming messages. In general, a WCF receiving application can build and listen on multiple endpoints, and each one requires an address, a binding, and a contract. The *System.ServiceModel.ServiceHost* type builds and hosts endpoints and manages other parts of the receiving infrastructure such as threading and object lifetime. The following code snippet demonstrates how to instantiate the *ServiceHost* type, how to add an endpoint, and how to begin listening for incoming messages:

```
// File: HelloWCFApp.cs
static void Main(){
  // define where to listen for messages
  Uri address = new Uri("http://localhost:4000/IHelloWCF");
  // define how to exchange messages
  BasicHttpBinding binding = new BasicHttpBinding();
  // instantiate a ServiceHost, passing the type to instantiate
  // when the application receives a message
  ServiceHost svc = new ServiceHost(typeof(HelloWCF));
  // add an endpoint, passing the address, binding, and contract
  svc.AddServiceEndpoint(typeof(IHelloWCF), binding, address);
  // begin listening
  svc.Open();
  // indicate that the receiving application is ready and
  // keep the application from exiting immediately
  Console.WriteLine("The HelloWCF receiving application is ready");
  Console.ReadLine();
  // close the service host
  svc.Close();
}
```

Also notice the argument in the call to the *ServiceHost* constructor. The *ServiceHost* constructor is overloaded several times, and each overload accepts, in some form or fashion, the type definition of the object that the WCF infrastructure dispatches incoming messages to. The *ServiceHost* constructor shown in the preceding code snippet indicates that the messaging infrastructure dispatches received messages to an instance of the *HelloWCF* type.

Also notice in the preceding code snippet the call to *svc.AddServiceEndpoint* and *svc.Open*. The *AddServiceEndpoint* instance method on the *ServiceHost* type sets the state of the *ServiceHost* object so that it will listen for incoming messages in a manner consistent with the address, the binding, and the contract parameters. It is important to note that the *AddServiceEndpoint* method does not begin the listening loop; it simply changes the state of the *ServiceHost* object (more on this in Chapter 10). The *Open* instance method on the *ServiceHost* type builds the messaging infrastructure and then begins the listening loop. The implementation of the *Open* method validates the state of the *ServiceHost* object, builds the endpoints from that state, and then begins the listening loop for each endpoint.

Mapping Received Messages to a *HelloWCF* Member

In its current form, our application will compile, but it will throw an *InvalidOperationException* when the application attempts to build the endpoint. The reason is fairly straightforward: in the constructor of the *ServiceHost* type, we passed the *HelloWCF* type as an argument, thereby signaling our intent for the messaging infrastructure to dispatch received messages to *HelloWCF* objects. For this to happen, there must be a mapping that associates received messages to members on the *HelloWCF* type. The simplest way to create this mapping is to change the *HelloWCF* type to implement the service contract defined by the *IHelloWCF* interface, as shown here:

```
// File: HelloWCFApp.cs
using System;
using System.ServiceModel;
using System.ServiceModel.Channels;

// implement the IHelloWCF service contract
sealed class HelloWCF : IHelloWCF {
  // indicate when a HelloWCF object is created
  HelloWCF() { Console.WriteLine("HelloWCF object created"); }

  static void Main(){
    // define where to listen for messages
    Uri address = new Uri("http://localhost:4000/IHelloWCF");
    // define how to exchange messages
    BasicHttpBinding binding = new BasicHttpBinding();
    // instantiate a ServiceHost, passing the type to instantiate
    // when the application receives a message
    ServiceHost svc = new ServiceHost(typeof(HelloWCF));
    // add an endpoint, passing the address, binding, and contract
    svc.AddServiceEndpoint(typeof(IHelloWCF), binding, address);
    // begin listening
    svc.Open();
    // indicate that the receiving application is ready and
    // keep the application from exiting immediately
    Console.WriteLine("The HelloWCF receiving application is ready");
    // wait for incoming messages
    Console.ReadLine();
    // close the service host
    svc.Close();
  }

  // received messages are dispatched to this instance
  // method as per the service contract
  public void Say(String input){
    Console.WriteLine("Message received, the body contains: {0}", input);
  }
}

[ServiceContract]
public interface IHelloWCF {
  [OperationContract]
  void Say(String input);
}
```

Changing the *HelloWCF* type definition in this manner causes the messaging infrastructure to dispatch received messages to the *Say* instance method on the *HelloWCF* type, thereby outputting a simple statement to the console.

Compiling, Running, and Verifying the Receiver

We are now ready to compile and run the application with the following command lines:

```
C:\temp>csc /nologo /r:"c:\WINDOWS\Microsoft.Net\Framework\v3.0\Windows Communication
Foundation\System.ServiceModel.dll" HelloWCFApp.cs

C:\temp>HelloWCFApp.exe
The HelloWCF receiving application is ready
```

At this point, the receiving application is passively waiting for incoming messages. We can verify that the application is indeed listening by running netstat.exe, as shown here:

```
c:\temp>netstat -a -b
TCP    kermit:4000             0.0.0.0:0              LISTENING       1104
[HelloWCFApp.exe]
```

This will no doubt produce more output than is shown in this example, but you should see two lines that look similar to these. (The name of my computer is Kermit.)

Sending a Message to the Receiver

The sending infrastructure relies on the address, binding, and contract constructs in much the same way the receiving infrastructure does. It is typically the sender's responsibility to use an address, a binding, and a contract that are compatible with the ones the receiver uses. Given the simplicity of our application, the sender can simply reuse the address, binding, and contract that the receiving infrastructure uses.

The sending code, however, uses different types than the receiver does. Conceptually, this makes sense because the sender and receiver have distinctly different roles in the message exchange. Instead of using the *Uri* type directly, most senders rely on the *System.Service-Model.EndpointAddress* type as a means for expressing the target of a message. As you'll see in Chapter 5, "Messages," the *EndpointAddress* type is the WCF abstraction of a WS-Addressing endpoint reference. Furthermore, the sender does not use the *ServiceHost* type, but rather uses the *ChannelFactory<T>* type (where *T* is the service contract type). The *ChannelFactory<T>* type builds the sending infrastructure in much the same way that the *ServiceHost* type builds the receiving infrastructure. The following code snippet shows how to use the *EndpointAddress* type and the *ChannelFactory<T>* type to build the sending infrastructure:

```
// File: HelloWCFApp.cs
using System;
using System.ServiceModel;
using System.ServiceModel.Channels;

// implement the IHelloWCF service contract
sealed class HelloWCF : IHelloWCF {
  // indicate when a HelloWCF object is created
  HelloWCF() { Console.WriteLine("HelloWCF object created"); }
```

```
static void Main(){
  // define where to listen for messages
  Uri address = new Uri("http://localhost:4000/IHelloWCF");
  // define how to exchange messages
  BasicHttpBinding binding = new BasicHttpBinding();
  // instantiate a ServiceHost, passing the type to instantiate
  // when the application receives a message
  ServiceHost svc = new ServiceHost(typeof(HelloWCF));
  // add an endpoint, passing the address, binding, and contract
  svc.AddServiceEndpoint(typeof(IHelloWCF), binding, address);
  // begin listening
  svc.Open();
  // indicate that the receiving application is ready and
  // keep the application from exiting immediately
  Console.WriteLine("The HelloWCF receiving application is ready");

  // begin the sender code
  // create a channelFactory<T> with binding and address
  ChannelFactory<IHelloWCF> factory =
    new ChannelFactory<IHelloWCF>(binding,
                                  new EndpointAddress(address));
  // use the factory to create a proxy
  IHelloWCF proxy = factory.CreateChannel();
  // use the proxy to send a message to the receiver
  proxy.Say("Hi there WCF");
  // end the sender code

  Console.ReadLine();
  // close the service host
  svc.Close();
}

// received messages are dispatched to this instance
// method as per the service contract
public void Say(String input){
  Console.WriteLine("Message received, the body contains: {0}", input);
}
}

[ServiceContract]
public interface IHelloWCF {
  [OperationContract]
  void Say(String input);
}
```

Notice that we call the *CreateChannel* instance method on the *ChannelFactory<T>* object and use the object returned to invoke a method on our service contract interface. At a high level, the *ChannelFactory<T>* object is a type that can manufacture the sending infrastructure required to generate and send a message to the receiver (hence the need to pass the binding and address in the constructor). The *CreateChannel* instance method on the *ChannelFactory<T>* type actually creates the sending infrastructure and returns a reference to that infrastructure via an object whose type implements the service contract interface. We interact with this sending infrastructure by invoking the methods on our service contract interface. Keep in mind that there are several other ways to accomplish the same work, and we will explore these later in this chapter and again in Chapter 6, "Channels."

Compiling, Running, and Verifying the Sender

Now that we have our receiving and sending infrastructure in place, it's time to compile and run the application, as shown here:

```
c:\temp>csc /nologo /r:"c:\WINDOWS\Microsoft.Net\Framework\v3.0\Windows Communication
Foundation\System.ServiceModel.dll" HelloWCFApp.cs

c:\temp>HelloWCFApp.exe
The HelloWCF receiving application is ready
HelloWCF object created
Message received, the body contains: HelloWCF!
```

As expected, our application does the following at run time:

1. Builds the infrastructure required to listen for incoming messages on *http://localhost:4000/IHelloWCF*

2. Begins listening for incoming messages on *http://localhost:4000/IHelloWCF*

3. Builds the infrastructure required to send a message to *http://localhost:4000/IHelloWCF*

4. Generates and sends a message to *http://localhost:4000/IHelloWCF*

5. Receives the message, instantiates a new *HelloWCF* object, and dispatches that message to the *Say* method on the *HelloWCF* object

Looking at the Message

On close inspection, none of the code in our HelloWCF example interacts with anything that even remotely resembles a message. To the application developer, a WCF application looks and feels much like any object-oriented or component-oriented application. At run time, however, a WCF application is fully engaged in the work of generating, sending, receiving, or otherwise processing messages. We can see the message that the WCF infrastructure generates by changing the implementation of the *Say* method to the following:

```
public void Say(String input){
  Console.WriteLine("Message received, the body contains: {0}", input);
  // Show the contents of the received message
  Console.WriteLine(
    OperationContext.Current.RequestContext.RequestMessage.ToString());
}
```

The change to the *Say* method changes the application output to the following:

```
The HelloWCF receiving application is ready
HelloWCF object created
Message received, the body contains: HelloWCF!
<s:Envelope xmlns:s="http://schemas.xmlsoap.org/soap/envelope/">
  <s:Header>
    <To s:mustUnderstand="1"
        xmlns="http://schemas.microsoft.com/ws/2005/05/adessing/none">
     http://localhost:8000/IHelloWCF
    </To>
    <Action s:mustUnderstand="1"
            xmlns="http://schemas.microsoft.com/ws/2005/05/addressing/none">
        http://tempuri.org/IHelloWCF/Say
      </Action>
  </s:Header>
  <s:Body>
    <Say xmlns="http://tempuri.org/">
      <input>HelloWCF!</input>
    </Say>
  </s:Body>
</s:Envelope>
```

Notice that the SOAP message is printed and the body of the SOAP message contains the *String* we passed to the *Say* method on the *channel* local variable. At the macroscopic level, this sending part of our application takes this *String*, uses it build a SOAP message, and then sends that SOAP message to the receiving part of our application. The receiving part of our application, on the other hand, receives the SOAP message, creates a *HelloWCF* object, extracts the contents of the SOAP body, and invokes the *Say* method on the *HelloWCF* object, passing the *String* as an argument.

A Slight Change with a Major Impact

The WCF infrastructure does most of the messaging work for us, and the normal object model does not always reveal the fact that our WCF application is actually passing messages between the sender and receiver. In fact, from the developer's perspective, the code shown in our example looks more like an application that uses distributed objects than a messaging application. We can, however, very easily see that our HelloWCF application is indeed a messaging application by changing one line of code and observing the impact that change has on message composition.

If we change the line

```
BasicHttpBinding binding = new BasicHttpBinding();
```

to the following:

```
WSHttpBinding binding = new WSHttpBinding();
```

we see the following output:

```
The HelloWCF receiving application is ready
Creating and sending a message to the receiver
HelloWCF object created
Message received, the body contains: HelloWCF!
<s:Envelope xmlns:a="http://www.w3.org/2005/08/addressing"
            xmlns:s="http://www.w3.org/2003/05/soap-envelope">
  <s:Header>
    <a:Action s:mustUnderstand="1" u:Id="_2"
              xmlns:u="http://docs.oasis-open.org/wss/2004/01/oasis-200401-
              wss-wssecurity-utility-1.0.xsd">
        http://tempuri.org/IHelloWCF/Say
      </a:Action>
    <a:MessageID u:Id="_3"
                 xmlns:u="http://docs.oasis-open.org/wss/2004/01/oasis-
                 200401-wss-wssecurity-utility-1.0.xsd">
      urn:uuid:2acf3d19-dac6-4f8f-8c5d-b2ca104cd3a0
    </a:MessageID>
    <a:ReplyTo u:Id="_4"
               xmlns:u="http://docs.oasis-open.org/wss/2004/01/oasis-
               200401-wss-wssecurity-utility-1.0.xsd">
      <a:Address>http://www.w3.org/2005/08/addressing/anonymous</a:Address>
    </a:ReplyTo>
    <a:To s:mustUnderstand="1" u:Id="_5" xmlns:u="http://docs.oasis-open.org/wss/2004/01/
oasis-200401-wss-wssecurity-utility-1.0.xsd">
      http://localhost:8000/IHelloWCF
    </a:To>
    <o:Security s:mustUnderstand="1" xmlns:o="http://docs.oasis-open.org/wss/2004/01/oasis-
200401-wss-wssecurity-secext-1.0.xsd">
      <u:Timestamp u:Id="uuid-a4e930a1-1fc5-4450-8140-754a98690449-12"
                   xmlns:u="http://docs.oasis-open.org/wss/2004/01/oasis-
                   200401-wss-wssecurity-utility-1.0.xsd">
        <u:Created>2006-08-29T01:57:50.296Z</u:Created>
        <u:Expires>2006-08-29T02:02:50.296Z</u:Expires>
      </u:Timestamp>
      <c:SecurityContextToken u:Id="uuid-a4e930a1-1fc5-4450-8140-754a98690449-6"
xmlns:c="http://schemas.xmlsoap.org/ws/2005/02/sc" xmlns:u="http://docs.oasis-open.org/wss/
2004/01/oasis-200401-wss-wssecurity-utility-1.0.xsd">
        <c:Identifier>
          urn:uuid:9cb35fed-f9cb-47b5-810b-54cd96970695
        </c:Identifier>
      </c:SecurityContextToken>
      <c:DerivedKeyToken
        u:Id="uuid-a4e930a1-1fc5-4450-8140-754a98690449-10"
        xmlns:c="http://schemas.xmlsoap.org/ws/2005/02/sc"
        xmlns:u="http://docs.oasis-open.org/wss/2004/01/oasis-200401-wss-
        wssecurity-utility-1.0.xsd">
        <o:SecurityTokenReference>
          <o:Reference
            ValueType="http://schemas.xmlsoap.org/ws/2005/02/sc/sct"
                URI="#uuid-a4e930a1-1fc5-4450-8140-754a98690449-6" />
        </o:SecurityTokenReference>
        <c:Offset>0</c:Offset>
        <c:Length>24</c:Length>
```

```xml
      <c:Nonce>A170b1nKz88AuWmWYONX5Q==</c:Nonce>
    </c:DerivedKeyToken>
    <c:DerivedKeyToken
      u:Id="uuid-a4e930a1-1fc5-4450-8140-754a98690449-11"
      xmlns:c="http://schemas.xmlsoap.org/ws/2005/02/sc"
      xmlns:u="http://docs.oasis-open.org/wss/2004/01/oasis-200401-wss-
        wssecurity-utility-1.0.xsd">
      <o:SecurityTokenReference>
        <o:Reference
          ValueType="http://schemas.xmlsoap.org/ws/2005/02/sc/sct"
            URI="#uuid-a4e930a1-1fc5-4450-8140-754a98690449-6" />
      </o:SecurityTokenReference>
      <c:Nonce>I8M/H2f3vFuGkwZVV1YwOA==</c:Nonce>
    </c:DerivedKeyToken>
    <e:ReferenceList xmlns:e="http://www.w3.org/2001/04/xmlenc#">
      <e:DataReference URI="#_1" />
      <e:DataReference URI="#_6" />
    </e:ReferenceList>
    <e:EncryptedData Id="_6"
      Type="http://www.w3.org/2001/04/xmlenc#Element"
      xmlns:e="http://www.w3.org/2001/04/xmlenc#">
      <e:EncryptionMethod
        Algorithm="http://www.w3.org/2001/04/xmlenc#aes256-cbc" />
      <KeyInfo xmlns="http://www.w3.org/2000/09/xmldsig#">
        <o:SecurityTokenReference>
          <o:Reference
            ValueType="http://schemas.xmlsoap.org/ws/2005/02/sc/dk"
            URI="#uuid-a4e930a1-1fc5-4450-8140-754a98690449-11" />
        </o:SecurityTokenReference>
      </KeyInfo>
      <e:CipherData>
        <e:CipherValue>
vQ+AT5gioRS6rRiNhWw2UJmvYYZpA+cc1DgC/K+6Dsd2enF4RUcwOG2
xqfkD/
EZkSFRKDzrJYBz8ItHLZjsva4kqfx3UsEJjYPKbxih12GFrXdPwTmrHWt35UwOL2rTh8kU9rtj44NfULS59CJbXE6PC7
Af1qWvnobcPXBqmgm4NA8wwSTuR3IKHPfD/Pg/
3WABob534WD4T1DbRr5tXwNr+yQl2nSWN8C0aaP9+LCKymEK7AbeJXAaGoxdGu/
t6l7Bw1lBsJeSJmsd4otXcLxt976kBEIjTl8/
6SVUd2hmudP2TBGDbCCvgOl4c0vsHmUC1SjXE5vXf6ATkMj6P3oOeMqBiW1G26RWiYBZ3OxnC1fDs60uSvfHtfF8CD0I
LYGHLgnUHz5CFYOrPomT73RCkCfmgFuheCgB9zHZGtWedY6ivNrZe2KPx0ujQ2Mq4pv4bLns2qoykwKO3ma7YGiGExGc
ZBfkZ2YAkYmHWXJ0Xx4PJmQRAWIKfUCqcrR6lwyLjl5Agsrt0xHA5WEk3hapscW3HZ8wOgwvOfcHlZ1e3EAmOdZr5Ose
3TAKMXf7FC1tMy5u0763flA6AZk9l7IpAQXcTLYicriH5hzf1416xbTJCtt2rztiItSkYizkiJCUMJLanc6ST5i+GVHz
J5oRCEWgfOTcQpHmri8y1P1+6jYe9ELla8Mj
        </e:CipherValue>
      </e:CipherData>
    </e:EncryptedData>
  </o:Security>
</s:Header>
<s:Body u:Id="_0" xmlns:u="http://docs.oasis-open.org/wss/2004/01/oasis-
  200401-wss-wssecurity-utility-1.0.xsd">
  <Say xmlns="http://tempuri.org/">
    <input>HelloWCF!</input>
  </Say>
</s:Body>
</s:Envelope>
```

As you can see, one simple change has a dramatic impact on the structure of the messages that our application produces. Changing from the *BasicHttpBinding* to the *WSHttpBinding* shifts our application from one that uses simple SOAP messages over HTTP to one that engages in a patchwork of WS-* protocols and choreographies over HTTP. The impact is more than just a more verbose and descriptive message, because our application is now sending and receiving multiple messages based on the WS-Security, WS-SecureConversation, and other specifications.

> **Note** In effect, the macroscopic programming model for WCF completely removes all perspective that a WCF application is indeed a messaging application, and provides more of a distributed object "feel." This is, in my opinion, a tremendous benefit of the platform, but it is, at the same time, fraught with danger. As developers, we must resist the temptation to lull ourselves into the idea that we can approach WCF as we would a distributed object platform, and embrace the concepts of messaging instead. Furthermore, as application and infrastructure developers, we must comprehend how changes in the way we use WCF types impact the messages that our application processes.

Exposing Metadata

Our Hello WCF application takes a very simplistic approach to creating compatibility between the receiver and the sender. Since both the receiver and the sender reside in the same *AppDomain* and the objects that the receiver uses are visible to the sender, we simply reuse the address, binding, and contract in the sender. In most messaging applications, however, this approach is not feasible. In most cases, we can expect the sender and receiver to reside in different *AppDomains* on different computers. In these scenarios, the receiver typically dictates the messaging requirements, and the senders attempt to adhere to those requirements.

The WS-MetadataExchange specification dictates the terms of how the sender and receiver can exchange this information in a vendor agnostic manner. In more specific terms, the WS-MetadataExchange specification dictates message schemas and choreographies that facilitate the exchange of information about a messaging endpoint or endpoints. In most real-world applications (or at least ones that are more complex than our Hello WCF application), there is a need to expose this information in a way that a sender can interrogate a receiver's endpoint to extract metadata and use that metadata to build the infrastructure necessary to send a compatible message to that endpoint.

By default, our Hello WCF application does not expose any metadata—at least, not in its most commonly accepted form of Web Services Description Language (WSDL) and Extensible Schema Definition (XSD). (Don't confuse messaging application metadata with assembly or type metadata, even though one can be used to create the other.) In fact, WCF applications by default do not expose metadata, and the reason for this default is rooted in concerns for security. The information exposed by metadata often includes the security requirements for that application. In the name of protecting secrets, the team opted to turn this feature off by default.

If, however, we decide to expose our application's metadata, we can build an endpoint specifically for exchanging metadata, and we approach building a metadata endpoint in much the same way that we approach building any endpoint: by starting with an address, a binding, and a contract. Unlike the endpoints you've seen so far, however, the service contract for a metadata endpoint is already defined for us in the WCF API.

The first step in building a metadata endpoint is to change the state of the *ServiceHost* in such a way that it expects to host metadata. We do this by adding a *System.ServiceModel. Description.ServiceMetadataBehavior* object to the behavior collection of the *ServiceHost*. A behavior is special information that the WCF infrastructure uses to change local message processing. The following code demonstrates how to add a *ServiceMetadataBehavior* object to the active *ServiceHost*:

```
// instantiate a ServiceHost, passing the type to instantiate
// when the application receives a message
ServiceHost svc = new ServiceHost(typeof(HelloWCF), address);

// BEGIN NEW METADATA CODE
// create a ServiceMetadataBehavior
ServiceMetadataBehavior metadata = new ServiceMetadataBehavior();
metadata.HttpGetEnabled = true;
// add it to the servicehost description
svc.Description.Behaviors.Add(metadata);
```

The next step is to define the *Binding* for the metadata endpoint. The object model for a metadata *Binding* is very different from other bindings—namely, we create the metadata *Binding* by calling a factory method on the *System.ServiceModel.Description. MetadataExchangeBindings* type, as shown here (other parts of our Hello WCF application have been omitted for clarity):

```
// instantiate a ServiceHost, passing the type to instantiate
// when the application receives a message
ServiceHost svc = new ServiceHost(typeof(HelloWCF));

// BEGIN NEW METADATA CODE
// create a ServiceMetadataBehavior
ServiceMetadataBehavior metadata = new ServiceMetadataBehavior();
// add it to the servicehost description
svc.Description.Behaviors.Add(metadata);
// create a TCP metadata binding
Binding mexBinding = MetadataExchangeBindings.CreateMexTcpBinding();
```

As a result of previous conditioning with ASMX, you might have the notion that metadata is expressible only over the HTTP transport. In reality, metadata is transmittable over a wide variety of transports, and WS-MetadataExchange states this flexibility. In our example, however, we call the *CreateMexTcpBinding* method, and it returns a reference to a *Binding*-derived type that uses the TCP transport. Since we are using the TCP transport, we must also ensure the the metadata address we choose uses the TCP scheme, as shown here:

```
// instantiate a ServiceHost, passing the type to instantiate
// when the application receives a message
ServiceHost svc = new ServiceHost(typeof(HelloWCF));

// BEGIN NEW METADATA CODE
// create a ServiceMetadataBehavior
ServiceMetadataBehavior metadata = new ServiceMetadataBehavior();
// add it to the servicehost description
svc.Description.Behaviors.Add(metadata);
// create a TCP metadata binding
Binding mexBinding = MetadataExchangeBindings.CreateMexTcpBinding();
// create an address to listen on WS-Metadata exchange traffic
Uri mexAddress = new Uri("net.tcp://localhost:5000/IHelloWCF/Mex");
```

Now that we have defined the address and the binding we want to use for our metadata endpoint, we must add the endpoint to the *ServiceHost*, in much the same way we did the first messaging endpoint. When adding a metadata endpoint, however, we use a service contract already defined in the WCF API named *System.ServiceModel.Description.IMetadataExchange*. The following code snippet shows how to add a metadata endpoint to the *ServiceHost*, using the appropriate address, binding, and contract:

```
// instantiate a ServiceHost, passing the type to instantiate
// when the application receives a message
ServiceHost svc = new ServiceHost(typeof(HelloWCF));

// BEGIN NEW METADATA CODE
// create a ServiceMetadataBehavior
ServiceMetadataBehavior metadata = new ServiceMetadataBehavior();
// add it to the servicehost description
svc.Description.Behaviors.Add(metadata);
// create a TCP metadata binding
Binding mexBinding = MetadataExchangeBindings.CreateMexTcpBinding();
// create an address to listen on WS-Metadata exchange traffic
Uri mexAddress = new Uri("net.tcp://localhost:5000/IHelloWCF/Mex");
// add the metadata endpoint
svc.AddServiceEndpoint(typeof(IMetadataExchange),
                       mexBinding,
                       mexAddress);
// END METADATA CODE
```

If we build and run our new Hello WCF application, we see that the application is indeed listening on two different addresses. One address is for servicing metadata requests, and the other is for the *IHelloWCF.Say* functionality. Let's now turn our attention to how we can extract metadata from the metadata endpoint and use it to build the sending infrastructure in our application.

Consuming Metadata

The Microsoft .NET Framework SDK installs a highly versatile tool named svcutil.exe, and one of its capabilities is to interrogate a running messaging application and generate a proxy based on the information it collects. Internally, svcutil.exe uses the WS-MetadataExchange protocol, as well as the WSDL "get" semantics popularized with ASMX. Since our receiving application now exposes a metadata endpoint, we can point svcutil.exe to that running endpoint, and svcutil.exe will autogenerate a proxy type and configuration information compatible with the endpoints referred to in the metadata endpoint. When used in this way, svcutil.exe sends messages to a receiving application in a manner consistent with WS-MetadataExchange and transforms the ensuing reply into .NET Framework types that facilitate the development of a sending application.

Generating the Proxy with Svcutil.exe

Before you run svcutil.exe, verify that the HelloWCFApp.exe receiving application is started and listening for incoming messages. Next open a new Windows SDK Command Prompt window, and enter the following command:

```
C:\temp>svcutil /target:code net.tcp://localhost:5000/IHelloWCF/Mex
```

Svcutil.exe will create two files: HelloWCFProxy.cs and output.config. If you examine the HelloWCFProxy.cs file, you'll see that svcutil.exe generated a source file that contains definitions for the *IHelloWCF* interface, an interface named *IHelloWCFChannel*, and a type named *HelloWCFClient*.

> **Note**   Of all the types autogenerated by svcutil.exe, the *HelloWCFClient* type is intended for the most frequent use. In my opinion, appending the word *Client* to the name of this type is a mistake in style that will undoubtedly surface as misunderstandings in the developer community. Without a doubt, *Client* connotes the phrase *Client and Server*. The *HelloWCFClient* type helps build a messaging infrastructure, not a traditional client/server infrastructure. Keep in mind that even though the name of this type ends in *Client*, we are still building a messaging application.

Together, these type definitions help us write sending code that is compatible with the receiver. Notice that there is no information in the HelloWCF.cs file about the address that the receiving application is listening on, nor a binding that is compatible with the receiving application in the HelloWCF.cs source file. This information is stored in the other file generated by svcutil.exe (output.config). WCF has a rich configuration infrastructure that allows us to configure many facets of a sending or receiving application through XML configuration files. To illustrate how to take advantage of the data created for us by svcutil, let's create another console application that sends messages to the receiver. We will name this application HelloWCFSender. To do this, we we will have to rename the output.config file so that our new sending application reads the config file (change to HelloWCFSender.exe.config).

Coding HelloWCFSender with Svcutil.exe-Generated Types

In short, svcutil.exe has generated most of the source code and configuration settings we will need to write our new sending application. Creating this sending application is very similar to the one in HelloWCF.exe.

```
using System;
using System.ServiceModel;

sealed class HelloWCFSender {

  static void Main(){
    // wait for the receiver to start
    Console.WriteLine("Press ENTER when the Receiver is ready");
    Console.ReadLine();

    // print to the console that we are sending a message
    Console.WriteLine("Sending a message to the Receiver");
    // create the HelloWCFClient type created by svcutil
    HelloWCFClient proxy = new HelloWCFClient();
    // invoke the Say method
    proxy.Say("Hi there from a new Sender");
    proxy.Close();
    // print to the console that we have sent a message
    Console.WriteLine("Finished sending a message to the Receiver");
  }
}
```

Notice that we only have to instantiate the *HelloWCFClient* type and call the *Say* method. The real heavy lifting has been done by the types that svcutil.exe created and the WCF configuration infrastructure. After we have written this source code, we can compile it to an assembly with the following command line:

```
C:\temp>csc /r: "C:\WINDOWS\Microsoft.Net\v3.0\Windows Communication
Foundation\System.ServiceModel.dll" HelloWCFProxy.cs HelloWCFSender.cs
```

Next we start the receiving application (HelloWCFApp.exe) and then start the sender (HelloWCFSender.exe), and we see output like the following on the sender:

```
C:\temp>HelloWCFSender.exe
Press ENTER when the Receiver is ready

Sending a message to the Receiver
Finished sending a message to the Receiver
```

In a nutshell, the output from our application confirms that the sending part of our application is working as it did before, without reusing the objects we used to build the receiving part of our application. We can check the receiving application to verify that the recever did indeed receive a new message.

Now that we have two fully functioning WCF applications, let's take a look at the architecture of WCF as a whole.

WCF Gross Anatomy from the Outside

Even though WCF is a very complex platform, it appears remarkably simple to the casual observer. As you saw in our Hello WCF examples, building a receiving application with WCF can be as simple as using an address, a binding, and a contract to build one or more endpoints. Building a sending application can be as simple as using a binding, a contract, and an address to send a message to that receiving endpoint. If, however, we want to modify local processing on the sender or the receiver, we are free to do so by either creating our own behaviors or using the behaviors that ship with WCF (like adding metadata support). Figure 4-1 shows the relationship between endpoints, addresses, bindings, contracts, and behaviors.

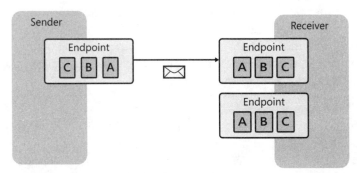

Figure 4-1   Endpoints, addresses, bindings, contracts, and behaviors

The Address

All applications that send or receive messages must make use of an address at some point in time. For example, receiving applications listen for incoming messages at some address, whereas sending applications direct messages to some target address. The WCF receiving infrastructure relies on the *System.Uri* type to build the receiving endpoint. The WCF sending infrastructure, on the other hand, relies on the *System.ServiceModel.EndpointAddress* type for directing messages to an ultimate receiver. An *EndpointAddress* type is the CLR abstraction of a WS-Addressing endpoint reference, and senders use this type to both add endpoint reference information to outbound messages and make the transport-level connection to the receiving endpoint (if there is one). Chapter 5 covers, among other things, the *EndpointAddress* type in detail.

In the context of WCF, an address is, in some form or fashion, a URI (an *EndpointAddress* object wraps a *System.Uri* object). One vital part of a URI is the scheme name. A scheme is an abstraction of the type of identifier that the URI represents, and the scheme name is a way to identify that scheme. In many cases, the scheme name matches the protocol that can be used to locate the resource, thereby using a URI as a URL. For example, the URI *http://localhost:5000/IHelloWCF* identifies *http* as the scheme name, and it just so happens that *http (Hypertext Transfer Protocol)* is also a transport. Internally, the WCF infrastructure must be able to use the URI to build either the sending or the listening infrastructure.

The Binding

Bindings are the primary way we express how a messaging application processes, sends, and receives messages. More specifically, it is the primary way we express the transport, WS-* protocols, security requirements, and transactional requirements an endpoint uses. WCF ships with nine bindings that cover a wide spectrum of transports, WS-* protocols, security requirements, and transactional requirements. If the capabilities do not fit the requirements of our application, we can define a custom binding that fits our particular needs.

In general, a binding is a type that defines much of our messaging infrastructure; it is a layer of abstraction around the transport and protocols that our application supports. To the developer, this abstraction means that the code required to send a message over the TCP/IP transport looks very similar to code that sends a message over MSMQ, thereby loosely coupling our application to a particular transport or set of protocols. Loose coupling in this manner means that application developers will be able to develop, adapt, and customize an application to fit customer demands more quickly than before.

All bindings subclass the *System.ServiceModel.Channels.Binding* type, and as a result, all bindings share common characteristics. One common characteristic of all bindings is that they maintain a private list of *System.ServiceModel.Channels.BindingElement* objects. A *BindingElement* is an abstraction of a particular facet of message exchange, like a transport or a WS-* protocol. All bindings expose a method named *CreateBindingElements* that builds and returns the list of binding elements for that particular binding. Shown here is a simple application that iterates over the nine default bindings in WCF and shows their *BindingElement* lists:

```
using System;
using System.ServiceModel;
using System.ServiceModel.Channels;
using System.Reflection;
using System.Collections.Generic;
using System.ServiceModel.MsmqIntegration;

sealed class BindingElementsShow
{
  static void Main(){
    List<Binding> bindings = new List<Binding>();
    bindings.Add(new BasicHttpBinding());
    bindings.Add(new NetNamedPipeBinding());
    bindings.Add(new NetTcpBinding());
    bindings.Add(new WSDualHttpBinding());
    bindings.Add(new WSHttpBinding());
    bindings.Add(new NetMsmqBinding());
    bindings.Add(new MsmqIntegrationBinding());
    bindings.Add(new WSFederationHttpBinding());
    // throws if Peer Networking not installed
    bindings.Add(new NetPeerTcpBinding());

    ShowBindingElements(bindings);
```

```
    }

    private static void ShowBindingElements(List<Binding> bindings){
      foreach (Binding binding in bindings){
        Console.WriteLine("Showing Binding Elements for {0}",
          binding.GetType().Name);
        foreach (BindingElement element in binding.CreateBindingElements()){
          Console.WriteLine("\t{0}", element.GetType().Name);
        }
      }
    }
  }
}
```

This program generates the following output:

```
Showing Binding Elements for BasicHttpBinding
        TextMessageEncodingBindingElement
        HttpTransportBindingElement
Showing Binding Elements for NetNamedPipeBinding
        TransactionFlowBindingElement
        BinaryMessageEncodingBindingElement
        WindowsStreamSecurityBindingElement
        NamedPipeTransportBindingElement
Showing Binding Elements for NetTcpBinding
        TransactionFlowBindingElement
        BinaryMessageEncodingBindingElement
        WindowsStreamSecurityBindingElement
        TcpTransportBindingElement
Showing Binding Elements for WSDualHttpBinding
        TransactionFlowBindingElement
        ReliableSessionBindingElement
        SymmetricSecurityBindingElement
        CompositeDuplexBindingElement
        OneWayBindingElement
        TextMessageEncodingBindingElement
        HttpTransportBindingElement
Showing Binding Elements for WSHttpBinding
        TransactionFlowBindingElement
        SymmetricSecurityBindingElement
        TextMessageEncodingBindingElement
        HttpTransportBindingElement
Showing Binding Elements for NetMsmqBinding
        BinaryMessageEncodingBindingElement
        MsmqTransportBindingElement
Showing Binding Elements for MsmqIntegrationBinding
        MsmqIntegrationBindingElement
Showing Binding Elements for WSFederationHttpBinding
        TransactionFlowBindingElement
        SymmetricSecurityBindingElement
        TextMessageEncodingBindingElement
        HttpTransportBindingElement
Showing Binding Elements for NetPeerTcpBinding
        PnrpPeerResolverBindingElement
        BinaryMessageEncodingBindingElement
        PeerTransportBindingElement
```

As this output illustrates, the object returned from the *CreateBindingElements* method on a *Binding* is an ordered list of *BindingElements*. Notice that the last entry in the *BindingElement* list is always a transport *BindingElement* and that each *BindingElement* list contains a *BindingElement* that represents the message encoding. Several of the default bindings create *BindingElement* lists that contain additional *BindingElements*, but the transport *BindingElements* must always appear in this list.

In our output, you can also see that each *Binding*-derived type represents a set of messaging characteristics. At run time, the contents of the *BindingElement* list determine the messaging characteristics of an endpoint in our application. In other words, the *Binding* we choose for our endpoint has a direct impact on the way our application sends and receives messages. As a result, understanding the messaging characteristics of a particular *Binding* is vital to a success-ful WCF implementation. Table 4-1 shows the important characteristics of each binding that ships with WCF.

Table 4-1   Default Binding characteristics

	Interop	Security	Session	Transactions	Duplex	Streaming	Encoder
BasicHttpBinding	BP 1.1	T				O	TX
WSHttpBinding	WS-*	M	O	O	O	O	TX/MT
WSDualHttpBinding	WS-*	TM	O	O	O		TX/MT
NetTcpBinding	WCF	TM	O	O	O	O	B
NetMsmqBInding	WCF	TM	O	O			B
MsmqIntegrationBinding	MSMQ	T					TX
NetNamedPipeBinding	WCF	TM	O	O	O	O	B
NetPeerTcpBinding	WCF	T					B
WSFederationHttpBinding	WS-*	M	O				TX

BP 1.1 = Basic Profile 1.1, T = Transport, M = Message, TX = Text, MT = MTOM, B = Binary

When one first approaches the default WCF bindings, it is easy to become confused by the spectrum of messaging options that these bindings provide. Keep in mind that when deciding on a binding, you are really deciding on a binding for a particular endpoint, and an applica-tion can host multiple endpoints. If we build and deploy a receiving application that receives text-encoded messages over HTTP, we can easily add another endpoint so that the application also receives binary-encoded messages over TCP. For the most part, the *Binding* implemented at an endpoint is the primary means we use to express the messaging infrastructure of an endpoint. Chapter 8 describes bindings in detail.

The Contract

Contracts map object-oriented constructs to messaging constructs. More specifically, contracts define the endpoints in a receiving application, the MEP used by those endpoints, and the structure of the messages that an endpoint processes. For example, a contract helps to map the schema of a message body to a .NET Framework type definition, thereby simplifying the code required to generate a message whose contents match that schema. Three types of contracts are possible in WCF: service contracts, data contracts, and message contracts. Service contracts describe the operations in an endpoint. This description includes the name, the MEP, session-specific information, the action header block of both the request and the reply messages, and security information for each operation. Data contracts, on the other hand, map the structure of the body of a message to one or more operations. Message contracts map the structure of both the body and the header blocks of a message to one or more operations.

> **Note**   All contracts are annotated type and type member definitions, and the attribute used in the annotation controls whether the type definition represents a service, data, or message contract. It is important to remember that annotating a type or member definition simply adds information to the metadata of that type definition. As a result, all attribute definitions are inert. Performing work as a result of the presence of a specific attribute requires other code to interrogate the metadata of the type definition via the Reflection API. In the case of WCF contracts, the WCF infrastructure interrogates the metadata of a contract definition and takes action based on the contents of that metadata. It is possible to perform similar work manually, so contracts are optional. Practically speaking, the WCF infrastructure performs quite a bit of tedious work based on contract defintions, so virtually all the WCF applications you write should use contracts. I cover contracts in detail in Chapter 9.
>
> Constructing a contract by annotating a type definition is inherently late-bound. Although this is one of the primary means by which WCF provides extensibility and adaptability for the developer, it also means that inconsistencies or incompatibilities might not be caught until run time.

Service Contracts

Service contracts represent the operations exposed by an endpoint and are used by both the sender and the receiver in a message exchange. Receiving applications can use a service contract to build the messaging infrastructure that listens for incoming messages. A sending application can use a service contract to build the messaging infrastructure that sends messages to a receiving endpoint. The information contained in a service contract includes the name of each operation, the parameters in that operation, the action header block associated with that operation, and session-specific information about that operation.

At the elemental level, a service contract is a class or an interface definition annotated with the *ServiceContractAttribute* attribute and one or more *OperationContractAttribute* attributes. The *ServiceContractAttribute* attribute is legal on both classes and interfaces, whereas the *OperationContractAttribute* is legal on methods. Most methods annotated with the *OperationContractAttribute* are members of a type annotated with the *ServiceContractAttribute*, with the one notable exception being duplex service contracts. Once again, I will cover this topic in detail in Chapter 9.

Data Contracts

Data contracts map .NET Framework types to the body of a message. If SOAP is the chosen messaging structure, a data contract maps a .NET Framework type to the schema of a SOAP message body. Like any WCF contract, a data contract is an annotated type definition, and the operative attributes are the *DataContractAttribute* and the *DataMemberAttribute*. Most of the time, a service contract references a data contract, as shown in the following example:

```
[ServiceContract]
interface ISomeServiceContract {
  [OperationContract]
  void SomeOperation(SomeDataContract info); // notice the argument type
}

[DataContract()]
sealed class SomeDataContract {
  [DataMember]
  Int32? number;

  String status;

  [DataMember] // must have getter and setter
  internal String Status {
    get { return status; }
    set { status = value; }
  }

  internal Int32? Number {
    get { return number; }
  }

  internal SomeDataContract(Int32? number) : this(number, null)
  {
  }

  internal SomeDataContract(Int32? number, String status) {
    this.number = number;
    this.status = status; // consider the null case
  }
}
```

In this example, the *ISomeServiceContract* interface defines a method that accepts an argument of type *SomeDataContract*. Since the *SomeDataContract* type is annotated with the *DataContractAttribute*, the body of the message sent to the *SomeOperation* operation will have a schema dictated by the *SomeDataContract* type.

Message Contracts

Message contracts map .NET Framework types to the structure of a message. If XML is the messaging structure, a message contract maps a .NET Framework type to the schema of the message. This includes both the header blocks and body of a message, as shown here:

```
[ServiceContract]
interface ISomeServiceContract {
  [OperationContract]
  void SomeOperation(SomeDataContract info); // notice the argument type
  [OperationContract]
  void SomeOtherOperation(SomeMessageContract info); // notice the argument type
}

[DataContract()]
sealed class SomeDataContract {
  [DataMember]
  Int32? number;

  String status;

  [DataMember] // must have getter and setter
  internal String Status {
    get { return status; }
    set { status = value; }
  }

  internal Int32? Number {
    get { return number; }
  }

  internal SomeDataContract(Int32 number) : this(number, null)
  {
  }

  internal SomeDataContract(Int32 number, String status) {
    this.number = number;
    this.status = status; // consider the null case
  }
}

[MessageContract]
sealed class SomeMessageContract {

  SomeMessageContract() {  }  // must have default constructor

  [MessageHeader]
  Int32? SomeNumber;

  [MessageBodyMember]
  SomeDataContract messageBody;

  internal SomeMessageContract(Int32? someNumber) {
    SomeNumber = someNumber;
    messageBody = new SomeDataContract(someNumber);
  }
}
```

Notice from the preceding code snippet that the *SomeOtherOperation* method on the *ISomeServiceContract* interface accepts an argument of type *SomeMessageContract*. This is legal because the *SomeMessageContract* type definition has the *MessageContractAttribute* annotation. There is quite a bit of information to cover in contracts, and we'll do the topic justice in Chapter 9.

WCF Gross Anatomy from the Inside

When examining the outside of a WCF application (the address, binding, and contract), it is natural to wonder how WCF uses addresses, bindings, and contracts to send or receive messages. From the code we have seen so far, there has been little code directly related to sending and receiving messages. In fact, an address, a binding, and a contract do little on their own. When we take a closer look at a WCF application, we see another infrastructure that uses addresses, bindings, and contracts to send and receive messages. In large measure, the rest of this book is dedicated to explaining this infrastructure, so I will introduce only the major parts of the infrastructure in this chapter.

When we look through the world of addresses, bindings, and contracts, we see an infrastructure that is split into two major architectural layers. The names of these layers are the ServiceModel layer and the Channel layer. The ServiceModel layer is the bridge between user code and the Channel layer. In other words, it is part of the normal API. The Channel layer, on the other hand, does the real work of messaging. The Channel layer is the layer that understands the details of a particular transport and WS-* message choreographies. WCF ships with rich Channel layer functionality. In general, the Channel layer is the domain of infrastructure developers, so it is entirely possible to write a fully functional WCF application without ever writing code that belongs to the Channel layer.

 Note   Although the division might be a bit simplistic, I am splitting developers into two categories: application developers and infrastructure developers. Application developers write applications, while infrastructure developers write code that will be reused by application developers. An application developer might write a purchase order processing application, while an infrastructure developer may write a reusable component that is consumed by the purchase order processing system. In WCF, the application developer writes a messaging application, but an infrastructure developer writes a custom channel.

Figure 4-2 illustrates how the ServiceModel layer and the Channel layer fit together.

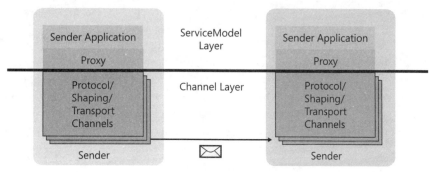

Figure 4-2 The ServiceModel layer and the Channel layer

Notice that the ServiceModel layer is called the Proxy (also called the Client) on the sender and the Dispatcher on the receiver. The Proxy and the Dispatcher have different roles, even though they are part of the same architectural layer. The Proxy is responsible for, among other things, creating messages to send to the Channel layer. The Dispatcher, on the other hand, is responsible for deserializing received messages, instantiating an object, and dispatching the deserialized message contents to that object. Both the Proxy and the Dispatcher serve more functions than these, and we will describe their roles more in Chapter 10.

The ServiceModel layer and the Channel layer are distinct from the simple world of the address, the binding, and the contract. In effect, the address, the binding, and the contract that are a part of the application developer API influence the creation of these two layers. When first approaching the WCF layers, it is often helpful to see which layers the address, binding, and contract influence. On the receiver, the address tells the Channel layer where to listen for incoming addresses. On the sender, the address tells the Channel layer where to connect to the receiving application. Bindings, on the other hand, are collections of factory objects that create the Channel layer. Contracts are used for message serialization and deserialization, and they are also used to determine the MEP of the receiving application. In general, the contract is a ServiceModel construct. Behaviors, on the other hand, can influence both the ServiceModel layer and the Channel layer. Figure 4-3 illustrates.

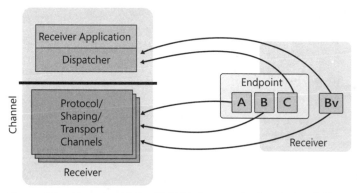

Figure 4-3 How the ABCs of WCF influence the ServiceModel layer and the Channel layer

Summary

In this chapter, we built a simple WCF application and decomposed it into its major components at run time. We saw that the application developer-facing WCF API is fairly straightforward but still offers considerable flexibility to the application developer. We also saw that the addresses, bindings, contracts, and behaviors that give WCF its simple API are used by two major architectural layers: the ServiceModel layer and the Channel layer. The remainder of this book covers both of these layers in detail.

Part II
WCF in the Channel Layer

Chapter 5
Messages

The *System.ServiceModel.Channels.Message* abstract type is the fundamental unit of communication in the Microsoft Windows Communication Foundation (WCF). Even though the *Message* type is used in every WCF application, access to it is largely abstracted away from the purview of the application developer. As a result, it is possible to write a feature-rich WCF application without ever directly interacting with an instance of a *Message* object. However, even if your code does not directly interact with *Message* objects, keep in mind that the WCF infrastructure is busy behind the scenes, creating, sending, receiving, or otherwise processing *Message* objects.

> **Note** Pay careful attention to the notation used in this chapter. When I use *Message*, I am referring to the *System.ServiceModel.Channels.Message* type. When I use *message*, I am referring to the abstract notion of data sent or received.

If the WCF infrastructure takes care of the *Message* processing for us, why should we spend the time and energy required to understand the *Message* type? In my opinion, there are two important reasons. First, many common WCF customizations (like behaviors and encoders) require direct interaction with the *Message* type. If you don't know anything about the *Message* type, these customizations will take longer than necessary, and you might do something that has drastic consequences for the rest of the WCF infrastructure. Second, I have found that a solid understanding of the *Message* type dramatically improves one's holistic understanding of WCF. On one level, most of the WCF infrastructure assists in the generation, sending, receiving, or other processing of *Message* objects, and as a direct result, understanding the *Message* type is fundamental in understanding the inner workings of WCF. For the purposes of enabling you to extend WCF and enhancing your general understanding of WCF, this chapter explains the core functionality of the *Message* type, as well as several other types that interact with *Message* objects.

Introduction to the *Message* Type

The *Message* reference type is the WCF abstraction of a SOAP message. As a result of this close association with a SOAP message, the *Message* type defines members that represent the SOAP version, envelope, header, header blocks, and body elements of a SOAP message. Like all XML-centric WCF types, the *Message* type is built on an XML Infoset. In effect, the *Message* type is really just a wrapper around a data store, and that data store is an XML Infoset.

The *Message* Type and SOAP

The relationship between the *Message* type and SOAP messages requires some explanation. When the architects at Microsoft designed WCF, they envisioned XML and SOAP as being the standard structure for all messaging applications. The industry has certainly trended in that direction. Most, if not all, modern messaging platforms have some support for sending and receiving XML messages. Many of these platforms have also embraced SOAP as the primary message structure. With this in mind, the architects at Microsoft drew the logical conclusion that SOAP and XML were the perfect choice for a message structure, and so the *Message* type fully embraces SOAP and has SOAP semantics baked into the object model.

The structure of the *Message* type adapts easily to non-SOAP-based XML messaging applications. The *Message* type is able to adapt to Plain Old XML (POX) messages by simply "rinsing off" the SOAP structure. Problems arise, however, when the *Message* type must adapt to a non-XML-based scenario. The most notable of these exceptions is JavaScript Object Notation (JSON). As its name implies, JSON is a way to represent an object in JavaScript, and is fully embraced by AJAX-enabling technologies like Microsoft ASP.NET AJAX.

Consider the following scenario as an example: A Web application needs to populate a drop-down list asynchronously with the values in an array. Assume also that the contents of the array are driven by the value of another control on the page. With Microsoft ASP.NET and ASP.NET AJAX, it is fairly trivial to retrieve this information and render it to the user without a full-page postback. What if, however, you wanted to retrieve the value of the array from a WCF service? In this case, the reply message must contain the array in JSON notation, not in XML. XML processing in browsers is too difficult and too complex for this type of application. Objects that are rendered as JSON, on the other hand, are easily transferable to the contents of the drop-down list via JavaScript.

At first glance, it might appear as though JSON could simply be another encoder that is applied to an instance of a *Message*, much like the Message Transmission Optimization Mechanism (MTOM). On closer inspection, several problems with this approach become apparent. For starters, JSON has no concept of XML namespaces and attributes. Our mythical JSON encoder would need to strip that information out of the XML. Furthermore, the order of strings is very important in JSON. In XML, the schema defines the order of elements. If a schema does not demand any order in the XML message, translating equivalent XML messages into the same JSON object is difficult, if not impossible. In an effort to solve this problem, the WCF team will release several additional types that assist in *Message* serialization.

Throughout its lifetime, a *Message* object must undergo several transformations before it can be transmitted to another messaging participant. From the sender's perspective, this transformation is a two-step process consisting of serialization and encoding. *Message* serialization is the act of transforming an instance of a *Message* into an XML Infoset, and encoding is the act of transforming an XML Infoset into a particular wire format. From the receiver's perspective, this transformation is the reverse of the one performed by the sender. In other words, the receiver must decode the received data into an Infoset and then deserialize that Infoset into an instance of a *Message*.

Much of the *Message* object model is dedicated to *Message* serialization and deserialization, and most of these members leverage other types in the WCF application programming interface (API). As a result, it is necessary to understand the types responsible for serialization and encoding before examing the *Message* type. The next section is devoted to examining the foundational types responsible for *Message* serialization and encoding. After we have looked at these serialization and encoding types, we will resume our examination of the *Message* type.

The WCF XML Stack

The Microsoft .NET Framework defines a rich set of types for general-purpose XML processing. As a messaging platform, WCF requires more functionality than what is normally required by other .NET applications. For example, you saw in Chapter 2, "Service Orientation," that WCF can generate, send, receive, and process binary and MTOM-encoded XML messages. Because the .NET Framework does not provide this capability, the WCF API defines types that do provide it, and we use these types to interact directly with the *Message* type. In other words, the WCF API defines types that transform a *Message* into a particular encoding. With this in mind, there are three key types defined in the WCF *System.Xml* namespace of the *System.Runtime.Serialization.dll* assembly that are fundamentally responsible for serializing and encoding the *Message* type: *XmlDictionary*, *XmlDictionaryWriter*, and *XmlDictionaryReader*. To keep the discussion of these types as simple as possible, I will illustrate these types by working with XML fragments rather than fully formed SOAP messages. Later in this chapter, you will see how these types can be used to serialize and encode instances of the *Message* type.

The *XmlDictionary* Type

As its name implies, an *XmlDictionary* object is a mapping of key-value pairs. Much like a language dictionary or vocabulary, an *XmlDictionary* can be used to substitute a simple expression for a complex one without losing any meaning. We use this type of mechanism in our everyday lives without even realizing it. Consider the following sentence I say to my friend Rusty: "I watched a movie last night about a *submarine.*" Rusty will hear this sentence and interpret it to mean "I watched a movie last night about a *vessel that functions on the surface and underwater.*" The first sentence is clearly shorter than the second sentence, and it requires less time to express. This compression and the resultant time savings are possible because Rusty and I share a vocabulary. As long as Rusty and I understand the same vocabulary, both of us can communicate efficiently. If, however, I say to Rusty: "This chapter was finished by sheer *elucubration,*" he might have no idea what I'm talking about. In this instance, I have ruined the overall time savings and efficiency by using a word that Rusty does not understand. In effect, a dictionary (or in this example, a vocabulary) increases efficiency only if it is known to all participants.

At the risk of flogging this analogy to death, there is one more lesson that it illustrates. When I say to Rusty, "I watched a movie last night about a submarine," the entire sentence itself symbolizes meaning that can be expressed several different ways, and in several different languages. If you know what the words *movie* and *submarine* mean, you probably envision, in your mind's eye, a dark theater (and maybe even the smell of $5.00 popcorn) and the silhouette of a submarine, respectively. In other words, the words in the sentence invoke images of "things" in the real world. In terms of the XML Infoset and encodings, you map the XML Infoset to these real-world "things," and you map the words used to express those "things" to a particular encoding.

In messaging applications, an *XmlDictionary* might be used to compress serialized and encoded message size, thereby decreasing the amount of bandwidth required to transmit the message. Just as humans must agree on a vocabulary before communication is effective, both the sender and the receiver must use compatible *XmlDictionary* objects when exchanging messages. Internally, an *XmlDictionary* defines a private list of key-value pairs that can represent the element names, attribute names, and XML namespace declarations of a SOAP message.

Before we work with the *XmlDictionary* directly, it is necessary to examine more closely the data stored inside an instance of an *XmlDictionary*. The key-value pairs stored internally in an instance of an *XmlDictionary* are of type *XmlDictionaryString*. An *XmlDictionaryString* is simply a type that defines, among other things, a *Key* property that is of type *Int32* and a *Value* property that is of type *String*. Even though the *XmlDictionaryString* type defines public constructors, an *XmlDictionaryString* is not typically created directly by user code, but by adding entries to a collection of *XmlDictionaryString* objects stored in an instance of an *XmlDictionary*. (We will see examples of creating an *XmlDictionaryString* later in this section.)

XmlDictionary defines a parameterless constructor and a seldom-used constructor that accepts an *Int32* that represents the maximum number of entries in the *XmlDictionaryString* collection. After construction, *XmlDictionaryString* entries can be added to the internal *XmlDictionaryString* collection of the *XmlDictionary* by calling the *Add* instance method defined by the *XmlDictionary* type. The *Add* method accepts a parameter of type *String* and returns an instance of type *XmlDictionaryString*, as shown in the following code snippet:

```
XmlDictionary dictionary = new XmlDictionary();
List<XmlDictionaryString> stringList = new List<XmlDictionaryString>();
// add element names to the dictionary and store in stringList
stringList.Add(dictionary.Add("ReleaseDate"));
stringList.Add(dictionary.Add("GoodSongs"));
stringList.Add(dictionary.Add("Studio"));
```

Because the *XmlDictionary.Add* method returns an instance of an *XmlDictionaryString*, the *dictionary* local variable contains three *XmlDictionaryString* objects that represent "*ReleaseDate*", "*GoodSongs*", and "*Studio*". Furthermore, the *stringList* local variable contains the same three *XmlDictionaryString* objects stored in the *dictionary* local variable. It is worth noting that the entries stored in the *dictionary* local variable are not publicly accessible—hence the need to store a list of these objects in another local variable. We can, however, see the *Key* and *Value* properties of each *XmlDictionaryString* by iterating over the *stringList* local variable as shown here:

```
Console.WriteLine("entries in Collection:");
foreach (XmlDictionaryString entry in stringList) {
  Console.WriteLine("Key = {0}, Value = {1}", entry.Key, entry.Value);
}
```

When the preceding code executes, we see that a value for the *Key* property is automatically assigned to each *XmlDictionaryString*:

```
entries in Collection:
Key = 0, Value = ReleaseDate
Key = 1, Value = GoodSongs
Key = 2, Value = Studio
```

Notice that the value of the *Key* property of each *XmlDictionaryString* is assigned by the *XmlDictionary.Add* method.

An *XmlDictionary* is useless on its own; it must be combined with other types in the WCF XML stack to perform syntactic compression. For that, let's turn our attention to the *XmlDictionaryWriter*, and then refocus our attention on how to leverage the *XmlDictionary-Writer* and an *XmlDictionary* to see how to compress a serialized and encoded XML Infoset.

The *XmlDictionaryWriter* Type

The *XmlDictionaryWriter* type is designed for *Message* serialization and encoding. It is derived from *System.Xml.XmlWriter*, and as such, it inherits many of its characteristics from the *XmlWriter*. Like the *XmlWriter*, the *XmlDictionaryWriter* is abstract, defines several factory methods that return instances of types derived from the *XmlDictionaryWriter*, wraps a *System.IO.Stream,* and defines many methods that begin with the word *Write*. In effect, using an *XmlDictionaryWriter* in an application is conceptually very similar to using an *XmlWriter*.

Unlike the *XmlWriter*, however, the purpose of the *XmlDictionaryWriter* type is to serialize and encode *Message* objects and optionally leverage an instance of an *XmlDictionary* for the purpose of syntactic compression. To this end, the *XmlDictionaryWriter* type defines some members that are different from the ones defined on *XmlWriter*. Let's further our exploration of the *XmlDictionaryWriter* by examining these unique members. First we will examine the creational methods on the *XmlDictionaryWriter* type, and then we will see how to serialize and encode XML data to the underlying *Stream*.

Creating an *XmlDictionaryWriter* Object

The *XmlDictionaryWriter* defines several factory methods, and all of them accept, either directly or indirectly, a reference to a *System.IO.Stream*. These methods are, for the most part, overloads of the following four methods: *CreateDictionaryWriter*, *CreateTextWriter*, *CreateMtomWriter*, and *CreateBinaryWriter*.

CreateDictionaryWriter   One of the *CreateDictionaryWriter* factory methods on the *XmlDictionaryWriter* type accepts a reference to an *XmlWriter*. Internally, the instance returned from these methods simply wraps the *XmlWriter* passed as a parameter. Since the object returned from these two methods is simply a wrapper around an *XmlWriter*, these methods are of little value, except when an *XmlDictionaryWriter* is required somewhere else in the API. For example, it is possible that you need to call a method that accepts an *XmlDictionaryWriter*, but you have only an *XmlWriter* local variable. In this case, you can create an *XmlDictionaryWriter* from an *XmlWriter* by calling the *CreateDictionaryWriter* factory method, passing the *XmlWriter* as a parameter as shown here:

```
MemoryStream stream = new MemoryStream();
XmlWriter xmlWriter = XmlWriter.Create(stream);
XmlDictionaryWriter writer =
  XmlDictionaryWriter.CreateDictionaryWriter(xmlWriter);
```

CreateTextWriter   The *XmlDictionaryWriter* type defines three *CreateTextWriter* factory methods. These methods return an instance of a type derived from *XmlDictionaryWriter*, and the purpose of this object is to generate text-encoded XML. All three of these methods accept a *Stream* as a parameter. Two methods accept a *Stream* and a *System.Text.Encoding* as parameters. One method accepts a *Stream*, an *Encoding*, and a *Boolean* as parameters. The *Encoding* parameter, as you might expect, dictates the *Encoding* used when encoding to the underlying

Stream. While there are many encoding choices, only UTF-8 and Unicode (UTF-16) little-endian and big-endian are supported by the *CreateTextWriter* methods. If none is specified, the encoding defaults to UTF-8. The *Boolean* parameter specifies whether the *XmlDictionary-Writer* owns the underlying *Stream*. If this parameter is set to *true*, calling *Close* or *Dispose* on the *XmlDictionaryWriter* will call *Close* on the underlying *Stream*, thereby preventing subsequent access to the *Stream*. If this parameter is not specified, it defaults to *true*. The following code snippet shows the *CreateTextWriter* method in action:

```
MemoryStream stream = new MemoryStream();
using (XmlDictionaryWriter writer =
  XmlDictionaryWriter.CreateTextWriter(stream, Encoding.UTF8, false)) {
      writer.WriteStartDocument();
      writer.WriteElementString("SongName",
                                "urn:ContosoRockabilia",
                                "Aqualung");
      writer.Flush();
}

Console.WriteLine("XmlDictionaryWriter (Text-UTF8) wrote {0} bytes",
                  stream.Position);
  stream.Position = 0;
  Byte[] bytes = stream.ToArray();
  Console.WriteLine(BitConverter.ToString(bytes));
  Console.WriteLine("data read from stream:\n{0}\n",
    new StreamReader(stream).ReadToEnd());
```

When this code runs, it generates the following output:

```
XmlDictionaryWriter (Text-UTF8) wrote 97 bytes
3C-3F-78-6D-6C-20-76-65-72-73-69-6F-6E-3D-22-31-2E-30-22-20-65-6E-63-6F-64-69-6E-67-3D-22-
75-74-66-2D-38-22-3F-3E-3C-53-6F-6E-67-4E-61-6D-65-20-78-6D-6C-6E-73-3D-22-75-72-6E-3A-43-
6F-6E-74-6F-73-6F-52-6F-63-6B-61-62-69-6C-69-61-22-3E-41-71-75-61-6C-75-6E-67-3C-2F-53-6F-
6E-67-4E-61-6D-65-3E
data read from stream:
<?xml version="1.0" encoding="utf-8"?>
<SongName xmlns="urn:ContosoRockabilia">Aqualung</SongName>
```

Notice that the *XmlDictionaryWriter* is wrapped in a *using* statement, thereby ensuring that the *Dispose* method is called. Also notice that the underlying *Stream* is available after the *using* block; this is possible because the *Boolean* parameter in the *CreateTextWriter* method call is set to *false*. It is also worth mentioning that the byte order mark (BOM) is omitted when UTF-8 is the chosen encoding. If Unicode encoding is selected, the output includes the standard UTF-16 little-endian BOM (FF FE).

CreateMtomWriter   The *XmlDictionaryWriter* defines two *CreateMtomWriter* methods. These methods return an instance of a type derived from *XmlDictionaryWriter* that will generate MTOM-encoded XML. Both of these methods accept a *Stream* as a parameter and several other parameters that control the way the XML Infoset is encoded. These parameters set the *Encoding*, the *ContentType* SOAP header, the Multipurpose Internet Mail Extensions (MIME) boundary, and the Uniform Resource Identifier (URI) for the MIME section, as well as whether the message headers are written to the underlying *Stream*. As with the *CreateTextWriter* methods, the supported encodings are UTF-8 and Unicode (UTF-16) little-endian and big-endian. The following code snippet demonstrates how to call the the *CreateMtomWriter* method:

```
MemoryStream stream = new MemoryStream();
using (XmlDictionaryWriter writer =
  XmlDictionaryWriter.CreateMtomWriter(stream, Encoding.UTF8, 1000,
                                       "Application/soap+xml")) {
  writer.WriteStartDocument();
  writer.WriteElementString("SongName",
                            "urn:ContosoRockabilia",
                            "Aqualung");
  writer.Flush();
}
Console.WriteLine("XmlDictionaryWriter (MTOM-UTF8) wrote {0} bytes",
                  stream.Position);
stream.Position = 0;
Byte[] bytes = stream.ToArray();
Console.WriteLine(BitConverter.ToString(bytes));
Console.WriteLine("data read from stream:\n{0}\n",
    new StreamReader(stream).ReadToEnd());
```

When this code executes, it generates the following output. (Most of the bytes have been elided for clarity.)

```
XmlDictionaryWriter (MTOM-UTF8) wrote 576 bytes
4D-49-4D-45-2D-56-65-72-73-69-6F-6E-3A-20-31-2E-30-0D-0A-43-6F-6E-74-65-6E-74-2D-54-79-70-
65-3A-20-6D-75-6C-74-69-70-61-72-74-2F-72-65-6C-61-74-65-64-3B-74-79-70-65-3D-22-61-70-70-
6C-69-63-61-74-69-6F-6E-2F-78-6F-70-2B-78-6D-6C-22-3B-62-6F-75-6E-64-61-72-79-3D-22-37-31-
65-37-62-35-32-61-2D-37-61-34-36-2D-34-37-32-36-2D-62-61-62-64-2D-31-37-37-32-32-39-65-32-
38-66-30-33-2B-69-64-3D-31-22-3B-73-74-61-72-74-3D-22-3C-68-74-74-70-3A-2F-2F-74-65-6D-70-
75-72-69-2E-6F-72-67-2F-30-2F-36-33-32-38-37-31-37-34-35-30-37-30-38-39-31-
data read from stream:
MIME-Version: 1.0
Content-Type: multipart/related;
  type="application/xop+xml";
  boundary="71e7b52a-7a46-4726-babd-177229e28f03+id=1";
  start="<http://tempuri.org/0/632871745070891488>";
  start-info="Application/soap+xml"

--71e7b52a-7a46-4726-babd-177229e28f03+id=1
Content-ID: <http://tempuri.org/0/632871745070891488>
Content-Transfer-Encoding: 8bit
Content-Type: application/xop+xml; charset=utf-8;
  type="Application/soap+xml"

<?xml version="1.0" encoding="utf-8"?>
  <SongName xmlns="urn:ContosoRockabilia">
    Aqualung
  </SongName>
--71e7b52a-7a46-4726-babd-177229e28f03+id=1-
```

The following code snippet demonstrates that calling the other *CreateMtomWriter* method produces very different output:

```
MemoryStream stream = new MemoryStream();
using (XmlDictionaryWriter writer =
   XmlDictionaryWriter.CreateMtomWriter(stream,
                                        Encoding.UTF8,
                                        1000,
                                        "startInfo",
                                        "boundary",
                                        "urn:startUri",
                                        false,
                                        false)){
   writer.WriteStartDocument();
   writer.WriteElementString("SongName",
                             "urn:ContosoRockabilia",
                             "Aqualung");
   writer.Flush();
}
Console.WriteLine("XmlDictionaryWriter (MTOM-UTF8) wrote {0} bytes",
   stream.Position);
stream.Position = 0;
Byte[] bytes = stream.ToArray();
Console.WriteLine(BitConverter.ToString(bytes));
Console.WriteLine("data read from stream:\n{0}\n",
   new StreamReader(stream).ReadToEnd());
```

When this code runs, it produces the following output. (Most of the bytes have been omitted for clarity.)

```
XmlDictionaryWriter (MTOM-UTF8) wrote 256 bytes
0D-0A-2D-2D-62-6F-75-6E-64-61-72-79-0D-0A-43-6F-6E-74-65-6E-74-2D-49-44-3A-20-3C-75-72-6E-
3A-73-74-61-72-74-55-72-69-3E-0D-0A-43-6F-6E-74-65-6E-74-2D-54-72-61-6E-73-66-65-72-2D-45-
6E-63-6F-64-69-6E-67-3A-20-38-62-69-74-0D-0A-
data read from stream:

--boundary
Content-ID: <urn:startUri>
Content-Transfer-Encoding: 8bit
Content-Type: application/xop+xml;charset=utf-8;type="startInfo"

<?xml version="1.0" encoding="utf-8"?>
<SongName xmlns="urn:ContosoRockabilia">
   Aqualung
</SongName>
--boundary-
```

Notice that the parameters of the second *CreateMtomWriter* method map to different locations in the MTOM-encoded data. Notice also that setting the penultimate parameter to *false* removes the multipart message headers at the beginning of the *Stream*.

Extreme care must be taken when calling the aforementioned *CreateMtomWriter* method. While both of the *CreateMtomWriter* methods serialize XML Infosets and encode them in an MTOM-compliant manner, the second method offers more control over the encoded data.

Clearly, the second method has benefits—namely, it allows more control over the formatting of the data. Certain applications might need this level of control. This control, however, introduces the possibility of breaking interoperability if the receiving application cannot interpret the information. As you saw in Chapter 2, one of the main motivators for MTOM is interoperability, so using the method might, if it is used incorrectly, subvert the very reason to use the MTOM encoding in the first place.

CreateBinaryWriter   The *XmlDictionaryWriter* type also defines four *CreateBinaryWriter* methods. These methods return an instance of a type derived from the *XmlDictionaryWriter* that generates binary-encoded XML. All of these methods accept a *Stream* as a parameter. Three of the methods accept an *XmlDictionary*, two of the methods also accept an *XmlBinary-WriterSession*, and one also accepts a *Boolean*. If specified, the *XmlDictionary* parameter indicates the *XmlDictionary* object used for syntactic compression. If no compression is required in an application, *null* can be passed for this parameter. In a manner consistent with the *CreateTextWriter* methods, the *Boolean* parameter in the *CreateBinaryWriter* method indicates whether the *XmlDictionaryWriter* owns the underlying *Stream*.

The *XmlBinaryWriterSession* parameter on the *CreateBinaryWriter* method allows the sender and receiver to automatically create and coordinate a dynamic *XmlDictionary*. As previously mentioned, the key-value pairs must be added to an *XmlDictionary* object before it is used, and the contents of the *XmlDictionary* must be shared among messaging participants (typically in an out-of-band mechanism). Sharing the contents of an *XmlDictionary* among messaging participants can be quite a challenge, and the *XmlBinaryWriterSession* addresses these challenges. The *XmlBinaryWriterSession* type emits the key-value pairs at the beginning of the *Stream*, thereby eliminating the need to explicity share an *XmlDictionary*. Internally, the *XmlBinary-WriterSession* maintains its own *XmlDictionary* and adds *XmlDictionaryString* objects as element names, attribute names, and XML namespaces appear in the content that is to be serialized. The *XmlBinaryWriterSession* generates data that is not as compact as data serialized via an equivalent *XmlDictionary* and a binary encoding, but the *XmlBinaryWriterSession* does not force us to know the contents of the *XmlDictionary* ahead of time or coordinate the *XmlDictionary* manually with the receiver. To decode the data in the underlying *Stream* at the receiving end of a message exchange, the receiver must use an *XmlBinaryReaderSession* object. The *XmlBinaryReaderSession* populates itself automatically from the dictionary emitted in the first part of the *Stream*. In effect, the *XmlBinaryWriterSession* type creates and coordinates an *XmlDictionary* dynamically, but does so with a performance cost.

> **Note**   Notice that this is the first mention of an *XmlDictionary* in the entire *XmlDictionaryWriter* type. As it turns out, binary-encoded XML is the only logical place to perform syntactical compression. All of the other factory methods are designed to generate some form of text. By their very nature, the UTF-8 and UTF-16 text encodings are well defined and do not lend themselves to compression in the same way that binary encodings do. There are other well-defined mechanisms for compressing text data (GZIP, the Huffman algorithm, and so on). It is also interesting that the *XmlDictionaryWriter* type is capable of a varied set of encodings, yet was named for one capability that is available only in the binary encoding.

The following code snippet shows how to call the *CreateBinaryWriter* method *without* using an *XmlDictionary*. (You will see how to leverage an *XmlDictionary* later in this chapter.)

```
MemoryStream stream = new MemoryStream();
using (XmlDictionaryWriter writer =
    XmlDictionaryWriter.CreateBinaryWriter(stream, null, null)) {
  writer.WriteStartDocument();
  writer.WriteElementString("SongName",
                            "urn:ContosoRockabilia",
                            "Aqualung");
  writer.Flush();
  Console.WriteLine(
    "XmlDictionaryWriter (Binary, no dictionary) wrote {0} bytes",
    stream.Position);
  stream.Position = 0;

  Byte[] bytes = stream.ToArray();
  Console.WriteLine(BitConverter.ToString(bytes));
}
```

When this code executes, it produces the following output:

```
XmlDictionaryWriter (Binary, no dictionary) wrote 43 bytes
3F-08-53-6F-6E-67-4E-61-6D-65-04-15-75-72-6E-3A-43-6F-6E-74-6F-73-6F-52-6F-63-6B-61-62-69-
6C-69-61-A1-08-41-71-75-61-6C-75-6E-67
```

Notice that the binary encoder generates output that is an order of magnitude smaller than the output of the MTOM encoder and half the size of the output of the text encoder. Also notice that access to the *stream* local variable is inside the block of a *using* statement. By default, the *CreateBinaryWriter* method puts the resultant *XmlDictionaryWriter* in control of the underlying *Stream*.

The *Write* Methods

Now that we have seen the different ways to create an *XmlDictionaryWriter* object, let's examine how to use this object to write XML. As previously mentioned, the *XmlDictionary-Writer* defines many methods for the purpose of writing XML to the underlying *Stream*, and all of these method names start with *Write*. Generally speaking, writing XML with an *XmlDictionaryWriter* is very similar to writing XML with the *XmlWriter*. The *XmlDictionary-Writer* does, however, define several unique methods that complement the needs of a messaging application. To prevent the risk of repeating documentation, this chapter does not elucidate the *XmlDictionaryWriter* methods that mimic the characteristics of the *XmlWriter* and instead focuses on a feature that is unique to the *XmlDictionaryWriter*: the ability to leverage the *XmlDictionary*.

Writing with an *XmlDictionary*

Many of the *Write* methods on the *XmlDictionaryWriter* type contain parameters of type *XmlDictionaryString*. These methods are typically paired with similar methods that accept parameters of type *String*. Consider the following method prototypes available in *XmlDictionaryWriter*:

```
// method accepting String objects
public void WriteElementString(String localName,
                               String ns,
                               String value);

// method accepting XmlDictionaryString and String objects
public void WriteElementString(XmlDictionaryString localName,
                               XmlDictionaryString namespaceUri,
                               String value);
```

Notice that both of these methods contain three parameters and that the second method simply accepts two *XmlDictionaryString* parameters for local name and namespace. It is important to note that the first method is defined on the *XmlWriter* type and the second method is defined on the *XmlDictionaryWriter* type. Given this tuple, you might wonder how they differ. For the answer, let's test both methods and then compare the results. The following code snippet uses the *WriteElementString* method that accepts three *String* parameters:

```
private static void UseTextWriter() {
  MemoryStream stream = new MemoryStream();

  using (XmlDictionaryWriter writer =
      XmlDictionaryWriter.CreateTextWriter(stream, Encoding.UTF8, true)) {
    writer.WriteElementString("SongName",
                              "urn:ContosoRockabilia",
                              "Aqualung");
    writer.Flush();
    Console.WriteLine("XmlDictionaryWriter (Text-UTF8) wrote {0} bytes",
                      stream.Position);
    stream.Position = 0;
    Byte[] bytes = stream.ToArray();

    Console.WriteLine(BitConverter.ToString(bytes));
    Console.WriteLine("data read from stream:\n{0}\n",
      new StreamReader(stream).ReadToEnd());
  }
}
```

This code generates the following output when it runs:

```
XmlDictionaryWriter (Text-UTF8) wrote 59 bytes
3C-53-6F-6E-67-4E-61-6D-65-20-78-6D-6C-6E-73-3D-22-75-72-6E-3A-43-6F-6E-74-6F-73-6F-52-6F-
63-6B-61-62-69-6C-69-61-22-3E-41-71-75-61-6C-75-6E-67-3C-2F-53-6F-6E-67-4E-61-6D-65-3E
data read from stream:
    <SongName xmlns="urn:ContosoRockabilia">Aqualung</SongName>
```

Next let's run a similar code snippet, but this time, call the *WriteElementString* method that accepts *XmlDictionaryString* parameters:

```
private static void UseTextWriterWithDictionary() {
  MemoryStream stream = new MemoryStream();

  // build the dictionary and populate
  XmlDictionary dictionary = new XmlDictionary();
  List<XmlDictionaryString> stringList = new List<XmlDictionaryString>();
  stringList.Add(dictionary.Add("SongName"));
  stringList.Add(dictionary.Add("urn:ContosoRockabilia"));

  using (XmlDictionaryWriter writer =
      XmlDictionaryWriter.CreateTextWriter(stream, Encoding.UTF8, true)) {
    writer.WriteElementString(stringList[0], stringList[1], "Aqualung");
    writer.Flush();
    Console.WriteLine("XmlDictionaryWriter (Text-UTF8) wrote {0} bytes",
                      stream.Position);
    stream.Position = 0;
    Byte[] bytes = stream.ToArray();

    Console.WriteLine(BitConverter.ToString(bytes));
    Console.WriteLine("data read from stream:\n{0}\n",
                      new StreamReader(stream).ReadToEnd());
  }
}
```

This code generates the following output:

```
XmlDictionaryWriter (Text-UTF8) wrote 59 bytes
3C-53-6F-6E-67-4E-61-6D-65-20-78-6D-6C-6E-73-3D-22-75-72-6E-3A-43-6F-6E-74-6F-73-6F-52-6F-
63-6B-61-62-69-6C-69-61-22-3E-41-71-75-61-6C-75-6E-67-3C-2F-53-6F-6E-67-4E-61-6D-65-3E
data read from stream:
<SongName xmlns="urn:ContosoRockabilia">Aqualung</SongName>
```

Both methods generate the same output! The syntactical compression that we expect when using an *XmlDictionary* did not occur. As stated in the discussion of *XmlDictionaryWriter* factory methods, the *XmlDictionary* is useful only when the *XmlDictionaryWriter* is going to generate binary-encoded XML. However, the ability to use an *XmlDictionary* is not limited to *XmlDictionaryWriter* methods that generate binary-encoded XML. This characteristic is intentional. To see why, consider the following method:

```
// assume that stringList contains XmlDictionaryString objects
// and is populated before this method is called
private static void WriteSomeXml(XmlDictionaryWriter writer) {
  writer.WriteElementString(stringList[0], stringList[1], "Aqualung");
}
```

The *WriteSomeXml* method will accept any parameter that derives from the *XmlDictionary-Writer* type. This includes an *XmlDictionaryWriter* that produces binary-encoded XML, as well as one that produces text-encoded XML. As a result of the encoding flexibility of the *XmlDic-tionaryWriter* type, the *WriteSomeXml* method can be used to write XML that adheres to a wide variety of encodings. In other words, the inclusion of the *WriteElementString* overload that accepts parameters of type *XmlDictionaryString* in all concrete *XmlDictionaryWriter* types results in a more flexible API.

If we create an *XmlDictionaryWriter* by calling the *CreateBinaryWriter* factory method and then call a *Write* method, we see a very different set of data in the underlying *Stream*. The following code snippet demonstrates:

```
// create the dictionary and add dictionary strings
XmlDictionary dictionary = new XmlDictionary();
List<XmlDictionaryString> stringList = new List<XmlDictionaryString>();
stringList.Add(dictionary.Add("SongName"));
stringList.Add(dictionary.Add("urn:ContosoRockabilia"));

MemoryStream stream = new MemoryStream();
using (XmlDictionaryWriter writer =
    XmlDictionaryWriter.CreateBinaryWriter(stream, dictionary, null)) {

    // write using the dictionary - element name, namespace, value
    writer.WriteElementString(stringList[0], stringList[1], "Aqualung");
    writer.Flush();
    Console.WriteLine("Using XmlDictionary w/Binary , wrote {0} bytes",
                    stream.Position);
    stream.Position = 0;
    Byte[] bytes = stream.ToArray();
    Console.WriteLine(BitConverter.ToString(bytes));
}
```

When this code runs, the following output is generated:

```
Using XmlDictionary w/Binary, wrote 14 bytes
42-00-0A-02-99-08-41-71-75-61-6C-75-6E-67
```

Notice that the combination of an *XmlDictionary* with binary-encoded XML results in over a 75 percent reduction in the size of the data produced with the text encoding (14 bytes vs. 59 bytes). The substitution of the *XmlDictionaryString* integer keys for the string values in the underlying *Stream* provides this compression. Keep in mind that the preceding code snippet substitutes the text of both the element name (*SongName*) and the namespace (*urn:ContosoRockabilia*). To further emphasize this point, the following code snippet shows how to generate binary-encoded XML without the assistance of an *XmlDictionary*:

```
private static void UseBinaryWriter() {
  MemoryStream stream = new MemoryStream();
  using (XmlDictionaryWriter writer =
      XmlDictionaryWriter.CreateBinaryWriter(stream, null, null)) {
    writer.WriteElementString("SongName",
                      "urn:ContosoRockabilia",
                      "Aqualung");
```

```
        writer.Flush();
        Console.WriteLine("Not Using XmlDictionary w/Binary, wrote {0} bytes",
                            stream.Position);
        stream.Position = 0;
        Byte[] bytes = stream.ToArray();
        Console.WriteLine(BitConverter.ToString(bytes));
    }
}
```

When this code executes, it generates the following output:

```
Not Using XmlDictionary w/Binary, wrote 43 bytes
3F-08-53-6F-6E-67-4E-61-6D-65-04-15-75-72-6E-3A-43-6F-6E-74-6F-73-6F-52-6F-63-6B-61-62-69-
6C-69-61-A1-08-41-71-75-61-6C-75-6E-67
```

In our test, the combination of an *XmlDictionary* and binary-encoded XML resulted in a 67 percent reduction in data size when compared with using binary-encoded XML with no *Xml-Dictionary*. To further understand the *XmlDictionary* and its purpose with the *XmlDictionary-Writer*, let's take another look at the byte sequences generated when the text encoder, binary encoder with no dictionary, and binary encoder with dictionary are used:

```
XML to be encoded:
<SongName xmlns="urn:ContosoRockabilia">Aqualung</SongName>

XmlDictionaryWriter (Text-UTF8) wrote 59 bytes
3C-53-6F-6E-67-4E-61-6D-65-20-78-6D-6C-6E-73-3D-22-75-72-6E-3A-43-6F-6E-74-6F-73-6F-52-6F-
63-6B-61-62-69-6C-69-61-22-3E-41-71-75-61-6C-75-6E-67-3C-2F-53-6F-6E-67-4E-61-6D-65-3E

XmlDictionaryWriter (binary) No XmlDictionary wrote 43 bytes
3F-08-53-6F-6E-67-4E-61-6D-65-04-15-75-72-6E-3A-43-6F-6E-74-6F-73-6F-52-6F-63-6B-61-62-69-
6C-69-61-A1-08-41-71-75-61-6C-75-6E-67

XmlDictionaryWriter (binary), With XmlDictionary wrote 14 bytes
41-00-06-02-A1-08-41-71-75-61-6C-75-6E-67
```

Notice the bold byte sequences. If we translate these byte sequences to ASCII characters, we see the following ASCII-to-byte mapping:

```
SongName
53-6F-6E-67-4E-61-6D-65

urn:ContosoRockabilia
75-72-6E-3A-43-6F-6E-74-6F-73-6F-52-6F-63-6B-61-62-69-6C-69-61

Aqualung
41-71-75-61-6C-75-6E-67
```

As evidenced by the preceding examples, an *XmlDictionaryWriter* that generates binary-encoded XML but does not use an *XmlDictionary* writes the element names, XML namespaces, attribute values, and element values directly to the underlying *Stream*. Likewise, an *XmlDictionaryWriter* that generates binary-encoded XML with the assistance of an *XmlDictionary* directly writes the element and attribute values, but substitutes single bytes for the element names and XML namespaces in the underlying *Stream*.

> **Note**   In my view, this sort of compression is a *huge* benefit. In distributed computing, one aspect of performance is the size of the transmitted data. In general, smaller data transmissions result in more highly performing applications. To relate this directly to messaging applications, smaller messages imply smaller data transmisstions, which in turn, imply more highly performing applications. Typically, developers and architects are so used to thinking about text-encoded XML that they assume that SOAP messages have a large footprint on the wire and perform poorly as a result. With WCF, this assumption is simply not true, because WCF can generate very compact XML. It is important to note, however, that the binary encoding discussed here does not interoperate with other platforms. Over time, I expect the industry to adopt standard binary encodings.

Now that we have seen how to instantiate an *XmlDictionaryWriter* and use it to write XML to a *Stream*, let's take a look at how to read encoded XML from a *Stream* using the *XmlDictionaryReader*.

The *XmlDictionaryReader* Type

The *XmlDictionaryReader* abstract type derives from *System.Xml.XmlReader*, and as such, inherits many of its characteristics from *XmlReader*. Like the *XmlReader*, the *XmlDictionaryReader* type defines several factory methods that return instances of types derived from *XmlDictionaryReader*. Furthermore, the *XmlDictionaryReader* wraps a *Stream* and defines many methods that begin with the word *Read*. As a result of its derivation hierarchy, using an *XmlDictionaryReader* is very similar to using an *XmlReader*.

Unlike the *XmlReader*, the purpose of the *XmlDictionaryReader* type is to read serialized and encoded XML Infosets and optionally leverage an instance of an *XmlDictionary* for the purpose of reversing syntactic compression. In effect, the *XmlDictionaryReader* is the converse of the *XmlDictionaryWriter*, and the object models of these two types are similar. Let's start our exploration of the *XmlDictionaryReader* by examining its creational methods and then examine how to use the *Read* methods. Because of the similarities between the *XmlDictionaryReader* and the *XmlDictionaryWriter*, this section will be shorter than the section on the *XmlDictionaryWriter* type.

Creating an *XmlDictionaryReader* Object

The *XmlDictionaryReader* type defines several factory methods, and all of them accept, either directly or indirectly, a reference to a *Stream* or a *Byte[]*. In general, the stream-oriented methods are similar to the buffer-oriented methods. For the most part, all of these factory methods are overloads of the four methods *CreateDictionaryReader*, *CreateTextReader*, *CreateMtomReader*, and *CreateBinaryReader*, and they mirror the behavior of the similarly named *XmlDictionaryWriter* factory methods. To keep repetition to a minimum, we will focus on the traits of the factory methods that are unique to the *XmlDictionaryReader*.

Several of the factory methods accept a reference to a *Stream*. Other parameters used in these stream-oriented factory methods include a reference to an *XmlDictionaryQuotas* object and a reference to an *OnXmlDictionaryReaderClose* delegate. In all cases, the former calls the latter, passing *null* for the *XmlDictionaryQuotas* and *OnXmlDictionaryReaderClose* parameters.

The *XmlDictionaryQuotas* type is a state container that describes the maximum values for important thresholds related to XML deserialization. For example, this type defines several properties that signify the maximum node depth to deserialize, maximum *String* length of a deserialized *Message*, maximum *Array* length of the body, and so on.

The *OnXmlDictionaryReaderClose* delegate is invoked near the end of the *Close* method implementation on the *XmlDictionaryReader* type. By the time this delegate is invoked, most of the state of the *XmlDictionaryReader* has been set to *null*. As a result, this delegate can be used as a notification mechanism (much like an event), but it cannot provide any valuable information about the state of the *XmlDictionaryReader* (unless of course, *null* is valuable). Message encoders use the *OnXmlDictionaryReaderClose* delegate to pool *XmlDictionaryReader* objects. These encoders rely on the *OnXmlDictionaryReaderClose* delegate as a notification that returns an instance of the *XmlDictionaryReader* to the resource pool.

The following code snippet illustrates how to instantiate an *XmlDictionaryReader*:

```
private static void CreateTextReader() {
  Console.WriteLine("==== Creating XML Dictionary Text Reader ====");
  MemoryStream stream = new MemoryStream();

  // create an XmlDictionaryWriter and serialize/encode some XML
  XmlDictionaryWriter writer = XmlDictionaryWriter.CreateTextWriter(stream,
    Encoding.BigEndianUnicode, false);
  writer.WriteStartDocument();
    writer.WriteElementString("SongName",
                              "urn:ContosoRockabilia",
                              "Aqualung");
  writer.Flush();
  stream.Position = 0;

  // create an XmlDictionaryReader to decode/deserialize the XML
  XmlDictionaryReader reader = XmlDictionaryReader.CreateTextReader(
    stream, Encoding.BigEndianUnicode, new XmlDictionaryReaderQuotas(),
    delegate { Console.WriteLine("closing reader"); } );
  reader.MoveToContent();
  Console.WriteLine("Read XML Content:{0}",reader.ReadOuterXml());

  Console.WriteLine("about to call reader.Close()");
  reader.Close();
  Console.WriteLine("reader closed");
}
```

When the preceding code snippet runs, the following output is generated:

```
==== Creating XML Dictionary Text Reader ====
Read XML Content:
<SongName xmlns="urn:ContosoRockabilia">Aqualung</SongName>
about to call reader.Close()
closing reader
reader closed
```

It is important to note that the other factory methods on the *XmlDictionaryReader* accept parameters that map very closely to the factory methods defined on the *XmlDictionaryWriter* type. These parameters have the same function as they do in the *XmlDictionaryWriter* type.

Round-Tripping XML with an *XmlDictionary*

Now that you've seen how to instantiate both the *XmlDictionaryWriter* and the *XmlDictionaryReader*, let's examine how to read binary-encoded XML with an *XmlDictionary*. As shown in the following code snippet, this is similar to what you've seen with the *XmlDictionaryWriter*:

```
MemoryStream stream = new MemoryStream();

// create the dictionary and add dictionary strings
XmlDictionary dictionary = new XmlDictionary();
List<XmlDictionaryString> stringList = new List<XmlDictionaryString>();
stringList.Add(dictionary.Add("SongName"));
stringList.Add(dictionary.Add("urn:ContosoRockabilia"));

// use an XmlDictionaryWriter to serialize some XML
using (XmlDictionaryWriter writer =
    XmlDictionaryWriter.CreateBinaryWriter(stream, dictionary, null)) {

  // write using the dictionary - element name, namespace, value
  writer.WriteElementString(stringList[0], stringList[1], "Aqualung");
  writer.Flush();
  Console.WriteLine("Using Dictionary, wrote {0} bytes",
                    stream.Position);
  stream.Position = 0;
  Byte[] bytes = stream.ToArray();
  Console.WriteLine(BitConverter.ToString(bytes));

  // create an XmlDictionaryReader passing the Stream
  // and an XmlDictionary
  XmlDictionaryReader reader =
    XmlDictionaryReader.CreateBinaryReader(stream, dictionary, new
      XmlDictionaryReaderQuotas());
  reader.Read();
  Console.WriteLine("data read from stream:\n{0}\n",
    reader.ReadOuterXml());
}
```

When this code executes, the following output is generated:

```
XmlDictionaryWriter (Binary w/dictionary) wrote 14 bytes
42-00-0A-02-99-08-41-71-75-61-6C-75-6E-67
data read from stream:
<SongName xmlns="urn:ContosoRockabilia">Aqualung</SongName>
```

Notice that the same *XmlDictionary* passed to the *CreateBinaryWriter* method on the *XmlDictionaryWriter* is also passed to the *CreateBinaryReader* method on the *XmlDictionaryReader*. Admittedly, passing a reference to the same *XmlDictionary* object is a crude way to ensure that both the *XmlDictionaryWriter* and the *XmlDictionaryReader* are using the same vocabulary, but nonetheless, it illustrates that the *XmlDictionaryReader* is able to interpret the compression performed by an *XmlDictionaryWriter* and an *XmlDictionary*.

Back to the *Message*

Now that we have explored the types fundamental in serializing and encoding a *Message*, it is time to refocus our attention on the *Message* type. The *Message* object model contains roughly 45 members that are either public or protected. Among these members are factory methods that return an instance of a *Message*, methods that serialize a *Message*, methods that deserialize a *Message*, properties that return information about a *Message*, properties to work with the header blocks of a *Message*, and methods that clean up a *Message*.

Creating a *Message*

A *Message* object can be created via one of the numerous *CreateMessage* factory methods it defines. For the most part, these methods accept the content of the SOAP body as a parameter to the method. It is important to note that the body of a *Message* cannot be changed after it has been created. SOAP header blocks, on the other hand, can be added or changed after the *Message* has been created. Broadly speaking, the factory methods on the *Message* type are categorized as methods that populate the body of the *Message* by serializing a graph of objects, methods that pull data into a *Message* from an *XmlReader*, methods that push data into a *Message*, and methods that generate a *Message* representing a SOAP Fault. Before we examine the different categories of factory methods, let's look at some of the context around *Message* serialization and deserialization.

A Word about *Message* Serialization and Deserialization

The words *serialization* and *deserialization* are common in distributed computing, and as a result, it is necessary to clarify their meaning as it relates to messaging applications. Let's consider the basic serialization and deserialization steps when sending and receiving *Message* objects. When a sending application needs to send a *Message* to another messaging participant, it must first create a *Message* object that contains the appropriate information, then serialize and encode the contents of that *Message* to a *Stream* or *Byte*, and then transmit that

Stream or *Byte* to the intended messaging participant. When a receiving application receives a *Message*, it is, for all practical purposes, in the form of a *Stream* or *Byte* (just as it left the sender). The receiving application must then decode and deserialize the *Stream* or *Byte[]* into a *Message* object and might need to optionally deserialize the contents of the header or the body of the *Message* into other objects.

As you can see, the serialization is generally associated with sender-specific tasks, and deserialization is generally associated with receiver-specific tasks. Both the sender and the receiver create *Message* objects, but the sender creates a *Message* from other objects in memory, while the receiver creates *Message* objects by decoding and deserializing a *Stream* or *Byte* into a *Message*. Once a receiving application decodes and deserializes a *Stream* or *Byte* into a *Message*, it can then transform the contents of the *Message* into another object, or a graph of objects. This transformation is, for all practical purposes, another deserialization step.

Message Versions

Because a *Message* object is the common language runtime abstraction of a SOAP message and there are multiple versions of SOAP in use, there is a need to express the SOAP version that a *Message* object is implementing. In the *Message* object model, the SOAP message version is applied when the *Message* object is created and cannot change afterward. The SOAP and WS-* specifications are living documents, and as a result, we should expect these documents to version over time. As they change, it is reasonable to assume that the qualifying namespaces and message structures they represent will change. To account for these inevitable changes, WCF provides several types that wrap SOAP-specific and WS-*-specific XML message semantics. Instances of these types are passed to the factory methods to indicate the intended SOAP version of the resultant *Message* object, and most of the factory methods defined on the *Message* type accept these types as parameters.

When applied to a *Message*, the *System.ServiceModel.Channels.EnvelopeVersion* type represents a SOAP specification that the *Message* will adhere to. Likewise, the *System.ServiceModel. Channels.AddressingVersion* type represents the WS-Addressing specification that the *Message* header blocks will adhere to when serialized. At the first release of WCF, there are two SOAP specifications (1.1 and 1.2) and two WS-Addressing specifications (August 2004 and 1.0).

The *System.ServiceModel.Channels.MessageVersion* type wraps both the *EnvelopeVersion* and the *AddressingVersion* types. *MessageVersion* has several static properties that represent the possible combinations of *EnvelopeVersion* and *AddressingVersion*. The following code snippet shows all of the publicly visible members of the *MessageVersion* type:

```
namespace System.ServiceModel.Channels {
  public sealed class MessageVersion {
    public AddressingVersion Addressing { get; }
    public static MessageVersion Default { get; }
    public EnvelopeVersion Envelope { get; }
    public static MessageVersion Soap11 { get; }
    public static MessageVersion Soap12 { get; }
```

```
    public static MessageVersion None { get; }
    public static MessageVersion Soap11WSAddressing10 { get; }
    public static MessageVersion Soap11WSAddressingAugust2004 { get; }
    public static MessageVersion Soap12WSAddressing10 { get; }
    public static MessageVersion Soap12WSAddressingAugust2004 { get; }
    public static MessageVersion CreateVersion(
      EnvelopeVersion envelopeVersion);
    public static MessageVersion CreateVersion(
      EnvelopeVersion envelopeVersion,
      AddressingVersion addressingVersion);
    public override bool Equals(object obj);
    public override string ToString();
  }
}
```

Most of these members are self-explanatory; a few require some explanation. In the version 3 release of WCF, the *MessageVersion.Default* property returns the equivalent of the *MessageVersion.Soap12WSAddressing10* static property. As you can see from the name, this property prepresents the infrastructure compliant with the SOAP 1.2 and WS-Addressing 1.0 specifications. The *MessageVersion.Soap11* and *MessageVersion.Soap12* properties set the *AddressingVersion* to *AddressingVersion.None* and set the *EnvelopeVersion* according to the name of the property. This is useful if you are creating a messaging application that needs to send SOAP messages but that does not implement WS-Addressing. The *MessageVersion.None* property returns a *MessageVersion* that indicates *EnvelopeVersion.None* and *AddressingVersion.None*. As you might expect, *MessageVersion.None* is useful in POX messaging scenarios.

Important   When either of these specifications evolve (and they inevitably will), code that builds a *Message* with the *MessageVersion.Default* might silently change in subsequent versions of WCF. This can be good or bad, depending on the messaging scenario. For example, upgrading to a future version of WCF might update the XML plumbing generated by the *MessageVersion.Default* property. If this update occurs, all of the messaging participants that interact with the updated message must understand the new message semantics. If all participants upgrade simultaneously, there shouldn't be any problems. If, however, we want to achieve independence in our versioning practices, accommodations must be made to interact with both the old and the new messages. In other words, an application that uses the *MessageVersion.Default* property might very well create a breaking change simply by upgrading WCF, and as a result, the *MessageVersion.Default* property should be used with caution.

The following code shows the the differences in the SOAP and WS-Addressing versions referenced by these properties of the *MessageVersion* type:

```
using System;
using System.ServiceModel.Channels;
using System.Xml;

class Program {
  static void Main(string[] args){
    MessageVersion version = MessageVersion.Default;
```

```
        PrintMessageVersion("Default",version);

        version = MessageVersion.Soap11WSAddressing10;
        PrintMessageVersion("Soap11WSAddressing10",version);

        version = MessageVersion.Soap11WSAddressingAugust2004;
        PrintMessageVersion("Soap11WSAddressingAugust2004",version);

        version = MessageVersion.Soap12WSAddressing10;
        PrintMessageVersion("Soap12WSAddressing10",version);

        version = MessageVersion.Soap12WSAddressingAugust2004;
        PrintMessageVersion("Soap12WSAddressingAugust2004", version);
    }
    private static void PrintMessageVersion(String name,
                                            MessageVersion version) {
      Console.WriteLine("Name={0}\nEnvelope={1}\nAddressing={2}\n",
                        name,
                        version.Envelope.ToString(),
                        version.Addressing.ToString());
    }
}
```

When this code runs, it generates the following output:

```
Name=Default
Envelope=Soap12 (http://www.w3.org/2003/05/soap-envelope)
Addressing=Addressing10 (http://www.w3.org/2005/08/addressing)

Name=Soap11WSAddressing10
Envelope=Soap11 (http://schemas.xmlsoap.org/soap/envelope/)
Addressing=Addressing10 (http://www.w3.org/2005/08/addressing)

Name=Soap11WSAddressingAugust2004
Envelope=Soap11 (http://schemas.xmlsoap.org/soap/envelope/)
Addressing=Addressing200408 (http://schemas.xmlsoap.org/ws/2004/08/addressing)

Name=Soap12WSAddressing10
Envelope=Soap12 (http://www.w3.org/2003/05/soap-envelope)
Addressing=Addressing10 (http://www.w3.org/2005/08/addressing)

Name=Soap12WSAddressingAugust2004
Envelope=Soap12 (http://www.w3.org/2003/05/soap-envelope)
Addressing=Addressing200408
  (http://schemas.xmlsoap.org/ws/2004/08/addressing)
```

Serializing an *Object* Graph

Several of the *CreateMessage* methods are designed to serialize an *Object* graph into the body of a *Message*. To that end, these methods accept a parameter of type *System.Object*. One of these methods uses the default WCF serializer, and another accepts a custom serializer as a parameter. (We will examine serialization in more detail in Chapter 9, "Contracts.") In addition to these parameters, these methods accept a parameter of type *String*. This parameter sets the value of the WS-Addressing *Action* header block in the resultant *Message* **object**. As shown here, these factory methods are fairly straightforward:

```
// pass a String into the factory method
Message msg = Message.CreateMessage(MessageVersion.Soap12WSAddressing10,
                                    "urn:SomeAction",
                                    "Hello There");
// the ToString() method returns the entire Message
Console.WriteLine(msg.ToString());
```

When this code executes, the following output is generated:

```
<s:Envelope xmlns:a="http://www.w3.org/2005/08/addressing"
    xmlns:s="http://www.w3.org/2003/05/soap-envelope">
  <s:Header>
    <a:Action s:mustUnderstand="1">urn:SomeAction</a:Action>
  </s:Header>
  <s:Body>
    <string xmlns="http://schemas.microsoft.com/2003/10/Serialization/">
      Hello There
    </string>
  </s:Body>
</s:Envelope>
```

As you can see from the preceding example, the *String* "Hello There" was automatically assigned to the body of the *Message*. Let's change the *Object* parameter from a *String* to a *PurchaseOrder*, as shown in the following code snippet, and see what happens:

```
sealed class MyApp {
  static void Main() {
    VendorInfo vInfo = new VendorInfo(5, "Contoso");
    PurchaseOrder po = new PurchaseOrder(50, vInfo);
    Message msg = Message.CreateMessage(
      MessageVersion.Soap12WSAddressing10,
      "urn:SomeAction",
      po);
    // the ToString() method returns the entire Message
    Console.WriteLine(msg.ToString());
  }

  private sealed class PurchaseOrder {
    Int32 poNumber;
    VendorInfo vendorInfo;

    internal PurchaseOrder(Int32 poNumber, VendorInfo vendorInfo) {
      this.poNumber = poNumber;
      this.vendorInfo = vendorInfo;
    }
  }
```

```
    private sealed class VendorInfo {
      Int32 vendorNumber;
      String vendorName;

      internal VendorInfo(Int32 vendorNumber, String vendorName) {
        this.vendorNumber = vendorNumber;
        this.vendorName = vendorName;
      }
    }
  }
}
```

When this code runs, the default serializer used by the *CreateMessage* method throws an *InvalidDataContractException*. We will examine data contracts and serialization in more detail in Chapter 9. If we want to pass an object graph to these methods, it must be serializable, and all the objects it refers to must also be serializable. The first example of passing a *String* to the *CreateMessage* method succeeded because C# primitive types are implicitly serializable. There are many types that are implicitly serializable, and there are several ways to make a type explicitly serializable. You will learn more about implicit and explicit serialization in Chapter 9. For the moment, let's annotate both the *PurchaseOrder* and *VendorInfo* types with the *SerializableAttribute* attribute, thereby making them serializable. If we run the preceding example with serializable types, we see the following output:

```
<s:Envelope xmlns:a="http://www.w3.org/2005/08/addressing"
    xmlns:s="http://www.w3.org/2003/05/soap-envelope">
  <s:Header>
    <a:Action s:mustUnderstand="1">urn:SomeAction</a:Action>
  </s:Header>
  <s:Body>
    <MyApp.PurchaseOrder
      xmlns:i="http://www.w3.org/2001/XMLSchema-instance" xmlns=
"http://schemas.datacontract.org/2004/07/CreatingMessageBySerialization">
      <poNumber>50</poNumber>
      <vendorInfo>
        <vendorName>Contoso</vendorName>
        <vendorNumber>5</vendorNumber>
      </vendorInfo>
    </MyApp.PurchaseOrder>
  </s:Body>
</s:Envelope>
```

Notice that a *PurchaseOrder* object (and a *VendorInfo* object) are serialized to the body of the SOAP message.

Pulling Data from a Reader

Several of the *CreateMessage* methods accept either an *XmlReader* or an *XmlDictionaryReader*. These methods "pull" either the entire contents of the *XmlDictionaryReader* into the returned *Message* or the contents of the *XmlDictionaryReader* into the body of the *Message*. It is important to note that the *CreateMessage* methods that accept an *XmlReader* as a parameter create an *XmlDictionaryReader* object by calling the *CreateDictionaryReader* factory method on the *XmlDictionaryReader* type.

These methods are most useful when you need to deserialize a *Message* from a *Byte[]* or a *Stream*, as is the case when a receiving application receives a *Stream* that contains a serialized and encoded *Message*. When building a *Message* using one of these methods, you must know whether the underlying *Byte[]* or *Stream* includes the entire contents of a *Message* or just the body. To accommodate both scenarios, *CreateMessage* is overloaded to include parameters that read the entire envelope and parameters that read just the body element.

To illustrate, the following file contains the contents of a message that has been serialized to a file named *entireMessage.xml:*

```
<s:Envelope xmlns:a="http://www.w3.org/2005/08/addressing" xmlns:s="http://www.w3.org/2003/
05/soap-envelope">
  <s:Header>
    <a:Action s:mustUnderstand="1">urn:SomeAction</a:Action>
  </s:Header>
  <s:Body>
    <string xmlns="http://schemas.microsoft.com/2003/10/Serialization/">
      Hello Message
    </string>
  </s:Body>
</s:Envelope>
```

Likewise, the following is a file named *bodyContent.xml* that contains the body of a message:

```
<string xmlns="http://schemas.microsoft.com/2003/10/Serialization/">
  Hello Message
</string>
```

The following code sample shows how to build messages using both of these sources:

```
const Int32 MAXHEADERSIZE = 500;

// ENVELOPE READER EXAMPLE
// Get data from the file that contains the entire message
FileStream stream = File.Open("entireMessage.xml", FileMode.Open);
XmlDictionaryReader envelopeReader =
    XmlDictionaryReader.CreateTextReader(stream, new
      XmlDictionaryReaderQuotas());
Message msg = Message.CreateMessage(envelopeReader,
                                MAXHEADERSIZE,
                                MessageVersion.Soap12WSAddressing10);
Console.WriteLine("{0}\n", msg.ToString());

//BODY READER EXAMPLE
// Get data from a file that contains just the body
stream = File.Open("bodyContent.xml", FileMode.Open);
XmlDictionaryReader bodyReader =
    XmlDictionaryReader.CreateTextReader(stream, new
      XmlDictionaryReaderQuotas());
msg = Message.CreateMessage(MessageVersion.Soap12WSAddressing10,
                        "urn:SomeAction", bodyReader);
Console.WriteLine("{0}\n", msg.ToString());
```

Notice that the first call to *CreateMessage* accepts an *Int32* as a parameter that indicates the maximum size in bytes of the *Message* header. This limit is necessary because we are deserializing the entire contents of the *Message* from a *Stream*. Since the header of a *Message* is always buffered, this parameter allows us to control the size of that buffer, and the resource demands placed on the application as that *Message* is processed. Because the second call to *CreateMessage* is reading only the contents of the body from the *Stream*, control over the size of the header buffer is not necessary.

Pushing Data into a *Message* with a *BodyWriter*

One of the *CreateMessage* overloads allows callers to "push" data into the *Message* by means of a *System.ServiceModel.Channels.BodyWriter*. A *BodyWriter* is an abstract type that exposes a protected abstract method named *OnWriteBodyContents* that accepts an *XmlDictionaryWriter* as a parameter. It is through this method that a *BodyWriter* derived type can exert control over the creation of the body of a *Message*, and therefore, a *BodyWriter* is useful for exerting control over *Message* deserialization. For the most part, the implementation of the *OnWriteBodyContents* method consists of calling various *Write* methods on the *XmlDictionaryWriter* parameter. The following example illustrates a *BodyWriter* derived type that is intended to read the contents of an XML file and push the contents of the file into the body of a *Message*:

```
sealed class MyBodyWriter : BodyWriter {
  private String m_fileName;

  internal MyBodyWriter(String fileName) : base(true) {
    this.m_fileName = fileName;
  }

  protected override void OnWriteBodyContents(XmlDictionaryWriter writer) {
    using (FileStream stream = File.Open(m_fileName, FileMode.Open)) {
      XmlDictionaryReader reader1 =
        XmlDictionaryReader.CreateTextReader(stream, new
          XmlDictionaryReaderQuotas());
      reader1.ReadStartElement();
      while (reader1.NodeType != XmlNodeType.EndElement) {
        writer.WriteNode(reader1, true);
      }
    }
  }
}
```

Once the *BodyWriter* is subclassed, it can be used in a *CreateMessage* method, as shown here:

```
Message pushMessage = Message.CreateMessage(
                        MessageVersion.Soap12WSAddressing10,
                        "urn:SomeAction",
                        new MyBodyWriter("bodyContent.xml"));
```

Messages and SOAP Faults

The *Message* type defines a few factory methods that create *Message* objects that represent a *SOAP Fault*. A SOAP Fault is a form of a SOAP message that carries error information. It is distinct from other SOAP messages in that the SOAP specifications (both 1.1 and 1.2) dictate the content of the body, and in some cases, a few of the header blocks of the SOAP message. By virtue of the fact that a *Message* is the common language runtime abstraction of a SOAP message, a *Message* can represent a SOAP Fault, just as it can represent a SOAP message. This section describes some of the basics of SOAP Faults, the types fundamental in creating a *Message* that represents a SOAP Fault, and how to create a *Message* that represents a SOAP fault.

SOAP Fault Anatomy

SOAP Fault anatomy is dictated by SOAP specifications (1.1 and 1.2). Fundamentally, a SOAP 1.1 Fault contains a SOAP body that wraps a mandatory *faultcode* element, a mandatory *faultstring* element, an optional *faultactor* element, and an optional *faultdetail* element. To avoid repeating the specification here, see *http://www.w3.org/TR/soap11* for more information about the rules that dictate when the optional elements should appear. At a high level, the *faultcode* element represents an identifier that can be used by the sender and receiver infrastructures to identify the type of error that occurred. The SOAP 1.1 specification defines a small set of *faultcode*s, but an application is free to define *faultcode*s that are unique to an application. The *faultstring* element is intended to be a human-readable representation of the *faultcode* and is not intended to be used by the receiving application (unless the contents of the *faultstring* are shown to the user). The *faultactor* element is a URI that describes the the source of the error.

The structure of a SOAP Fault changes dramatically from SOAP 1.1 to SOAP 1.2. Because SOAP 1.2 is built on the Infoset, a SOAP 1.2 Fault is fundamentally composed of a set of information items. In addition to this fundamental change in the representation of a SOAP Fault, the names of the parts of a SOAP Fault have been changed and expanded to include more descriptive information. SOAP 1.2 states that a SOAP Fault should contain a mandatory Code information item, a mandatory Reason information item, an optional Node information item, an optional Role information item, and an optional Detail information item. Information about the rules surrounding when an information item is needed can be found at *http://www.w3.org/TR/soap12-part1/#soapfault*. In general, the Code information item represents an identifier of the error that occurred, and allows nesting sub-Code information items to provide more granular information about the error. SOAP 1.2 defines a few Code information items and allows an application to define its own values. The Reason information item represents a human-readable explanation of the error. The Node information item represents the messaging participant that caused the SOAP Fault. The Role information item represents the SOAP Role that the messaging participant was participating in when the SOAP Fault was generated. The Detail information item is intended to be a bucket for other relevant information about the error.

SOAP 1.1 and 1.2 Faults, despite their differences, are similar in the type of information they describe. Both of these specifications define placeholders for an error code, a human-readable description of the error, a description of the messaging participant that caused the SOAP Fault, and a bucket that contains extra information about the error. To this end, WCF defines a type named *System.ServiceModel.Channels.MessageFault* that represents the information stored in SOAP 1.1 and SOAP 1.2 Faults. Before we look at how to express a SOAP Fault in a format described by SOAP 1.1 and SOAP 1.2, let's first examine how to generalize a SOAP Fault through the *MessageFault* type.

The *MessageFault* Type

The *MessageFault* type is a way to describe error information in a SOAP-version-agnostic manner. Keeping in mind that WCF has a highly layered architecture, the *MessageFault* type provides tremendous flexibility when processing SOAP messages and optionally generating exceptions.

Creating a *MessageFault* Object   Like many other types in WCF, *MessageFault* is an abstract type that defines several factory methods. These factory methods accept parameters that represent the information stored in a SOAP Fault. In addition to these parameters, the *MessageFault* also defines factory methods that accept a parameter identifying the messaging participant generating the SOAP Fault. It is worth noting that the *MessageFault* type defines one factory method that accepts a *Message* as a parameter. This method is quite useful when a WCF application receives a *Message* determined to be a SOAP Fault and needs to pass information about that fault to other parts of the WCF infrastructure for processing.

Information about the *faultcode* is represented by the *System.ServiceModel.FaultCode* type. This type defines constructors as well as factory methods. All of these creational methods allow the specification of a sub-Code. The factory methods on the *FaultCode* type, however, automate the generation of sender and receiver fault codes (as defined in both SOAP 1.1 and SOAP 1.2).

Information about the *faultreason* is represented by the *System.ServiceModel.FaultReason* type. In the simplest case, one constructor accepts a parameter of type *String*, where the *String* represents human-readable information about the error. Since humans do not all speak the same language (even Microsoft .NET developers can't agree on a language), the *FaultReason* type defines constructors and methods that allow an application to embed multiple translations of a *String* in the *FaultReason* and extract the appropriate *String* based on a *CultureInfo*.

All but one of the factory methods defined on the *MessageFault* type accept parameters of type *FaultCode* and *FaultReason*. As a result, these types must be instantiated before a *MessageFault* is created, except when creating a *MessageFault* from a *Message*. Several of the factory methods also accept an *Object* as a parameter, and this parameter represents extra information about the error. As with the *Object* parameter in the factory methods on the *Message* type, the type passed for this parameter must be serializable (more on serialization in Chapter 9). The existence of this parameter begs the question, "What type of object should I use for this parameter?" Since *System.Exception* is serializable, you might be tempted to pass an *Exception* for this parameter. I strongly encourage you to resist this temptation. I prefer creating a custom type whose purpose is passing error information to other messaging participants. As we will see in Chapter 9, this demands a change to the contract.

Creating a *Message* from a *MessageFault*   Once we have created a *MessageFault*, we can create a *Message* from it by calling one of the factory methods defined on the *Message* type. The following code snippet demonstrates how to use the *FaultCode*, the *FaultReason*, and an *Object* to create a *MessageFault*, as well as how to build a *Message* object from a *MessageFault* object:

```
static void Main() {
  // create a Receiver Fault Code
  FaultCode faultCode = FaultCode.CreateReceiverFaultCode("MyFaultCode",
                                                          "urn:MyNS");
  // create a meaningful FaultReason
  FaultReason faultReason = new FaultReason("The value must be > 10");

  // create an object that represents the SOAP Fault detail
  SomeFaultDetail faultDetail = new SomeFaultDetail("Contoso", "SomeApp");

  // create a MessageFault
  MessageFault messageFault = MessageFault.CreateFault(faultCode,
                                                       faultReason,
                                                       faultDetail);

  // Build a Message from the MessageFault, passing the MessageVersion
  CreateAndShowMessage(messageFault, MessageVersion.Soap11WSAddressing10);
  CreateAndShowMessage(messageFault, MessageVersion.Soap12WSAddressing10);
}

private static void CreateAndShowMessage(MessageFault messageFault,
                                         MessageVersion version) {
  // actually create the Message object w/version info
  Message message = Message.CreateMessage(version,
                          messageFault,
                                "urn:SomeFaultAction");
  // show the contents of the Message
  Console.WriteLine("{0}\n", message.ToString());
}

// a serializable type for storing Fault detail information
[Serializable]
sealed class SomeFaultDetail {
  String companyName;
  String applicationName;
  DateTime? dateOccurred;

  internal SomeFaultDetail(String companyName, String applicationName) {
    this.companyName = companyName;
    this.applicationName = applicationName;
    //this.dateOccurred = null;
    this.dateOccurred = DateTime.Now;
  }
}
```

When this code executes, the following output is generated:

```
<s:Envelope xmlns:a="http://www.w3.org/2005/08/addressing"
    xmlns:s="http://schemas.xmlsoap.org/soap/envelope/">
  <s:Header>
    <a:Action s:mustUnderstand="1">
      urn:SomeFaultAction
    </a:Action>
  </s:Header>
  <s:Body>
    <s:Fault>
      <faultcode xmlns:a="urn:MyNS">a:MyFaultCode</faultcode>
      <faultstring xml:lang="en-US">The value must be &gt; 10</faultstring>
      <detail>
        <Program.SomeFaultDetail xmlns:i="http://www.w3.org/2001/XMLSchema-instance"
xmlns="http://schemas.datacontract.org/2004/07/MessageFaults">
          <applicationName>SomeApp</applicationName>
          <companyName>Contoso</companyName>
          <dateOccurred>2006-06-14T12:34:44.52325-04:00</dateOccurred>
        </Program.SomeFaultDetail>
      </detail>
    </s:Fault>
  </s:Body>
</s:Envelope>

<s:Envelope xmlns:a="http://www.w3.org/2005/08/addressing"
    xmlns:s="http://www.w3.org/2003/05/soap-envelope">
  <s:Header>
    <a:Action s:mustUnderstand="1">
      urn:SomeFaultAction
    </a:Action>
  </s:Header>
  <s:Body>
    <s:Fault>
      <s:Code>
        <s:Value>s:Receiver</s:Value>
        <s:Subcode>
          <s:Value xmlns:a="urn:MyNS">a:MyFaultCode</s:Value>
        </s:Subcode>
      </s:Code>
      <s:Reason>
        <s:Text xml:lang="en-US">The value must be &gt; 10</s:Text>
      </s:Reason>
      <s:Detail>
        <Program.SomeFaultDetail xmlns:i="http://www.w3.org/2001/XMLSchema-instance"
xmlns="http://schemas.datacontract.org/2004/07/MessageFaults">
          <applicationName>SomeApp</applicationName>
          <companyName>Contoso</companyName>
          <dateOccurred>2006-06-14T12:34:44.52325-04:00</dateOccurred>
        </Program.SomeFaultDetail>
      </s:Detail>
    </s:Fault>
  </s:Body>
</s:Envelope>
```

The most striking feature this code snippet shows is how the *MessageFault* is truly SOAP version agnostic. The first call to *CreateAndShowMessage* passes the *MessageFault* and *MessageVersion.Soap11WSAddressing10* as parameters, and the result is a SOAP 1.1 Fault. The second call to *CreateAndShowMessage* passes the same *MessageFault* but changes the *MessageVersion* to *MessageVersion.Soap12WSAddressing10*. The result is a SOAP 1.2 Fault.

The preceding example also shows how to create a *Message* from a *MessageFault*. The *Message* type defines a factory method that accepts a *MessageFault* and several others that accept a *FaultCode*. These factory methods on the *Message* type allow an application to create a *MessageFault* or *FaultCode* indicating an error and then pass that object to another layer in the WCF infrastructure to generate a *Message* object.

> **Note**   This might seem like a subtle capability, but it provides tremendous benefit. In effect, the *MessageVersion*-agnostic capability of the *MessageFault* type allows the SOAP version decision to be deferred to another part of the WCF infrastructure. In other words, only one layer in the WCF infrastructure needs to know the SOAP version required for transmission, thereby creating a more pluggable and extensible framework.

Buffered vs. Streamed Messages

When we think of messages moving between endpoints, we instinctively think in terms of buffers. To put it another way, we typically assume that when our application has received a *Message*, it has knowledge of the *Message* in its entirety. This type of behavior is known as *buffering*. The converse of buffering is known as *streaming*, and there are two ways that streaming communication can occur. The first mechanism resembles a *push model*, where the sender is pushing bytes to the receiver at its own cadence. When streaming content is moved in this way, the sender writes data until its local buffer is full, the data is transmitted to the receiver, and the receiver reads data from its local buffer as it arrives. The second mechanism resembles a *pull model*. When streaming content is moved in this way, the receiver requests bytes from the sender, and upon receipt of this request, the sender sends the requested number of bytes. This process is repeated in a loop until the sender has no more bytes to send. The WCF infrastructure implements the latter streaming methodology.

In WCF, the header blocks of a *Message* are always buffered, and the body of a *Message* is either buffered or streamed. The default maximum size of this buffer is 64 KB. (You will see how to change this setting in Chapter 8.) If the body of a *Message* is streamed, its size is unbounded. In practical terms, this means that we can transmit streaming media in WCF. Not all messages have streamed body elements. For example, small messages do not need to be streamed; buffers effectively handle them. Furthermore, a large *Message* is inherently difficult to validate. Consider, as an example, the case of a sending a 30-minute home movie in a streamed body element. The movie probably has value on its own and can be shown to the end user before the end tags are received. If the stream ends and no end tags are sent, handling the error becomes nearly impossible, because the end user has probably already seen the data. Likewise, if an application applies a digital signature to the stream, the signature can be vaidated only after the entire stream has been received and buffered, thereby largely defeating the purpose of using a streamed body.

Serializing a *Message*

Now that you've learned how to create a *Message*, let's examine how to serialize all or part of a *Message*. For starters, all of the *Message* serialization methods on the *Message* type methods start with the word *Write*, and these methods accept parameters of type *XmlWriter* or *XmlDictionaryWriter*. The actual work of *Message* serialization is performed by the *XmlWriter* or *XmlDictionaryWriter* object, rather than directly by the *Message* object. Remembering the discussion of the *XmlDictionaryWriter*, this serialization is actually a two-step process of *Message* serialization and encoding. The available method prototypes for serializing a *Message* are listed here:

```
public void WriteStartEnvelope(XmlDictionaryWriter writer);
public void WriteStartBody(XmlDictionaryWriter writer);
public void WriteStartBody(XmlWriter writer);
public void WriteBody(XmlDictionaryWriter writer);
public void WriteBody(XmlWriter writer);
public void WriteBodyContents(XmlDictionaryWriter writer);
public void WriteMessage(XmlDictionaryWriter writer);
public void WriteMessage(XmlWriter writer);
```

The *WriteMessage* methods serialize the entire contents of the *Message* to the the *Stream* wrapped by the *XmlWriter* or *XmlDictionaryWriter*. Since these methods serialize the entire *Message*, they are more commonly used than any other *Write* method on the *Message* type.

The *Message* type also defines methods that allow more granular control over *Message* serialization. For example, the *WriteBody* methods serialize the body element tags and body element content to the *Stream* wrapped by the *XmlWriter* or *XmlDictionaryWriter*. The *WriteBodyContents* method, on the other hand, serializes the contents of the body element (and not the body tags) to the *Stream* wrapped by the *XmlDictionaryWriter*. The *WriteStartEvelope* method simply writes the <s:Envelope tag to the *Stream* wrapped by the *XmlDictionaryWriter*. Calling the *WriteStartBody* method immediately after calling *WriteStartEnvelope* writes the XML namespaces to the envelope and serializes the start of the body tag and completely omits the headers from the serialized content. In practice, if we need to exert control over *Message* serialization by using these methods, we will certainly want to serialize header block contents. This capability is indirectly available in the *Message* object model and is covered in the section "The *Message Headers* Type" later in this chapter. For now, keep in mind that if you want to serialize a *Message* manually, you must explicitly serialize the appropriate header blocks. There are no explicit methods for writing the end envelope or body tags. To write the end envelope and body tags, simply call the *XmlWriter*. *WriteEndElement* method as necessary.

Deserializing a *Message*

The one ubiquitous task in all receiving applications is *Message* deserialization. *Message* deserialization is another term for creating a *Message* from a serialized *Message*. Since we have already covered how to create a *Message* object, we have, for the most part, already covered parts of *Message* deserialization. More specifically, we have already covered how to create a *Message* from an underlying *Stream* or *Byte* via the *XmlDictionaryReader* type.

Remembering the discussion of the *Message* factory methods, one of the ways we can create the body of a *Message* is by passing an *Object* graph to a *Message* factory method. In a similar manner, we might need to deserialize an *Object* graph from an instance of a *Message*. To this end, the *Message* type defines members that deserialize the body of a *Message* object. The prototypes for these methods are shown here:

```
public T GetBody<T>();
public T GetBody<T>(XmlObjectSerializer serializer);
```

The *GetBody* generic methods allow the caller to deserialize the contents of the body into an object of type *T*. One of the *GetBody<T>* methods accepts an *XmlObjectSerializer*, thereby providing an extensibility point for body deserialization. Regardless of which *GetBody* generic method we call, we must have specific knowledge of the type contained in the body of the *Message*. If the generic parameter used in these methods is not compatible with the body of the *Message*, a *SerializationException* is thrown.

Checking Whether a *Message* Is a SOAP Fault

As you have seen, an instance of the *Message* type can represent a SOAP message or a SOAP Fault. When a receiving application deserializes a *Message*, it must be able to determine whether the *Message* represents a SOAP Fault, because it is often the case that the execution path for a SOAP Fault is different from that of a SOAP message. To this end, the *Message* type defines the *IsFault* read-only property. In short, once an instance of a *Message* has been deserialized from an incoming *Stream* or *Byte*, the *IsFault* property indicates whether the *Message* represents a SOAP Fault and is typically one of the first checks the WCF infrastructure performs on a deserialized *Message*. We can illustrate the functionality of this property by changing the *CreateAndShowMessage* method from the preceding example, as shown here:

```
private static void CreateAndShowMessage(MessageFault messageFault,
                                         MessageVersion version) {
  Message message = Message.CreateMessage(version,
                                    messageFault,
                                    "urn:SomeFaultAction");
  // commented out for clarity
  // Console.WriteLine("{0}\n", message.ToString());

  // ** New code begins here **
  MemoryStream stream = new MemoryStream();
  // write the Message to a Stream
```

```
XmlDictionaryWriter writer = XmlDictionaryWriter.CreateBinaryWriter(
    stream,null, null, false);
message.WriteMessage(writer);
writer.Flush();

stream.Position = 0;

// read the Message from the Stream
XmlDictionaryReader reader =
    XmlDictionaryReader.CreateBinaryReader(stream, new
        XmlDictionaryReaderQuotas());
message = Message.CreateMessage(reader, Int32.MaxValue, version);

// check if it is a Fault
Console.WriteLine("the message {0} a SOAP Fault",
    message.IsFault ? "is" : "is not");
}
```

When this code executes (as part of the earlier code snippet), the following is generated:

```
the message is a SOAP Fault
the message is a SOAP Fault
```

Notice that the *Message.IsFault* property returns *true* for both of the *Message* objects created. It is important to note that this property returns *true* for all *Message* objects that represent a SOAP Fault, regardless of their encoding on the wire or the *MessageVersion*.

Message State

Now that we have seen how to create, serialize, and deserialize a *Message*, let's turn our attention to an important read-only property of the *Message* type named *State*. The *Message* type is stateful, and *Message* state can be described through a variety of means. Like any reference type, the state of a *Message* is the combination of the values of its fields, but this is not strictly what the *State* property of a *Message* represents. The *State* property of a *Message* represents the value of one private field of type *MessageState* (called *state*). As shown here, *MessageState* is an enumerated type that defines five possible values: *Created*, *Read*, *Written*, *Copied*, and *Closed*.

```
namespace System.ServiceModel.Channels {
  public enum MessageState {
    Created = 0,
    Read    = 1,
    Written = 2,
    Copied  = 3,
    Closed  = 4,
  }
}
```

The value of the *State* property of a *Message* object changes when certain methods are called on that *Message* object. Internally, concrete implementations of the *Message* type use the *State* property to manage the order in which methods are called on a *Message* object. For example, anytime a message is created via one of the *Message.CreateMessage* factory methods, its *State* is set to *Created*; calling any of the methods that start with the word *Write* changes the *State* to *Written*; etc.

Working with Headers

As you saw in Chapter 2, header blocks are used by SOAP message processing infrastructures to, among other things, express addressing, routing, and security information. Since WCF is fundamentally a message processing infrastructure that fully supports SOAP, it has several facilities for creating, serializing, deserializing, and interrogating the header blocks of a SOAP message. Remembering that the *Message* type is a common language runtime abstraction of a SOAP message, it follows that the *Message* type defines members that allow the WCF infrastructure to work with the header blocks of an outgoing or a received *Message*. The aptly named *Headers* instance property of the *Message* type provides this capability. As with other key types in WCF, working with the *Headers* property requires us to interact with other types in the WCF API—namely, the *MessageHeader*, the *MessageHeaders*, and the *EndpointAddress* types. The names of these types gives hints of their purpose. For example, the *MessageHeader* type is a generalized common language runtime abstraction of a SOAP header block; the *MessageHeaders* type is, in a broad sense, a grouping of *MessageHeader* objects; and the *EndpointAddress* type is a common language runtime abstraction of a WS-Addressing endpoint reference. When used in concert, these types provide the ability to insert header blocks to a *Message*, serialize and encode the contents of those header blocks, deserialize and decode the header blocks of a received *Message*, and extract information from deserialized header blocks. In this section, we will examine these fundamental types and how they can be used with the *Message* type.

The *MessageHeader* Type

The fundamental building block for SOAP message header blocks in WCF is the *MessageHeader* type, and its object model is very similar to that of the *Message* type. Like the *Message* type, the *MessageHeader* type is an abstract class that exposes several factory methods that each return a new instance of a concrete *MessageHeader* derived type. The *MessageHeader* type also defines several methods for serializing the contents of a *MessageHeader* via an *XmlWriter* or an *XmlDictionaryWriter*.

Creating a *MessageHeader* Object

There are several *CreateHeader* factory methods defined on the *MessageHeader* type. Each of these factory methods accept different combinations of parameters, but three parameters signifying the name (*String*), namespace (*String*), and value (*Object*) of the header block are always present. The remaining parameters allow us to pass a custom serializer, as well as values for the *mustUnderstand*, *actor*, and *relay* SOAP header block attributes. The following code snippet demonstrates how to build a simple *MessageHeader* object that signifies the *MessageID* header block as defined in WS-Addressing:

```
String WSAddNS = "http://www.w3.org/2005/08/addressing";
MessageHeader header = MessageHeader.CreateHeader("MessageID",
  WSAddNS, new UniqueId().ToString());
Console.WriteLine(header.ToString());
```

The following output is generated when this code executes:

```
<MessageID xmlns="http://www.w3.org/2005/08/addressing">
  urn:uuid:4639e0a1-4373-4a3a-b1c4-639ea0e72c00
</MessageID>
```

Notice that the XML namespace and the name of the *MessageID* information item must be known to create a *MessageHeader* object that serializes to (or in this case, renders as a *String*) the WS-Addressing *MessageID* header block. I'm not sure about you, but I would rather not memorize the gaggle of namespaces and header block names defined in all of the WS-* specifications. The WCF architects felt the same way, and they have provided several mechanisms that create WS-*-compliant header blocks for us. We will look at these mechanisms at different points throughout this book, as well as in the section "The *MessageHeaders* Type" later in this chapter.

It is important to note that we can also build *MessageHeader* objects that represent custom header blocks not related to WS-*. For example, a purchase order processing application might need to add a header block named *PurchaseOrderInfo* to a *Message* before the *Message* is sent to another messaging participant. To do this, we simply change the XML namespace, header block name, and header block value from the preceding example to fit the needs of the application. An example of a custom *MessageHeader* is shown here:

```
MessageHeader header = MessageHeader.CreateHeader("PurchaseOrderDate",
  "http://wintellect.com/POInfo", DateTime.Now);
Console.WriteLine(header.ToString());
```

This code generates the following output:

```
<PurchaseOrderDate xmlns="http://wintellect.com/POInfo">
  2007-01-12T09:18:52.020824-04:00
</PurchaseOrderDate>
```

Note   As you'll see in Chapter 9, the WCF infrastructure can do this work for us through the use of a message contract. When we take this easier and less-error-prone approach, the WCF infrastructure is executing code that is fundamentally similar to the preceding code snippet. It is also important to point out that a *MessageHeader* object is of little value on its own. To have any meaning, we need to reference that *MessageHeader* object from a *Message* object. You'll learn more about adding a *MessageHeader* to a *Message* in the section "The *Message-Headers* Type" later in this chapter.

Serializing a *MessageHeader* Object

The *MessageHeader* type defines several members that serialize and encode the state of a *MessageHeader* object. Like the *Message* type, many of these members are methods that start with the word *Write* and accept either an *XmlWriter* or an *XmlDictionaryWriter* as a parameter. The *MessageHeader* type also defines the *OnWriteHeaderContents* protected abstract method and the *OnWriteStartHeader* protected virtual method to allow types derived from *Message-Header* to exert more control over *MessageHeader* serialization. In a manner befitting an extensible framework, the implementation of the *Write* methods in the *MessageHeader* type calls the appropriate protected methods, thereby passing the task of serialization to the derived type.

> **Note** It is hard for me to imagine a reason to serialize a *MessageHeader* object outside the greater context of *Message* serialization. To put it another way, the only time you will need to care about *MessageHeader* serialization is when you are serializing a *Message*. Since the *Write* methods defined on the *Message* type serialize only the SOAP envelope and the SOAP body of a *Message*, it is necessary to serialize *MessageHeader* objects when serializing a *Message* object. We will revisit this topic in the section "The *MessageHeaders* Type" later in this chapter.

The following code snippet illustrates how to call one of the *Write* methods to serialize a *MessageHeader* object via an *XmlDictionaryWriter*:

```
[Serializable]
sealed class PurchaseOrderInfo {
  internal Int32 PONumber;
  internal DateTime? IssueDate;
  internal Double? Amount;

  internal PurchaseOrderInfo(Int32 ponumber,
                             DateTime? issueDate,
                             Double? amount){
    PONumber = ponumber;
    IssueDate = issueDate;
    Amount = amount;
  }
}
class Program {
  static void Main(){
    // create an object to store in the MessageHeader
    PurchaseOrderInfo poinfo = new PurchaseOrderInfo(1000,
                                                     DateTime.Now,
                                                     10.92);
    // create the MessageHeader
    MessageHeader header = MessageHeader.CreateHeader(
      "PurchaseOrderInfo", "http://wintellect.com/POInfo", poinfo);

    MemoryStream stream = new MemoryStream();
    XmlDictionaryWriter writer = XmlDictionaryWriter.CreateTextWriter(
      stream, Encoding.UTF8, false);
```

```
    // Serialize the MessageHeader via an XmlDictionaryWriter
    header.WriteHeader(writer, MessageVersion.Soap12WSAddressing10);
    writer.Flush();
    stream.Position = 0;
    // Show the contents of the Stream
    Console.WriteLine(new StreamReader(stream).ReadToEnd());
  }
}
```

When this code executes, the following output is generated:

```
<PurchaseOrderInfo xmlns:i="http://www.w3.org/2001/XMLSchema-instance"
    xmlns="http://wintellect.com/POInfo">
  <Amount xmlns="http://schemas.datacontract.org/2004/07/">
    10.92
  </Amount>
  <IssueDate xmlns="http://schemas.datacontract.org/2004/07/">
    2007-01-11T15:06:25.515625-04:00
  </IssueDate>
  <PONumber xmlns="http://schemas.datacontract.org/2004/07/">
    1000
  </PONumber>
</PurchaseOrderInfo>
```

Notice that the output contains information items that are subordinate to the *PurchaseOrderInfo* information item. Nesting information items as shown here is a byproduct of the way the *PurchaseOrderInfo* object serializes, rather than a direct function of the *Message-Header* object. Why, you might ask, do we care about nested information items in a serialized header block? We care because many of the header blocks defined in WS-* and many custom headers are structured as nested information items. In a nutshell, if we need to create nested information items when a *MessageHeader* is serialized, we must either pass an object to the *MessageHeader* factory method that serializes appropriately or subclass the *MessageHeader* type and control serialization through the implementation. Subclassing the *MessageHeader* type offers more control than relying on the default serializer in WCF and is certainly easier that writing our own serializer. As a result, the WCF API internally uses subclassed *MessageHeader* types as a means to serialize WS-* header blocks.

WS-Addressing Endpoint References

As you saw in Chapter 2, WS-Addressing identifies and standardizes constructs used to address SOAP messages, and one of these core constructs is the endpoint reference. As it is defined in WS-Addressing, an endpoint reference has a general structure similar to the one shown here (and also shown in Chapter 2):

```
<wsa:EndpointReference xmlns:wsa="..." xmlns:wnt="...">
  <wsa:Address>http://wintellect.com/OrderStuff</wsa:Address>
  <wsa:ReferenceParameters>
    <wnt:OrderID>9876543</wnt:OrderID>
    <wnt:ShoppingCart>123456</wnt:ShoppingCart>
  </wsa:ReferenceParameters>
</wsa:EndpointReference>
```

The information items shown here are really just one header block in a SOAP message. Keeping in mind that the *MessageHeader* type is a common language runtime abstraction of a SOAP header block, we can assume that a *MessageHeader* object can be the common language runtime abstraction of an endpoint reference. Notice from the preceding structure that the reference parameters information item is subordinate to the endpoint reference as a whole, and as mentioned in the previous section, this presents some interesting serialization challenges.

If we try to build a *MessageHeader* object that will serialize to a full endpoint reference (that is, address and reference parameter information items), we have three options:

- Define a type that represents an endpoint reference and pass an instance of that type as the *Object* parameter in a *CreateHeader* factory method.

- Subclass *MessageHeader* in such a way that we can customize serialization.

- Define a type that represents an endpoint reference *and* subclass the *MessageHeader* type.

Upon trying the first option, we quickly find that it is, by itself, unworkable (you'll learn more about serialization in Chapter 9), thereby forcing us to take the second or third approach. We can make the second approach work, but if we refactor our design, we quickly see that other parts of our application need a type that represents an endpoint reference. In other words, we are presented with a situation that lends itself to defining a type that represents an endpoint reference. Due to these facts, the WCF team took the third approach. They defined the *EndpointAddress* type as a way to represent a WS-Addressing endpoint reference and subclassed the *MessageHeader* type. It is through this combination that we can represent an endpoint reference with a *MessageHeader* object and serialize it properly. You'll see this in more detail in the section "The *MessageHeaders* Type" on the next page.

MessageHeader Miscellany

Several other facets of the *MessageHeader* type are worth mentioning. The most striking aspect of the *MessageHeader* type is the lack of a way to extract the value of a *MessageHeader* after it is instantiated. At first glance, this appears to present a real problem, especially when we try to interrogate the header block contents of a deserialized SOAP message. The *Headers* property of the *Message* type provides us with the solution to this dilemma. The *Headers* property is of type *MessageHeaders*, and this type defines mechanisms to extract the contents of all *MessageHeader* objects present in the *Message*. We will examine this topic in more detail in the section "The *MessageHeaders* Type" on the next page.

Another curious member of the *MessageHeader* type is the *IsReferenceParameter* read-only property. Useful when interrogating the header blocks of a deserialized SOAP message, this property indicates whether a *MessageHeader* object is a WS-Addressing reference parameter or reference property. You might be saying to yourself, "Didn't you just say that a reference parameter/property is, in effect, *part* of a *MessageHeader* object that represents an endpoint reference?" Yes, I did, but that does not subjugate the need to know if a *MessageHeader* object is a reference parameter or reference property.

Consider the structure of the *To* message information item in a SOAP message, as shown here:

```
<S:Envelope xmlns:S="..." xmlns:wsa="..." xmlns:wnt="... ">
  <S:Header>
    ...
    <wsa:To>http://wintellect.com/OrderStuff</wsa:To>
    <wnt:OrderID wsa:IsReferenceParameter="true">9876543</wnt:OrderID>
    <wnt:ShoppingCart wsa:IsReferenceParameter="true">
      123456
    </wnt:ShoppingCart>
    ...
  </S:Header>
<S:Body>
```

As illustrated here, the *OrderID* and *ShoppingCart* information items are their own header blocks and represent the reference parameters of an endpoint reference. Combined with the *To* URI, they can be used to create an endpoint reference, and therefore, they are different from other application-specific header blocks. We can easily build *MessageHeader* objects that represent the *OrderID* and *ShoppingCart* information items of the logical *To* endpoint reference, but it is not quite as easy to distinguish those *MessageHeader* objects from other *MessageHeader* objects unless the *IsReferenceParameter* attribute is present. In other words, when we deserialize a SOAP message into a *Message* object and interrogate the *MessageHeader* objects, we can determine whether any of these objects are reference parameters by checking the value of the *IsReferenceParameter* property. Once we have determined which header blocks are reference parameters, we can combine them with the *To* URI, thereby effectively building a *To* endpoint reference. You'll learn more about this topic in the next section.

The *MessageHeaders* Type

Because a SOAP message is likely to contain many header blocks, we need a way to represent a group of *MessageHeader* objects in a *Message*. The *MessageHeaders* type serves this purpose, and the *Message* type defines a read-only instance property named *Headers* that is of type *MessageHeaders*. The *Headers* property is the primary way that we add, modify, interrogate, or remove a *MessageHeader* from an instance of a *Message*. In one sense, this section covers the *MessageHeaders* type, and virtually all of the information can be applied to the *Headers* property of the *Message* type. In contrast to the body of a *Message*, we are free to modify the contents of the *Headers* property after we instantiate a *Message*. The *MessageHeaders* type is a concrete class that defines no factory methods. This is worthy of note since many of the other types discussed in this chapter are abstract and define factory methods.

As previously mentioned, the *MessageHeaders* type is, on one level, a grouping of *Message-Header* objects. The object model of the *MessageHeaders* type, however, is curiously missing a member that returns a collection of *MessageHeader* objects. Instead, the *MessageHeaders* type implements the *IEnumerable<MessageHeaderInfo>* and *IEnumerable* interfaces. This means that we can simply iterate over the *MessageHeaders* type to see all of the header blocks (after the *MessageHeaders* object has been populated).

> **Note** For thoroughness, I have to mention that the *MessageHeaderInfo* type is the base type of *MessageHeader*. The *MessageHeaderInfo* type defines several properties representing SOAP header block attributes like *Actor*, *MustUnderstand*, and so on. Quite frankly, I see little reason for the existence of this type since the *MessageHeader* type is abstract.

Creating a *MessageHeaders* Object

The *MessageHeaders* type defines three publicly visible constructors. It is important to note that most developers will never use these constructors directly, because the existing infrastructure in the *Message* type (or its derived types) will call one of these constructors for you. If you choose, however, to subclass the *Message* type, you might need to call one of these constructors to populate the header of the resultant *Message* object.

One of these constructors accepts one parameter of type *MessageHeaders*. This constructor performs a deep copy of the contents of the *MessageHeaders* parameter and stores that copy internally in the new *MessageHeaders* instance.

Another constructor accepts a parameter of type *MessageVersion* and, as you might expect, sets the SOAP version and WS-Addressing versions of the resultant *MessageHeaders* instance accordingly. The last constructor accepts a parameter of type *MessageVersion* and an *Int32*. This constructor assigns the SOAP and WS-Addressing versions, as well as the initial number of elements in the internal list of header blocks. Keep in mind that the actual number of elements in the list can grow beyond the value of the *Int32* parameter. If we know the number of header blocks we are going to add to a *MessageHeaders* object, using this overload has a slight performance benefit since the internal storage mechanism can be sized properly early in the life cycle of the object.

Adding a *MessageHeader*

Once a *MessageHeaders* object is instantiated, we will often need to add one or more *MessageHeader* objects to it. The *MessageHeaders* type defines an *Add* method that accepts a *MessageHeader* object as a parameter. The *Add* method inserts the *MessageHeader* parameter to the end of the list of existing header blocks.

If we need to insert a *MessageHeader* object in a specifc order, we can use the *Insert* method. This method accepts a parameter of type *Int32* and another of type *MessageHeader*. The *Int32* parameter represents the index we want to insert the *MessageHeader* into, and the *Message-Header* parameter is, of course, the object whose value we want to store. It is interesting to note that a *MessageHeaders* object stores its header blocks as an array—hence the indexing semantics. If we pass an index value that is greater than the size of the array, the method throws an *ArgumentOutOfRangeException*.

Getting the Value of a *MessageHeader*

When an application receives, decodes, and deserializes a stream into a *Message* object, we frequently need to get the values of one or more header blocks. Since the *MessageHeader* type offers no way to do this, we must turn to the *MessageHeaders* type.

One way we can find a particular *MessageHeader* in a *MessageHeaders* object is to find it by index. To find the index of a particular header block, we can call one of the two *FindHeader* methods. Both of these methods accept *String* parameters that represent the name and namespace of the header block. One of these methods accepts a *String* that represents the actors that can interact with that header block. The return type of both of these methods is an *Int32*. If a matching header block is not found, the *FindHeader* method behaves badly—it returns a −1. If duplicate header blocks are present, the method returns the index of the first one found.

> **Note**   In my view, this is a bad design since it runs counter to the best practices outlined in all of the Microsoft documentation and internal standards regarding framework design. It would have been better to name these methods *TryFindHeader* or throw an exception of some sort if a matching header block is not found. Regardless of my opinion, we must now check for the value -1 when calling either of the *FindHeader* methods.

After we have found the index (as long as it isn't −1) of the header block, we must then retrieve the value of the header block. To do this, we call one of the *GetHeader<T>* methods. The overloads of this method accept a variety of parameters, including the index of the header block and a custom serializer. Three of these overloads accept *String* parameters that map to the parameters of the *FindHeader* methods. Internally, these overloads call the appropriate *FindHeader* method and check for the return value of −1 accordingly. In contrast to the *FindHeader* method, if a matching header block is not found, the *GetHeader<T>* methods throw an exception.

Copying a *MessageHeaders* Object

The *MessageHeaders* type provides several mechanisms to copy one or all of the header blocks from one *MessageHeaders* object to another. To see where this is useful, consider what is required to generate a *Message* that is a reply to a received *Message*. If the received *Message* contains a *PurchaseOrderInfo* header block, we might need to include a copy of that header block in the reply *Message*. While it is possible to simply create a new header block with the same values, it would be simpler to copy the existing header block into the new *Message*.

The two *CopyHeaderFrom* instance methods provide the capability to copy the value of one header block into the *MessageHeaders* instance. Both methods accept an *Int32* parameter that indicates the index of the source header block. Both *CopyHeaderFrom* methods add the header block to the end of the internal array of header blocks, and there is no way to specify the destination index. One of the *CopyHeaderFrom* methods accepts a *Message* object as a parameter, while the other one accepts a *MessageHeaders* object as a parameter. Internally, the former calls the latter by means of the *Headers* instance property in the *Message* type.

The two *CopyHeadersFrom* instance methods provide the ability to copy the entire contents of one *MessageHeaders* object into another. There is an overload that accepts a *Message* object as a parameter, and another that accepts a *MessageHeaders* object as a parameter. Source header blocks are added to the end of the destination header blocks. In other words, this operation is more of a concatenation to the existing header blocks, rather than a complete replacement. This can easily have some unintended consequences, as shown in the following code snippet:

```
// create a Message
Message message = Message.CreateMessage(
    MessageVersion.Soap12WSAddressing10,
    "urn:SomeAction",
    "Hello WCF");
// add two new headers to the Message
message.Headers.To = new Uri("http://wintellect.com/Original");
message.Headers.Add(MessageHeader.CreateHeader("test", "test", "test"));

// create a new Message
Message message2 = Message.CreateMessage(
    MessageVersion.Soap12WSAddressing10,
    "urn:SomeAction2",
    "Hello WCF2");
// add two new headers to the Message
message2.Headers.To = new Uri("http://wintellect.com/Test");
message2.Headers.Add(MessageHeader.CreateHeader("test", "test", "test"));

// copy the headers from the first Message into the second one
message2.Headers.CopyHeadersFrom(message);

// show the contents
Console.WriteLine(message2.ToString());
```

When this code executes, the following output is generated:

```
<s:Envelope xmlns:a="http://www.w3.org/2005/08/addressing"
  xmlns:s="http://www.w3.org/2003/05/soap-envelope">
  <s:Header>
    <a:Action s:mustUnderstand="1">urn:SomeAction2</a:Action>
    <a:To s:mustUnderstand="1">http://wintellect.com/Test</a:To>
    <test xmlns="test">test</test>
    <a:Action s:mustUnderstand="1">urn:SomeAction</a:Action>
    <a:To s:mustUnderstand="1">http://wintellect.com/Original</a:To>
    <test xmlns="test">test</test>
  </s:Header>
  <s:Body>
    <string xmlns="http://schemas.microsoft.com/2003/10/Serialization/">
      Hello WCF2
    </string>
  </s:Body>
</s:Envelope>
```

Oops. Clearly there is a problem with this *Message*. In reality, the *CopyHeaderFrom* methods suffer from the same malady (duplicate header blocks). In other words, copying header blocks is a fairly tricky business, and the onus is on the developer to check for duplicate header blocks in the destination *Message*.

Serializing a *MessageHeaders* Object

The *MessageHeaders* type defines several methods that serialize all or part of a *MessageHeaders* object. Like the *Message* and the *MessageHeader* types, the serialization methods on the *MessageHeaders* type start with the word *Write*. The simplest of these methods is the *WriteHeader* method. As implied from its name, this method serializes one header block. It accepts an *Int32* and an *XmlDictionaryWriter* as parameters. The *Int32* parameter represents the index of the header block to serialize, and the *XmlDictionaryWriter* is, as you might have guessed, the object that performs the actual serialization and encoding. The implementation of the *WriteHeader* method calls two other *MessageHeaders* serialization methods: the *WriteStartHeader* and the *WriteHeaderContents* methods. The *WriteStartHeader* method, as its name implies, serializes the start of the header block, while the *WriteHeaderContents* method serializes the contents of the header block.

There is no one-step mechanism to serialize the entire contents of a *MessageHeaders* object. The only way to serialize all of the header blocks is to iterate over the header blocks and serialize each one. In practice, we seldom have the need to serialize header blocks outside the context of serializing a *Message*. To this end, the *Message* type defines the *WriteMessage* methods that serialize the entire contents of the *Message*. The implementation of the *WriteMessage* method on the *Message* type, however, iterates over and serializes each header block one at a time.

WS-Addressing and the *MessageHeaders* Type

In the section "The *MessageHeader* Type" earlier in this chapter, we examined some of the considerations for using a *MessageHeader* to represent a WS-Addressing endpoint reference. We will seldom, if ever, need to manually work with a *MessageHeader* that represents an endpoint reference, because the *MessageHeaders* type defines several properties that represent an endpoint reference. In other words, the *MessageHeaders* type defines several properties that will add, change, or remove WS-Addressing header blocks and is primarily used to assign these header blocks to an instance of a *Message* (via the *Headers* property of a *Message*).

More specifically, the *MessageHeaders* type defines the following endpoint reference–related properties: *From*, *ReplyTo*, *FaultTo*, and *To*. The *From*, *ReplyTo*, and *FaultTo* properties are of type *EndpointAddress*. As previously mentioned, the *EndpointAddress* type is the common language runtime abstraction of a WS-Addressing endpoint reference. We will examine the *EndpointAddress* type in more detail in the next section. Following the letter of the law as stated in WS-Addressing, the *To* property is of type *Uri*.

The *MessageHeaders* type also defines properties that relate to other parts of the WS-Addressing specification. For example, the *Action*, *MessageId*, and *RelatesTo* properties map to the similarly named WS-Addressing header blocks. The *Action* property is of type *String* and is fairly straightforward. In a nutshell, when this property is set, a WS-Addressing *Action* header block is serialized when the *Message* is serialized.

The *MessageId* and *RelatesTo* properties are of type *UniqueId*, and are also fairly straightforward. The *UniqueId* type is a GUID-like construct, but it can also take the shape of other types through the use of the constructor overloads. Consider the following code snippet:

```
UniqueId uniqueId = new UniqueId();
Console.WriteLine(uniqueId.ToString());
uniqueId = new UniqueId("myuniquevalue");
Console.WriteLine(uniqueId.ToString());
```

When this code executes, the following output is generated:

```
urn:uuid:fa89c9eb-6ada-4465-8f89-a7405f4aad4d
myuniquevalue
```

Notice that the value of a *UniqueId* object can be either a GUID-like value or an arbitrary *String* value. This functionality is required since the the *MessageId* and *RelatesTo* WS-Addressing header blocks are of type *xs:Uri*. In other words, any value can be placed in these fields. Since WCF is WS-Addressing compliant, a *System.Guid* cannot be used to represent these properties.

The *EndpointAddress* Type

The *EndpointAddress* type serves two functions: it is an easy-to-use type that stores destination address information, and it is a means to serialize a WS-Addressing endpoint reference into a *Message*. In other words, the *EndpointAddress* type is part of the commonly used API, but it also plays a critical role in *Message* serialization and deserialization.

An *EndpointAddress* object wraps a *System.Uri* object. As a result, all of the *EndpointAddress* constructors accept a *System.Uri*, in some form or fashion, as a parameter. More specifically, five of the six constructors accept a *Uri* as a parameter, and one accepts a *String* as a parameter. The constructor that accepts a *String* internally generates a *Uri* from that *String* and then calls one of the other constructors. This feature of the *EndpointAddress* simply makes the type more usable, as shown here:

```
EndpointAddress address1 = new
  EndpointAddress("http://wintellect.com/OrderStuff");
Console.WriteLine("Address1: {0}",address1.ToString());

EndpointAddress address2 = new EndpointAddress(
  new Uri("http://wintellect.com/OrderStuff"));
Console.WriteLine("Address2: {0}", address2.ToString());

Console.WriteLine("address1 {0} address2",
  (address1 == address2) ? "equals" : "does not equal");
```

When this code executes, the following output is generated:

```
Address1: http://wintellect.com/OrderStuff
Address2: http://wintellect.com/OrderStuff
Address1 equals Address2
```

Notice that the *String* rendering of the *Uri* is returned from the *ToString* method, rather than the String representation of a serialized *EndpointAddress*. Also notice that both constructors create the equivalent *EndpointAddress* object. (The operator overload on the *EndpointAddress* type checks the internal state for equivalence.)

There are several other constructor overloads that accept parameters of type *AddressHeader*, *AddressHeaderCollection*, *EndpointIdentity*, and *XmlDictionaryReader*. The most notable of these parameters is the *AddressHeader* type, and that is where we will begin.

The *AddressHeader* Type

The *AddressHeader* type is the common language runtime abstraction of a WS-Addressing reference parameter, and it simplifies the work required to add a reference parameter to a *Message* before serialization, as well as read the value of a reference parameter after *Message* deserialization. When one first approaches the *AddressHeader* type, there is commonly some confusion surrounding the differences between it and the *MessageHeader* type. These types do not share a common hierarchy, but they still serialize to the header of a SOAP message. The main difference is in their purpose: the *AddressHeader* type models a reference parameter, and the *MessageHeader* type models more general purpose header blocks.

From an object model perspective, the *AddressHeader* type is similar to the *Message* and *MessageHeader* types in that it is an abstract type that defines several factory methods, *Write* methods, and *Get* methods. (*MessageHeader* does not define *Get* methods, however.) The purpose of these methods in the *AddressHeader* type is consistent with the purpose of these methods in the *Message* and *MessageHeader* types and does not warrant repetition. I will leave it to the reader to experiment with these methods, if you are compelled to do so.

Serializing an *EndpointAddress* Object

An *EndpointAddress* is most useful when referenced from a *Message* object. This is typically done through the *Headers* property of the *Message* type. For example, we can instantiate an *EndpointAddress* and assign that *EndpointAddress* to the *FaultTo* address of a *Message*, as shown here:

```
String uriValue = "http://wintellect.com/someService";
AddressHeader header = AddressHeader.CreateAddressHeader("ref param");
EndpointAddress address = new EndpointAddress(new Uri(uriValue),
  new AddressHeader[1] { header }); // notice the use of the AddressHeader

Message myMessage = Message.CreateMessage(
  MessageVersion.Soap12WSAddressing10, "urn:SomeAction", "Hello There");
myMessage.Headers.FaultTo = address;
Console.WriteLine(myMessage.ToString());
```

When this code executes, the following output is generated:

```
<s:Envelope xmlns:a="http://www.w3.org/2005/08/addressing" xmlns:s="http://www.w3.org/2003/
05/soap-envelope">
  <s:Header>
    <a:Action s:mustUnderstand="1">urn:SomeAction</a:Action>
    <a:FaultTo>
      <a:Address>http://wintellect.com/someService</a:Address>
      <a:ReferenceParameters>
       <string xmlns="http://schemas.microsoft.com/2003/10/Serialization/">
         ref param
       </string>
      </a:ReferenceParameters>
    </a:FaultTo>
  </s:Header>
  <s:Body>
    <string xmlns="http://schemas.microsoft.com/2003/10/Serialization/">
      Hello There
    </string>
  </s:Body>
</s:Envelope>
```

Notice that the *AddressHeader* is populated in the WS-Addressing *FaultTo* endpoint reference as a reference parameter.

Because the *To* message header in WS-Addressing is an *xs:uri*, it is reasonable to wonder how we can use the *EndpointAddress* type in this critically important header. As you saw previously, the *To* property of the *MessageHeaders* type accepts a *System.Uri*, so we cannot set the *To* property directly with an *EndpointAddress*. The *EndpointAddress* defines the *ApplyTo* instance method, and thereby solves our dilemma. The *ApplyTo* method accepts a parameter of type *Message* and adds the state of the *EndpointAddress* to the *Message* passed as a parameter, as shown here:

```
String uriValue = "http://wintellect.com/someService";
AddressHeader header = AddressHeader.CreateAddressHeader("ref param");
EndpointAddress address = new EndpointAddress(new Uri(uriValue),
  new AddressHeader[1] { header }); // notice the use of the AddressHeader

Message myMessage = Message.CreateMessage(
  MessageVersion.Soap12WSAddressing10, "urn:SomeAction", "Hello There");

address.ApplyTo(myMessage);
Console.WriteLine(myMessage);
```

When this code executes, the following output is generated:

```
<s:Envelope xmlns:a="http://www.w3.org/2005/08/addressing"
  xmlns:s="http://www.3.org/2003/05/soap-envelope">
  <s:Header>
    <a:Action s:mustUnderstand="1">urn:SomeAction</a:Action>
    <a:To s:mustUnderstand="1">http://wintellect.com/someService</a:To>
```

```
    <string a:IsReferenceParameter="true"
            xmlns="http://schemas.microsoft.com/203/10/Serialization/">
      ref param
    </string>
  </s:Header>
  <s:Body>
    <string xmlns="http://schemas.microsoft.com/2003/10/Serialization/">
      Hello There
    </string>
  </s:Body>
</s:Envelope>
```

Notice that the *EndpointAddress* (including the *AddressHeader*) was assigned to the *Message* object and that the reference parameter attribute is flagged as per the WS-Addressing specification.

Copying Messages

In some cases it might be necessary to create a buffered copy of an existing message. The *Message* type contains the following instance method for this purpose:

```
public MessageBuffer CreateBufferedCopy(Int32 maxBufferSize) { ... }
```

Creating a copy of a *Message* is fairly straightforward, but it does cause a state change within the *Message* being copied. If not properly used, this state change can cause problems when working with the *Message* object that was just copied. When the *CreateBufferedCopy* method is invoked, the state property of the calling instance must be *MessageState.Created*. If the state property is set to any other value, the method will throw an *InvalidOperationException*. By the time the call to *CreateBufferedCopy* returns, the state of the calling instance has changed to *MessageState.Copied*. If the method call succeeds, an instance of a *System.ServiceModel. Channels.MessageBuffer* is returned. *MessageBuffer* defines a *CreateMessage* instance method that returns a *Message*. The newly created *Message* has a state of *Message.Created*. The following code snippet demonstrates how to copy a message:

```
Message msg = Message.CreateMessage(MessageVersion.Default,
                                    "urn:SomeAction",
                                    "Something in the body");

Console.WriteLine("Starting Message state: {0}\n", msg.State);
Console.WriteLine("Message:\n{0}\n", msg.ToString());

MessageBuffer buffer = msg.CreateBufferedCopy(Int32.MaxValue);
Console.WriteLine("Message state after copy: {0}\n", msg.State);
Message msgNew = buffer.CreateMessage();
Console.WriteLine("New Message State: {0}\n",msgNew.State);
Console.WriteLine("New Message:\n{0}\n", msgNew.ToString());
```

When this code executes, the following output is generated:

```
Starting Message state: Created

Message:
<s:Envelope xmlns:a="http://www.w3.org/2005/08/addressing"
  xmlns:s="http://www.w3.org/2003/05/soap-envelope">
  <s:Header>
    <a:Action s:mustUnderstand="1">urn:SomeAction</a:Action>
  </s:Header>
  <s:Body>
    <string xmlns="http://schemas.microsoft.com/2003/10/Serialization/">
      Something in the body</string>
  </s:Body>
</s:Envelope>

Message state after copy: Copied

New Message State: Created

New Message:
<s:Envelope xmlns:a=http://www.w3.org/2005/08/addressing
  xmlns:s="http://www.w3.org/2003/05/soap-envelope">
  <s:Header>
    <a:Action s:mustUnderstand="1">urn:SomeAction</a:Action>
  </s:Header>
  <s:Body>
    <string xmlns="http://schemas.microsoft.com/2003/10/Serialization/">
      Something in the body
    </string>
  </s:Body>
</s:Envelope>
```

Notice the state of the *Message* right after the *CreateBufferedCopy* method call and the state of the new *Message*. The *CreateBufferedCopy* method has limited uses, and the culprit is the state changes within the copied *Message*. It does prove useful, however, in the case of multiparty messaging scenarios, like the one in PeerChannel. In PeerChannel, one *Message* object must be copied several times, and the copies are sent to the various neighbors in the mesh.

Message Cleanup

The *Message* type implements *IDisposable* and defines a *Close* method. In a strange twist of architectural decision making, the *Dispose* member of the *Message* type is implemented explicitly, thereby preventing its use directly from the *Message* type. Calling the *Dispose* method on a *Message* object requires first casting the *Message* object to an *IDisposable* object and then calling *Dispose* through that reference. Further complicating this twist is the fact that the *Close* method is implemented as a publicly visible instance method. In essence, you can call the *Close* method on a *Message* object, but you cannot call the *Dispose* method directly. Internally, the *Dispose* method calls the *Close* method, so it functionally works, and you can still wrap *Message* instantiation in the C# *using* statement.

> **Note**   In my view, *IDisposable* is not implemented properly in the *Message* type. All standards that I know of, including the ones stated in the Framework Design Guidelines, state that interface methods should seldom be implemented explicitly, and I know of no standard that accepts a *Close* method without a similarly visible *Dispose* method. Although this was done with the aim of reducing developer confusion about *Close/Dispose*, I think that the *Message* type makes an existing problem worse, not better. Developers have come to expect to see a *Dispose* method on types, and occasionally a *Close* method. I know of no other type in the Microsoft .NET Framework that hides *Dispose* and exposes *Close*.

Summary

There is more to the *Message* type than is apparent at first glance; *Message* is one of the richer types in WCF. Even though the *Message* type is not visible in many WCF applications, it is always present, and it is the fundamental unit of communication in WCF. Because of its central position in WCF, it is my opinion that understanding the *Message* type is critical to understanding WCF as a whole. In this chapter, you've seen the various ways to create a *Message* object; how to serialize, encode, decode, and deserialize *Message* objects; how to work with header blocks; and much more. For the remainder of this book, as we examine different layers in WCF, it is important to remember that those layers are busy, behind the scenes, performing the work described in this chapter.

Chapter 6
Channels

Channels send and receive messages. Channels are responsible for work at the transport layer and for WS-* protocol implementations, security, and transactional processing. Channels are highly composable—in other words, they can be stacked in various ways to create the functionality required for a given application. Channels are extensible, and the WCF application programming interface (API) is intentionally designed in a way that allows framework developers to create custom channels when necessary.

For the most part, channels are hidden from the mainstream application developer API. Framework developers, on the other hand, will frequently create custom channels as a means to allow messaging over custom transport or via a custom protocol that is not supported by WCF out of the box. Learning about channel internals is important for both the application developer and the framework developer. After all, channels are a key part of the internal plumbing in all WCF applications. This chapter explains channel essentials and is targeted to both the application developer and the framework developer.

Tip As you've probably seen, the WCF API is fairly complex, and the channel layer is no exception. As with other parts of WCF, learning to use channels consists of two major phases: learning the type hierarchies and learning the execution environment. In my experience, the best way to learn to use channels is to spend some time learning the type hierarchies, and then build a simple channel and plug that channel into the WCF infrastructure. Spending too much time in the type hierarchies early on tends to be disorienting, and starting by building a custom channel without knowledge of the type hierarchies is virtually impossible and a sure path to frustration.

It is also important to note that production quality channels must have an asynchronous interface. If asynchronous programming is new to you, it is probably beneficial to brush up on asynchronous programming before writing your own production quality channel. In my view, a great reference is Jeffrey Richter's *CLR via C#* (Microsoft Press, 2006).

Channels in Perspective

A channel typically relates to one aspect of the messaging functionality in an application. If a WCF application is secure, reliable, and transactionally capable, that application will use one channel for security, another for reliability, and another for transactional capability. Because each channel has a discrete set of functionality and most applications need more functionality than one channel can provide, WCF applications arrange channels in a stack and leverage the functionality across the stack. Very seldom does a production application use a channel in isolation.

A WCF application references the topmost channel in the stack only. When stacked, a channel in the stack is responsible for doing some work *and* invoking the next channel in the stack (or invoking the next channel and *then* doing its work when the previous call returns). The important point here is that once a message is sent to the channel stack, the channel stack itself pulls or pushes messages through the stack. There is no outside engine that manages the transition of a *Message* from one channel in the stack to the next. Once an application builds a channel stack, the channel stack is an opaque entity. As you'll see later in this chapter, it is possible to query the channel stack for certain capabilities, but this is a far cry from the full transparency one might expect when first approaching a topic as important as channels.

When channels are arranged in a stack, the composition of the stack dictates many of the features of the application, and each channel in the stack has a distinct role in the overall functionality of the application. For the most part, channel stacks accept or return a *Message* at the topmost channel in the stack, and the channel at the bottom of the stack emits or receives bytes at the transport level. Channel stacks on a sending application accept a message at the top of the stack and emit bytes at the bottom of the stack. Channel stacks on a receiving application, on the other hand, accept bytes at the bottom of the channel stack and return a *Message* at the top of the stack. What happens in the middle of the stack depends on the channels residing there. Typically, the channels in the middle of a channel stack are the physical implementations of a WS-* protocol or security toll gates. Figure 6-1 illustrates the composition of a typical channel stack on a sending application.

Notice that the bottom channel in the stack accepts a Message as input and outputs bytes on the wire. This bottom channel in the stack is also responsible for the mechanics of communication on a particular transport. If the transport is TCP, this channel is responsible for the socket connection and sending bytes to that socket. If the transport is MSMQ, the bottom channel is responsible for connecting to an MSMQ queue and sending the message to that queue. Notice also in Figure 6-1 that the channels arranged above the transport channel have distinct roles in message processing (for example, transactions, security, and reliability).

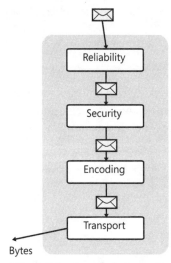

Figure 6-1   A typical channel stack

There is no concrete, one-size-fits-all channel type definition. The WCF type system abounds with channel type definitions, and each channel type definition results in a channel object with a stated purpose. For example, all supported transports in WCF have at least one channel type definition in the WCF type system that provides a WCF application the physical means to communicate over that transport. Likewise, the WCF type system contains many channel definitions that are the physical means of providing the venerated features of reliability, transactional processing, and security.

Instantiating a Channel

Factory objects instantiate channel objects. In most cases, there is a one-to-one correlation between factory objects and channel objects. In other words, each channel type has a corresponding factory type. Just as there is no one-size-fits-all channel type, there is no one-size-fits-all factory type. Because channels are frequently arranged in a stack at run time, the factory objects that create the channel stack are also frequently arranged in a stack. In one sense, the arrangement of factory objects in the factory object stack dictates the arrangement of the channels in the channel stack. You'll learn more about the channel factory members in Chapter 7, "Channel Managers." For now, it is enough to know that channels are not directly instantiated by user code, but rather through a channel factory.

The Channel State Machine

Channels and channel factories share common characteristics that are independent of their run-time functionality. One of the most important characteristics of these different constructs is their common state machine. Every channel and channel factory in a WCF application has a predefined set of states and a predefined set of methods that drive the channel or channel factory through those states.

The *ICommunicationObject* Interface

At the object-oriented level, one of the ways the WCF type system enforces the uniformity of a common state machine is by mandating that all channels and channel factories implement the *System.ServiceModel.ICommunicationObject* interface. The *ICommunicationObject* interface is fairly straightforward:

```
public interface ICommunicationObject {
  event EventHandler Closed;
  event EventHandler Closing;
  event EventHandler Faulted;
  event EventHandler Opened;
  event EventHandler Opening;

  void Abort();
  IAsyncResult BeginClose(AsyncCallback callback, object state);
  IAsyncResult BeginClose(TimeSpan timeout, AsyncCallback callback,
                          Object state);
  IAsyncResult BeginOpen(AsyncCallback callback, object state);
  IAsyncResult BeginOpen(TimeSpan timeout, AsyncCallback callback,
                         Object state);
  void Close();
  void Close(TimeSpan timeout);
  void EndClose(IAsyncResult result);
  void EndOpen(IAsyncResult result);
  void Open();
  void Open(TimeSpan timeout);

  CommunicationState State { get; }
}
```

Note   For brevity in this section, I will refer to objects that implement the *ICommunication-Object* interface as channels, even though channel factories also implement the interface.

Let's talk first about the methods. As you can see in the interface definition, the *ICommunicationObject* interface defines methods for opening, closing, and aborting the channel. Notice that the interface definition overloads the synchronous *Open* and *Close* methods with methods that accept a *TimeSpan*. In theory, the parameterless *Open* and *Close* methods block until the channel eventually opens or closes. In practice, this is never a good idea, and the overloads that accept a *TimeSpan* represent a way to dictate the amount of time a caller is willing to wait for the object to open or close. Since it is never a good idea to block indefinitely, waiting for a channel to open or close, it is a good idea for the parameterless *Open* and *Close* methods to call the *Open* and *Close* methods that do accept a *TimeSpan*, passing a default *TimeSpan* as an argument.

Notice also that the *ICommunicationObject* interface defines asynchronous *BeginOpen* and *BeginClose* methods that match the Microsoft .NET Asynchronous Programming Model (APM) pattern. Because opening or closing a channel might result in I/O, it is a good idea to use asynchronous programming for opening and closing a channel. Doing so means that the application uses the thread pool for efficient resource management and the calling thread does not have to block while the actual work of opening or closing the channel is taking place. Notice also that even the *BeginOpen* and *BeginClose* methods are overloaded to include a *TimeSpan*. Like their synchronous cousins, these methods allow the caller to dictate how long they are willing to wait for a channel to open or close. When opening or closing a channel, I greatly prefer and encourage the use of the asynchronous-capable members defined in *ICommunicationObject*.

The *ICommunicationObject* interface also defines a read-only property of type *Communication-State*. This member is simply a means to query a channel for its location in the channel state machine. You'll learn more about the channel state machine in the next section, "The *CommunicationObject* Type." For now, it is enough to know the possible states, as shown here:

```
public enum CommunicationState {
    Created,
    Opening,
    Opened,
    Closing,
    Closed,
    Faulted
}
```

The *ICommunicationObject* interface also defines several events. Like any .NET Framework event, the events defined in *ICommunicationObject* are a means for other objects to receive notifications of some or all channel state transitions. Notice that the event names correlate to the *CommunicationState* enumerated type. We'll look at the timing of these events in the next section.

The *CommunicationObject* Type

By itself, implementing the *ICommunicationObject* interface does nothing to enforce consistent state transitions across all channels or channel factories. Instead, it ensures that all channels and channel factories have common members. In practical terms, enforcing consistent behavior across a set of types compels the use of a common base type for implementation inheritance, rather than interface inheritance alone. The *System.ServiceModel.Channels. CommunicationObject* abstract type serves this purpose.

> **Note**   For brevity in this chapter, I will once again refer to objects that subclass the *CommunicationObject* type as channels, even though other types are also derived from this *CommunicationObject*.

CommunicationObject is a base type for all channels, and the *CommunicationObject* type implements the *ICommunicationObject* interface. The *Open*, *Close*, and *Abort* methods on *CommunicationObject* drive channels through their various states in a consistent manner, as shown in Figure 6-2. More than just an implementation of *ICommunicationObject*, *CommunicationObject* also raises *ICommunicationObject* events at the appropriate time, invokes abstract and virtual methods for derived type implementation, and provides several helper methods for consistent error handling. The next section of this chapter describes the manner in which the *CommunicationObject* drives channels through different states.

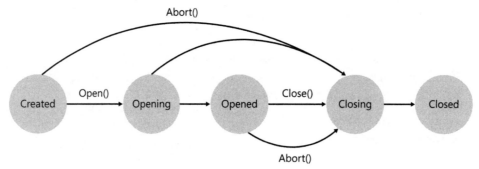

Figure 6-2   The channel state machine embodied in *CommunicationObject*

CommunicationObject-Derived Types

In practice, types derived from *CommunicationObject* should work with the state machine defined in *CommunicationObject*, should leverage some of its other members for error handling, and of course, should add implementation that fits the needs of that particular derived type. As with any type hierarchy, blindly inheriting from a base type does not by itself ensure the proper use of the base type functionality. When building a channel, it is extremely important to add functionality in the appropriate place and to call methods on the base type correctly.

The *CommunicationObject* type defines several virtual methods. When a derived type overrides these virtual methods, it is extremely important that the derived type call its base because it is the *CommunicationObject* implementation that drives state changes and raises events. Failing to make this call means that the state of the derived type will not transition properly, events will not be raised, and the channel will be of little value. It is not required that a type derived from *CommunicationObject* override these members. Instead, a *CommunicationObject*-derived type should override these virtual members only when that derived type needs to perform some work in its own implementation.

The following code snippet shows the virtual methods in the *CommunicationObject* type and how they must be overridden:

```
public abstract class CommunicationObject : ICommunicationObject {
  // virtual methods shown, others omitted
  protected virtual void OnClosed();
  protected virtual void OnClosing();
  protected virtual void OnFaulted();
  protected virtual void OnOpened();
  protected virtual void OnOpening();
}

sealed class CommunicationObjectDerivedType : CommunicationObject {
  // other methods omitted for clarity
  protected override void OnClosed() {
    // implementation can occur before or after
    // the call to the base implementation
    base.OnClosed();
  }

  protected override void OnClosing() {
    // implementation can occur before or after
    // the call to the base implementation
    base.OnClosing();
  }

  protected override void OnOpened() {
    // implementation can occur before or after
    // the call to the base implementation
    base.OnOpened();
  }

  protected override void OnOpening() {
    // implementation can occur before or after
    // the call to the base implementation
    base.OnOpening();
  }

  protected override void OnFaulted() {
    // implementation can occur before or after
    // the call to the base implementation
    base.OnFaulted();
  }
}
```

The *CommunicationObject* type also defines several abstract members that are the primary means by which a channel performs specialized work. The following code snippet describes these members:

```
public abstract class CommunicationObject : ICommunicationObject {

  // abstract members shown, others omitted
  protected abstract void OnOpen(TimeSpan timeout);
  protected abstract IAsyncResult OnBeginOpen(TimeSpan timeout,
    AsyncCallback callback, Object state);
  protected abstract void OnEndOpen(IAsyncResult result);

  protected abstract void OnClose(TimeSpan timeout);
  protected abstract IAsyncResult OnBeginClose(TimeSpan timeout,
    AsyncCallback callback, Object state);
  protected abstract void OnEndClose(IAsyncResult result);

  protected abstract void OnAbort();

  protected abstract TimeSpan DefaultCloseTimeout { get; }

  protected abstract TimeSpan DefaultOpenTimeout { get; }
}
```

The only members in the preceding code snippet that should come as a surprise are the *DefaultCloseTimeout* and *DefaultOpenTimeout* properties. As a rule, when deciding which overloaded member to call, always choose the one with a *TimeSpan* parameter. This provides explicit control over the time-out. As it turns out, even the members that do not have a *TimeSpan* parameter call the member that does have a *TimeSpan* parameter. In that case, the value used is the value of the *DefaultOpenTimeout* and *DefaultClosedTimeout*, accordingly.

The *OnOpen*, *OnClose*, and *OnAbort* methods and their asynchronous siblings are, as their name implies, the place where much of the initialization and cleanup implementation goes in a *CommunicationObject*-derived type. For example, if you are writing a custom transport channel that uses the User Datagram Protocol (UDP) transport, the code required to initialize the socket should reside in the *OnOpen* and *OnBeginOpen* methods. Likewise, the code to tear down the socket should reside in the *OnClose*, *OnBeginClose*, and *OnAbort* methods.

One of the areas that can be confusing when first approaching channels and the channel state machine is the way in which the *CommunicationObject* interacts with types derived from the *CommunicationObject*. In my view, understanding these interactions is one of the most important first steps in understanding how channels work. The next sections describe the collaboration between the *CommunicationObject* base type and derived types for the *Open*, *Close*, *Abort*, and *Fault* methods. For the sake of simplicity, the following code snippet defines the context for these sections:

```
sealed class App {
  static void Main() {
    MyCommunicationObject myCommObject = new MyCommunicationObject();
```

```
      // method invocations here
  }
}
sealed class MyCommunicationObject : CommunicationObject {
  // implementatation omitted for brevity
}
```

The *Open* and *BeginOpen* Methods

As you saw earlier in this chapter, the *CommunicationObject* defines the *Open* and *BeginOpen* methods that open the *CommunicationObject*-derived type. This section describes what happens as a result of the following code:

```
MyCommunicationObject myCommObject = new MyCommunicationObject();
myCommObject.Open();
```

CommunicationObject: Check Whether State Transition to *Open* Is Permissible

The *Open* and *BeginOpen* methods throw an exception if the *State* state property is anything other than *CommunicationObject.Created*. The *CommunicationObject* type performs these checks by calling the *ThrowIfDisposedOrImmutable* protected method. If the *CommunicationState* is *CommunicationState.Opened* or *CommunicationState.Opening*, the *Open* and *BeginOpen* methods throw an *InvalidOperationException*. Likewise, if the *State* is *CommunicationState.Closed* or *CommunicationState.Closing*, the *Open* and *BeginOpen* methods throw an *ObjectDisposedException*. It is worth noting that this state check happens in a thread safe manner. The following code snippet describes the implementation of the *CommunicationObject.Open* method:

```
lock (this.thisLock){
  // check the state, throw an exception if transition is not OK
  this.ThrowIfDisposedOrImmutable();
    // other implementation shown in the next section
  }
```

CommunicationObject: If So, Transition State to *Opening*

If the current state is *CommunicationState.Created*, the *State* property transitions to *CommunicationState.Opening*. The following code snippet shows the code in the *CommunicationObject.Open* method that transitions the state to *CommunicationState.Opening*:

```
lock (this.thisLock){
  // check the state, throw an exception if transition is not OK
  this.ThrowIfDisposedOrImmutable();
    // transition the CommunicationState
    this.state = CommunicationState.Opening;
  }
```

MyCommunicationObject: *OnOpening* Virtual Method Invoked

If the *CommunicationState* property transitions to *Opening* without throwing an exception, the *CommunicationObject.Open* method invokes the *CommunicationObject.OnOpening* virtual method. If the *CommunicationObject* derived type has overridden this method, the *OnOpening* method on the derived type is invoked. As mentioned earlier, the *OnOpening* implemention in the derived type must call the *OnOpening* method on the *CommunicationObject* type.

CommunicationObject: Opening Event Raised, Delegates Invoked

The *OnOpening* method on the *CommunicationObject* type raises the *Opening* event and invokes the delegates referred to in that event. This is one reason the derived type must call the *OnOpening* method on the *CommunicationObject*. The *CommunicationObject.Open* method will throw an *InvalidOperationException* if this collaboration does not occur.

MyCommunicationObject: *OnOpen* Virtual Method Invoked

If the *OnOpening* method does not throw an exception, the *CommunicationObject.Open* method invokes the *OnOpen* method in the derived type. Because the *CommunicationObject* type defines *OnOpen* as an abstract method, derived types must implement this method. As mentioned earlier, this is the method that contains the bulk of the work required to initialize the *CommunicationObject*-derived type.

MyCommunicationObject: *OnOpened* Virtual Method Invoked

If the *OnOpen* method returns without throwing an exception, the *CommunicationObject.Open* method invokes the *OnOpened* virtual method. If the derived type implements the *OnOpened* method, the implementation in that derived type is invoked. As with the *OnOpening* method, it is absolutely critical that the derived type invoke the *CommunicationObject.OnOpened* method. Failing to do so results in the *CommunicationObject.Open* method throwing an *InvalidOperationException*.

CommunicationObject: State Transitions to *Opened*

The *CommunicationObject.OnOpened* method, among other things, transitions the *State* property of the *CommunicationObject* to *CommunicationState.Opened*. The only *CommunicationState* that is permissible before this state transition is *CommunicationState.Opening*.

CommunicationObject: Opened Event Raised, Delegates Invoked

After the state transitions to *Opened*, the *CommunicationObject.OnOpened* method raises the *Opened* event, thereby invoking any referenced delegates.

The *Close* and *Abort* Methods

The *CommunicationObject* type exposes members that tear down the object. In general, the *Close* and *BeginClose* methods are intended for graceful *CommunicationObject* shutdown, and the *Abort* method is intended for immediate *CommunicationObject* shutdown. Notice that the *Close* method has an asynchronous sibling, whereas the *Abort* method does not. The reason stems from the different roles of the *Close* and *Abort* methods. For example, in the graceful shutdown initiated by invoking the *Close* (or *BeginClose*) method, the *CommunicationObject* can perform I/O while shutting down the object. To illustrate, consider the case of calling *Close* during a WS-ReliableMessaging (WS-RM) choreography. In this case, the Close method will cause the channel responsible for WS-RM to send a *TerminateSequence* message to the other participant. In other words, the *Close* method can trigger I/O.

On the other hand, the immediate shutdown initiated by invoking the *Abort* method will immediately shut down the *CommunicationObject* and will perform minimal I/O. As a result, there is no need for an asynchronous sibling to the *Abort* method. It is also worth mentioning that the *Abort* method does not accept a *TimeSpan* as a parameter, while the *Close* method does.

The collaboration pattern between the *CommunicationObject* and the *CommunicationObject*-derived type that occurs as a result of invoking the *Close* or *BeginClose* method is very similar to the collaboration pattern that occurs as a result of invoking the *Open* method. As shown earlier, invoking the *CommunicationObject.Open* method can lead to an invocation of the *OnOpening*, *OnOpen*, and *OnOpened* methods. Likewise, invoking the *Communication-Object.Close* method can cause the *OnClosing*, *OnClose*, and *OnClosed* methods to execute. The following code snippet illustrates the way the .NET Framework implements the *CommunicationObject.Close* method:

```
public void Close(TimeSpan timeout){
  // only general implementation shown
  this.OnClosing();
  this.OnClose(timeout);
  this.OnClosed();
}
```

Furthermore, the *CommunicationObject* raises the *Closing* and *Closed* events in a manner similar to the way it raises the *Opening* and *Opened* events.

The *Abort* method starts a different sort of collaboration. The following code snippet illustrates the way the .NET Framework implements the *CommunicationObject.Abort* method:

```
public void Abort(){
  // only general implementation shown
  this.OnClosing();
  this.OnAbort(); // only difference from Close
  this.OnClosed();
}
```

As the preceding code snippet shows, the *Abort* method invokes methods that are also in the normal execution path of the *Close* method. The *OnClosing* and *OnClosed* methods raise the *Closing* and *Closed* events, respectively. In effect, the *Abort* method shares some of the execution path of the *Close* method and raises the same events as the *Close* method.

Remembering that one of the primary jobs of the *CommunicationObject* type is to maintain a consistent state machine, it stands to reason that the execution paths of the *Close* and *Abort* methods change based on the *State* property of the object being closed or aborted. To illustrate, consider the case of calling *Close* when the state is *CommunicationState.Created*. If the *Open* method has not been called, should there be any difference in execution paths between *Close* and *Abort*? Remember that the real work of initializing the *CommunicationObject* results from calling the *Open* or *BeginOpen* method. Until one of these methods executes, the *CommunicationObject* is nothing more than an object on the heap. In the pre-open state, the *CommunicationObject.Close* method and *CommunicationObject.Abort* method perform the same work. However, after the *Open* or *BeginOpen* method executes, the *CommunicationObject* might have a reference to something like a connected socket, and the *CommunicationObject.Close* and *CommunicationObject.Abort* methods perform very different work. Table 6-1 describes how the state of the *CommunicationObject* impacts the way *Close* and *Abort* execute. As you review this table, remember that *Close* is the graceful way to tear down a *CommunicationObject* and *Abort* is the abrupt way to tear down a *CommunicationObject*.

Table 6-1   *CommunicationState, Close,* and *Abort*

State Property	Close	Abort
CommunicationState.Created	Calls *Abort*	Aborts normally
CommunicationState.Opening	Calls *Abort*	Aborts normally
CommunicationState.Opened	Closes normally	Aborts normally
CommunicationState.Closing	No action	Aborts normally
CommunicationState.Closed	No action	No action

The *Fault* Method

The protected *Fault* method is a way for a *CommunicationObject* to shut down, but it is not part of the *ICommunicationObject* interface. Because it is not visible to outside callers, the *Fault* method is a way for a *CommunicationObject*-derived type to sense an error condition and abruptly shut down the channel. Calling the *Fault* method transitions the *State* property to *CommunicationState.Faulted* and invokes the *OnFaulted* virtual method, thereby allowing a *CommunicationObject*-derived type to define its own behavior. In most cases, the *OnFaulted* method calls the *Abort* method.

About *CommunicationObject* Stacks

Remember that the *CommunicationObject* type is the base type for all channels and channel factories. Remember also that channels and channel factories are commonly arranged as a stack, and only the top of the stack is visible to a caller. In concept, this sort of arrangement is possible via a type such as the following:

```
internal sealed class MyCommunicationObject : CommunicationObject {
  private CommunicationObject _inner;
  internal MyCommunicationObject(CommunicationObject inner){
    this._inner = inner;
  }
  // other implementation omitted for brevity
}
```

Because *MyCommunicationObject* derives from *CommunicationObject*, it is subject to the state machine defined in *CommunicationObject*. Furthermore, *MyCommunicationObject* has the responsibility of synchronizing its transition through the state machine with the _inner member variable's transition through the state machine. For example, if a referent of a *MyCommunicationObject* object calls the *Open* method, the *MyCommunicationObject.Open* implementation must also call the *Open* method on its inner member variable, as shown here:

```
internal sealed class MyCommunicationObject : CommunicationObject {
  private CommunicationObject _inner;
  internal MyCommunicationObject(CommunicationObject inner){
    this._inner = inner;
  }   protected override void OnOpen(TimeSpan timeout) {
    // MyCommunicationObject.OnOpen implementation here
    // ...
    // Call Open on the inner member variable
    // NOTE: may want to reduce timeout
    _inner.Open(timeout);
  }
  // other implementation omitted for brevity
}
```

When arranged in this way, the referent that calls *MyCommunicationObject.Open* does not have to know all of the *CommunicationObject* nodes in the stack, and they all transition through the same state machine in a synchronized manner. For thoroughness, it is important to note that it does not matter whether the call to _inner.Open occurs before or after the *MyCommunication-Object.OnOpen* method. In practice, it is usually performed at the end of the method. It might be necessary to adjust the *TimeSpan* passed to the inner member variable to reflect the remaining time allowed in the operation.

Introduction to Channel Shape

Channel shape is one of the key means by which we categorize channels. Conceptually, a channel shape corresponds to one or more Message Exchange Patterns (MEPs), as discussed in Chapter 3, "Message Exchange Patterns, Topologies, and Choreographies." To illustrate, consider a sender and a receiver that are exchanging messages as prescribed by the Request/Reply MEP. In Request/Reply, the sender sends a message to the receiver, and the receiver sends a reply message back to the sender, and the correlation between the request and the reply is implicit. Because channels are the physical means by which senders and receivers send and receive messages, both the sender and receiver must build their own channels. When the sender and receiver are exchanging messages via the Request/Reply MEP, the sending and receiving channels must understand the rules of the Request/Reply MEP. Structurally, this means that the channels on the sender define members specific to sending a request message and receiving a reply message. On the other end of the message exchange, the channels on the receiver must define members specific to receiving a request message and sending a reply message. In addition, both the sender and the receiver define members that correlate the request and the reply.

At first glance, it might seem that the sender and the receiver have identical roles. For example, it is true that both the sender and the receiver send and receive messages. The logical difference between the sender and the receiver is the order in which they send and receive messages. This difference in order means that the channels on the sender and the receiver must be slightly different. This difference manifests itself structurally as different members in sending and receiving channels. Channel shapes are the way we name and group these structural differences. Because .NET interfaces are a natural way to enforce the existence of members in a .NET type, they are a great way to identify the shape of a channel.

The WCF type system defines several interfaces that describe the different channel shapes, and these interfaces map to the MEPs described in Chapter 3. Table 6-2 lists the MEP-to-interface mapping for the sender and receiver. All interfaces listed in Table 6-2 are a part of the *System.ServiceModel.Channels* namespace.

Table 6-2   MEPs and Channel Shapes

MEP	Sender	Receiver
Datagram	*IOutputChannel*	*IInputChannel*
Request/Reply	*IRequestChannel*	*IReplyChannel*
Duplex	*IDuplexChannel*	*IDuplexChannel*
P2P	*IDuplexChannel*	*IDuplexChannel*

Notice that the interfaces for Datagram and Request/Reply are different on the sender and the receiver. With the Datagram MEP, the sender sends a message and is not able to receive a message, while the receiver is able to receive a message only. With this in mind, the *IOutputChannel* defines a method named *Send* and the *IInputChannel* defines a method named *Receive*.

The Duplex MEP entry in Table 6-2 warrants some explanation. Remember that the Duplex MEP blurs the distinction between the sender and the receiver since both the sender and receiver are free to send and receive messages at will. At the member level, both the sender and the receiver can define a method named *Send* and a method named *Receive*. Since the members can be identical on both the sender and the receiver, it is natural that sending and receiving channels implement the same interface in the Duplex MEP.

In practice, messaging applications need to correlate multiple messages. For example, a purchasing application (sender) might need to send multiple messages to an accounting application (receiver) in such a way that all messages are related to one purchase order or product. The logical boundary for this correlation is called a *session*. When initially considering sessions, the tendency might be to assume that the receiver correlates messages based on the sender. With this mindset, it is natural to assume that a receiver servicing five senders will relate a message to a particular sender, as in the case of an ASP.NET application servicing multiple browsers. In a WCF application, however, this coupling is too narrow to work for many known messaging requirements. For example, one purchasing application (sender) might send messages that are related to several purchase orders, and the accounting application (receiver) might need to correlate these messages based on the purchase order rather than the instance of the purchasing application (sender).

WCF sessions are an optional channel-level construct. Because the concept of a session is nothing more than a means to correlate messages, each channel can have its own way of correlating messages. For example, a TCP/IP transport channel can correlate messages in a session based on the socket it uses to receive messages. In contrast, the channel that implements WS-ReliableMessaging can use the ID message header to correlate messages in a session, thereby removing the dependence on a particular socket or transport construct.

The one characteristic common to all session-capable channels is that they have an identifier, and different parts of the WCF infrastructure can use this identifier to correlate messages. Structurally, a channel supports sessions when it implements the *System.ServiceModel. Channels.ISessionChannel<T>* interface. The generic parameter in *ISessionChannel<T>* must implement the *System.ServiceModel.Channels.ISession* interface. The following code snippet shows the members in these interfaces:

```
public interface ISession {
  String Id { get; }
}
public interface ISessionChannel<T> where T: ISession {
  T Session { get; }
}
```

As the preceding code snippet shows, these interfaces expose a member named *Id*, and this member represents a session identifier. In WCF, channel types that implement the *ISessionChannel<T>* interface are said to be *sessionful channels*. For the sake of consistency, the WCF type system considers a sessionful channel as a variant on channel shape. In other words, the *IDuplexChannel* interface has a variant named *IDuplexSessionChannel*. From a shape perspective, the *IDuplexSessionChannel* has a different shape than the *IDuplexChannel*, even though they are both capable of duplex communication. The real difference between these interfaces is that the *IDuplexSessionChannel* implements the *ISessionChannel<T>* interface. Table 6-3 illustrates the sessionful channel shapes in the WCF type system.

Table 6-3   MEPs and Sessionful Channel Shapes

MEP	Sender	Receiver
Datagram	*IOutputSessionChannel*	*IInputSessionChannel*
Request/Reply	*IRequestSessionChannel*	*IReplySessionChannel*
Duplex	*IDuplexSessionChannel*	*IDuplexSessionChannel*
P2P	*IDuplexSessionChannel*	*IDuplexSessionChannel*

> **Note**   In contrast with the section "The Channel State Machine" earlier in this chapter, only channels implement the channel shape interfaces. Since channel factories create channels, they require a reference to the channel shape interface that describes the shape of the channels they create.

Channel Interfaces and Base Types

As mentioned at the beginning of this chapter, one of the key facets of learning about the WCF channel infrastructure is unfolding the list of interfaces and types that the WCF type system uses in the channel layer. This section condenses this complex type system into manageable chunks, making it more palatable to the newcomer.

The *IChannel* Interface

The *System.ServiceModel.Channels.IChannel* interface is deceptively simple, but its implementation is vital to the channel layer. All channels and channel factories must implement it. To put it another way, a type that derives from *CommunicationObject* usually also implements the *IChannel* interface. Before we delve into the purpose of the *IChannel* interface, let's examine its structure:

```
public interface IChannel : ICommunicationObject {
    T GetProperty<T>() where T: class;
}
```

You might ask yourself: "What's so important about that?" Remember that each *CommunicationObject* in a *CommunicationObject* stack supports some capability, and only the topmost *CommunicationObject* in the *CommunicationObject* stack is visible to the caller. When implemented properly, the *GetProperty<T>* method provides the means to query the *CommunicationObject* stack for certain capabilities. For example, you might want to query a *CommunicationObject* stack for its support of a particular channel shape, *MessageVersion*, or even security capabilities. The following code snippet shows how a caller can use the *IChannel.GetProperty<T>* method:

```
// assume channel stack (myChannelStack) created
MessageVersion messageVersion =
  myChannelStack.GetProperty<MessageVersion>();
if(MessageVersion != null){
  // do something
}
// app continues
```

Like many other members in a *CommunicationObject* stack, it is important that a *CommunicationObject* delegate the call to the next channel in the stack when a channel does not know the answer to the query. A simple implementation of the *GetProperty<T>* method is shown here:

```
public override T GetProperty<T>() where T: class {
    if (typeof(T) == typeof(MessageVersion)) {
        // this type knows only how to return MessageVersion
        return (T) this.MessageVersion;
    }
    // no other capabilities are known here, so
    // delegate the query to the next node
    return this.inner.GetProperty<T>();
}
```

As this example shows, this implementation of *GetProperty<T>* is able to return only the *MessageVersion*, and it delegates all other queries to the next node in the stack. If a capability is not known to any node in the stack, *GetProperty<T>* returns *null* instead of throwing an exception. As a result of this delegation paradigm, only the bottom node in the stack ever explicitly returns *null*.

Datagram Channels: *IInputChannel* and *IOutputChannel*

As mentioned in Chapter 3, the Datagram MEP is extremely powerful and scalable. In a Datagram MEP, the sender sends one message to the receiver, and the sender expects no message in response. More simply, a sender outputs (sends) a message, and the receiver receives the message as input. As a result, the interface that the WCF infrastructure defines for the sender in a Datagram MEP is named *System.ServiceModel.Channels.IOutputChannel*, and the interface for the receiver is named the *System.ServiceModel.IInputChannel*.

Sending: *IOutputChannel*

Like its role in the Datagram MEP, the *IOutputChannel* interface is simple, as shown here:

```
public interface IOutputChannel : IChannel, ICommunicationObject {
    IAsyncResult BeginSend(Message message, AsyncCallback callback,
                        Object state);
    IAsyncResult BeginSend(Message message, TimeSpan timeout,
                        AsyncCallback callback, Object state);
```

```
    void EndSend(IAsyncResult result);
    void Send(Message message);
    void Send(Message message, TimeSpan timeout);

    EndpointAddress RemoteAddress { get; }
    Uri Via { get; }
}
```

First, notice that the *IOutputChannel* interface implements the *IChannel* and *ICommunication-Object* interfaces. Any type that implements the *IOutputChannel* interface must also define members for the common channel state machine and the *GetProperty<T>* query method. Also notice that the interface defines both synchronous and asynchronous *Send* methods in a manner consistent with the APM.

The *RemoteAddress* property is a way to express the target of the message. It is important to note, however, that the target of the message does not have to be where the message is actually sent. Recalling the postal service example from Chapter 2, "Service Orientation," it is often useful to address the message to one recipient but deliver it via another address. The *Via* property on the *IOutputChannel* represents the other address and is intended to be used as the physical target address of the message.

Receiving: *IInputChannel*

Channels that receive datagram messages implement the *IInputChannel* interface. In keeping with the role of a receiver in datagram message exchanges, the *IInputChannel* interface defines members for receiving messages and does not define members for sending messages. The members in the *IInputChannel* interface are shown here:

```
public interface IInputChannel : IChannel, ICommunicationObject {
    EndpointAddress LocalAddress { get; }

    // Receive Methods
    IAsyncResult BeginReceive(AsyncCallback callback, Object state);
    IAsyncResult BeginReceive(TimeSpan timeout, AsyncCallback callback,
                              Object state);
    Message EndReceive(IAsyncResult result);
    Message Receive();
    Message Receive(TimeSpan timeout);

    // TryReceive Methods
    IAsyncResult BeginTryReceive(TimeSpan timeout, AsyncCallback callback,
                                 Object state);
    bool EndTryReceive(IAsyncResult result, out Message message);
    bool TryReceive(TimeSpan timeout, out Message message);

    // Waiting Methods
    IAsyncResult BeginWaitForMessage(TimeSpan timeout,
                                     AsyncCallback callback,
                                     Object state);
    bool EndWaitForMessage(IAsyncResult result);
    bool WaitForMessage(TimeSpan timeout);
}
```

In general, receiving applications passively wait for incoming messages. To this end, the *IInputChannel* interface defines three sets of methods that provide different ways to wait for an incoming message. There are no universal names for these different sets of methods, but for simplicity, let's classify them as the *Receive*, *TryReceive*, and *WaitForMessage* method groups. All of these method groups have synchronous and asynchronous variants.

The *Receive* methods wait for a period of time, and if a *Message* arrives within that period of time, the *Message* is returned from the method. If the period of time elapses without the arrival of a *Message*, these methods throw a *TimeoutException*. The *TryReceive* methods wait for a period of time and then return a *Message* as an *out* parameter. These methods return a *Boolean* that represents whether a *Message* arrived within the allotted period of time. The major difference between the *Receive* and the *TryReceive* methods is the way they indicate an expired time-out.

The *WaitForMessage* methods, in contrast to the *Receive* and *TryReceive* methods, do not return a *Message* as a return value or an *out* parameter. Instead, the *WaitForMessage* methods return a *Boolean* that indicates whether a *Message* has arrived. This is similar to the *Peek* functionality available in the other I/O infrastructures. Combining the use of a *WaitForMessage* method with a *Receive* or *TryReceive* method provides the capability to wait for a *Message* and then receive it.

The *WaitForMessage* methods can be useful when the arrival of a *Message* corresponds with some other activity that requires nontrivial overhead. As an example, consider the case when the arrival of a *Message* must correspond with the creation of a transaction. In this case, the call to *Receive* or *TryReceive* must be wrapped in a transaction. If a *Message* does not arrive, the caller must abort the transaction. If, however, the caller uses the *WaitForMessage* method, the call does not have to occur within the scope of a transaction. If *WaitForMessage* returns *false*, the caller can simply call *WaitForMessage* again. Once a *Message* does arrive, the caller can start a transaction and then call *Receive* or *TryReceive* and perform the necessary work on the *Message*.

Request/Reply Channels: *IRequestChannel* and *IReplyChannel*

In the Request/Reply MEP, both the messaging participants send and receive messages. The sender sends a message to the receiver and then awaits a reply, while the receiver receives incoming messages and sends a reply message after receipt of a message. As for channel shapes, the *IRequestChannel* and *IReplyChannel* interfaces reflect this highly structured form of message exchange for the sender and receiver, respectively.

Sending: *IRequestChannel*

The *IRequestChannel* interface defines several members related to sending a request to a receiving application and receiving a *Message* as a response to the request. As with many other members related to sending and receiving messages in the channel layer, there are both synchronous and asynchronous variants of these members, as shown here:

```
public interface IRequestChannel : IChannel, ICommunicationObject {
  // Request Methods
  IAsyncResult BeginRequest(Message message, AsyncCallback callback,
                            Object state);
  IAsyncResult BeginRequest(Message message, TimeSpan timeout,
                            AsyncCallback callback, Object state);
  Message EndRequest(IAsyncResult result);
  Message Request(Message message);
  Message Request(Message message, TimeSpan timeout);

  EndpointAddress RemoteAddress { get; }
  Uri Via { get; }
}
```

As the preceding code snippet shows, the *Request* methods accept a *Message* as a parameter and return a *Message*. The signature of these members ensures compliance with the Request/Reply MEP.

Receiving: *IReplyChannel*

Receiving applications that want to use the Request/Reply MEP implement the *IReplyChannel* interface as follows:

```
public interface IReplyChannel : IChannel, ICommunicationObject {
  RequestContext ReceiveRequest();
  RequestContext ReceiveRequest(TimeSpan timeout);
  IAsyncResult BeginReceiveRequest(AsyncCallback callback, Object state);
  IAsyncResult BeginReceiveRequest(TimeSpan timeout,
                                   AsyncCallback callback, Object state);
  RequestContext EndReceiveRequest(IAsyncResult result);

  Boolean TryReceiveRequest(TimeSpan timeout, out RequestContext context);
  IAsyncResult BeginTryReceiveRequest(TimeSpan timeout,
                                      AsyncCallback callback,
                                      Object state);
  Boolean EndTryReceiveRequest(IAsyncResult result,
                               out RequestContext context);

  Boolean WaitForRequest(TimeSpan timeout);
  IAsyncResult BeginWaitForRequest(TimeSpan timeout,
                                   AsyncCallback callback,
                                   Object state);
  bool EndWaitForRequest(IAsyncResult result);

  EndpointAddress LocalAddress { get; }
}
```

No member on the *IReplyChannel*, however, directly returns a *Message*. Instead, the *IReplyChannel* interface members provide access to the received *Message* via the *RequestContext* type. The next section discusses the *RequestContext* type in more detail. For now, it is enough to know that the received *Message* is visible via the *RequestContext* type, and it is through the *RequestContext* type that the *IReplyChannel* provides access to the received *Message*.

Like the *IInputChannel* interface, the *IReplyChannel* interface defines several categories of methods that provide different ways to receive a *Message*. The *ReceiveRequest* methods return a *RequestContext* object and will throw an exception if a time-out is exceeded. The *TryReceiveRequest* methods return a *Boolean* that indicates whether a *Message* was received in the allotted time. The *WaitForRequest* methods, like the *WaitForMessage* methods on the *IInputChannel* interface, return upon receipt of a request *Message* or the expiration of the time-out.

Request/Reply Correlation: The *RequestContext* Type

In the Request/Reply MEP, a request is tightly coupled to a reply. From the sender's perspective, a request always returns a *Message*. From the receiver's perspective, a received *Message* must always generate a reply *Message*. As shown in the preceding section, the *IReplyChannel* uses the *RequestContext* type as the return type from the *ReceiveRequest* methods. This type is the primary means by which a receiving channel that uses the Request/Reply MEP correlates a request with a reply.

At a high level, the *RequestContext* type wraps the request *Message* and provides the means to send a reply *Message* back to the sender. The request *Message* is visible in the *RequestContext* via the *RequestMessage* property. Likewise, the *Reply* methods on the *RequestContext* type provide the means to send a reply *Message* back to the sender. Like other methods in the channel type system, the reply methods are available in both synchronous and asynchronous variants. The following code snippet shows the *RequestContext* types members:

```
public abstract class RequestContext : IDisposable {
  protected RequestContext();

  public abstract void Abort();

  public abstract void Reply(Message message);
  public abstract void Reply(Message message, TimeSpan timeout);
  public abstract IAsyncResult BeginReply(Message message,
                                          AsyncCallback callback,
                                          Object state);
  public abstract IAsyncResult BeginReply(Message message,
                                          TimeSpan timeout,
                                          AsyncCallback callback,
                                          Object state);
  public abstract void EndReply(IAsyncResult result);

  public abstract void Close();
  public abstract void Close(TimeSpan timeout);

  protected virtual void Dispose(Boolean disposing);
  void IDisposable.Dispose();

  public abstract Message RequestMessage { get; }
}
```

As this code snippet shows, the *RequestContext* type implements the *IDisposable* interface. Because many other members in the channel layer do not implement *IDisposable*, it might not be obvious why the *RequestContext* type does. The *RequestContext* type implements *IDisposable* because the *RequestContext* type contains a *Message*. As discussed in Chapter 4, "WCF 101," the *Message* type might contain a *Stream* and therefore implements *IDisposable*. As a result of this association, the *Dispose* method on the *RequestContext* type calls the *Dispose* method on its *Message*, which in turn disposes the *Stream* owned by the *Message*. Keeping in mind that the *RequestContext* type is an abstract class, classes derived from *RequestContext* are free to add to this implementation as needed.

> **Note**   Like the *Message* type, the *RequestContext* type explicitly implements *IDisposable*.

Duplex Channels: *IDuplexChannel*

Duplex channels enable the Duplex MEP. Unlike the rigid structure of the Datagram and Request/Reply MEPs, the Duplex MEP allows the sender and receiver to freely send and receive messages with one another. As we saw in Chapter 3, the Duplex MEP closely resembles the communication exchange commonplace in telephone conversations. The sender and receiver must establish a communication context before open communication can begin. In the Duplex MEP, the sending and receiving channel shapes are the same, and as a result, the sender and receiver implement the same interface (assuming that both participants are WCF applications). Given the liberal nature of the Duplex MEP and the common interface for the sender and receiver, the only way to truly differentiate the sender from the receiver is to identify the messaging participant that initiated the communication (much the same way the person dialing the phone initiates a phone conversation).

Sending and Receiving: *IDuplexChannel*

The *IDuplexChannel* is actually the combination of the *IInputChannel* and *IOutputChannel* interfaces. As shown earlier, the *IInputChannel* interface is for implementing a datagram receiver, and the *IOutputChannel* interface is for implementing a datagram sender. Because a channel that implements the Duplex MEP must be able to send and receive messages, the logical choice for *IDuplexChannel* members is the combination of the interfaces used in the Datagram MEP. The definition of *IDuplexChannel* is shown here:

```
public interface IDuplexChannel : IInputChannel, IOutputChannel, IChannel,
  ICommunicationObject
{
}
```

The *IDefaultCommunicationTimeouts* Interface

Because channels are frequently hidden from the view of most application developers, there must be a way for layers above the channel layer to dictate the time-outs for a particular set of operations at the channel layer. When considering time-outs for a channel, there are four relevant time-sensitive operations: opening a channel, sending a message, receiving a message, and closing a channel. Like most functionality in the channel layer, the WCF type system contains an interface that describes these time-outs. The *System.ServiceModel. IDefaultCommunicationTimeouts* interface has the following members:

```
public interface IDefaultCommunicationTimeouts {
    TimeSpan CloseTimeout { get; }
    TimeSpan OpenTimeout { get; }
    TimeSpan ReceiveTimeout { get; }
    TimeSpan SendTimeout { get; }
}
```

The purpose of each member in the *IDefaultCommunicationTimeouts* interface is easily derived from the name of that member. Bindings, channel factories, and channels all implement this interface. Since a *Binding*, channel factory, and channel implement the same interface, these types can pass time-outs down the construction chain. For example, a user can specify a send time-out in a *Binding*. (The *Binding* also defines a setter property.) If the *Binding* is part of a message sender, the *Binding* passes the send time-out to the channel factory via the channel factory constructor. Similarly, the channel factory passes the send time-out to the channel via the channel constructor. In effect, this series of handoffs provides the user the ability to specify time-outs in a type that is part of the normal developer-facing API, and the impact trickles down to the channel layer.

The *ChannelBase* Type

All custom channels must implement the common state machine, expose the *GetProperty<T>* query mechanism, implement one or more channel shapes, and accept time-outs from a channel factory. The *System.ServiceModel.Channels.ChannelBase* abstract type serves as a single base type for channels and helps ensure that each channel defines the members compatible with the rest of the channel layer. The following code shows the *ChannelBase* type definition:

```
public abstract class ChannelBase : CommunicationObject,
                                    IChannel,
                                    ICommunicationObject,
                                    IDefaultCommunicationTimeouts {
    // Constructor with channel factory parameter
    protected ChannelBase(ChannelManagerBase channelManager);

    // IChannel implementation
    public virtual T GetProperty<T>() where T: class;

    // CommunicationObject members
    protected override TimeSpan DefaultCloseTimeout { get; }
```

```
protected override TimeSpan DefaultOpenTimeout { get; }
protected override void OnClosed();

protected TimeSpan DefaultReceiveTimeout { get; }
protected TimeSpan DefaultSendTimeout { get; }

// IDefaultCommunicationTimeouts implementation
TimeSpan IDefaultCommunicationTimeouts.CloseTimeout { get; }
TimeSpan IDefaultCommunicationTimeouts.OpenTimeout { get; }
TimeSpan IDefaultCommunicationTimeouts.ReceiveTimeout { get; }
TimeSpan IDefaultCommunicationTimeouts.SendTimeout { get; }

// reference to channel factory
protected ChannelManagerBase Manager { get; }
private ChannelManagerBase channelManager;
}
```

The members that are of type *ChannelManagerBase* represent ways to reference the factory that created the channel. The topic of channel factories is covered in greater detail in Chapter 7, "Channel Managers." For now, assume that the *ChannelManagerBase* references are ways to retrieve the time-outs from a channel factory. Notice the two sets of *TimeSpan* members in the *ChannelBase* type. The property names that start with the word *Default* retrieve the time-outs from the channel factory, and the explicitly implemented *IDefaultCommunicationTimeouts* members delegate to the *Default* members. The following code snippet illustrates:

```
protected override TimeSpan DefaultOpenTimeout {
  get {
    return ((IDefaultCommunicationTimeouts)this.channelManager).OpenTimeout;
  }
}
// delegate to DefaultOpenTimeout property TimeSpan
IDefaultCommunicationTimeouts.OpenTimeout {
  get {
    return this.DefaultOpenTimeout;
  }
}
```

The preceding code snippet describes only how the open time-out propagates through a channel. The close, send, and receive time-outs work in a similar manner.

Channel Flavors

Channels can perform a variety of functions. Virtually any type of messaging functionality can be written into a channel and plugged into the WCF runtime. We can, however, broadly categorize the types of tasks that a channel can perform. At the conceptual level, a channel can facilitate the use of a particular transport, messaging protocol, or channel shape.

Transport Channels

Transport channels are channels that interact with the network, file system, memory, or other application (like Microsoft SQL Server 2005, SAP, or Oracle). Each transport supported by WCF out of the box has at least one matching WCF transport channel. For example, WCF supports TCP/IP communication, and the means by which a WCF application interacts with sockets is a TCP/IP channel. Other supported transports are HTTP, Named Pipes, and MSMQ, and each of these transports has at least one transport channel associated with it.

While TCP/IP, HTTP, Named Pipes, and MSMQ represent the mainstream transports in use today, applications might require additional transports. Although the possibilities abound, some candidates are file system, Simple Mail Transfer Protocol (SMTP), Post Office Protocol 3 (POP3), and File Transfer Protocol (FTP). If one thinks a little outside the box, it is not too hard to conceive of other transports as well. Consider the SQL Server 2005 Service Broker. Although this is not a standard transport, treating it as such by creating a WCF transport channel provides WCF applications access to its features through the standard WCF programming model. With a Service Broker custom channel in place, application developers could leverage the Service Broker just as easily as they could leverage WS-* over HTTP. In effect, this type of custom transport channel allows the application developer to focus more on the business functionality of the application rather than the Service Broker access points or API. The same concept beneath writing a custom transport channel for the SQL Server 2005 Service Broker also applies to other enterprise computing applications like SAP and Oracle.

Transport channels are always the bottommost channel in a channel stack. From the sender's perspective, a transport channel is the last channel in the stack to interact with the data before it is sent to the chosen transport. From the receiver's perspective, a transport channel is the first channel in the stack to interact with the data before it is sent to other channels in the stack. In effect, other channels in the channel stack do not need to know the transport used in the application. A channel stack without a transport channel is of little or no value (except perhaps for a philosophical debate)—all channel stacks must contain at least one transport channel. As you'll see in the section "Shaping Channels" later in this chapter, some channel stacks can even contain more than one transport channel.

Protocol Channels

Protocol channels are the means by which WCF implements messaging protocols like WS-ReliableMessaging, WS-AtomicTransaction, and WS-SecureConversation. In fact, all

WS-* specifications supported by WCF are implemented as protocol channels. Since WS-* specifications frequently dictate that one application-level message exchange can actually generate more than one message at the transport layer, WS-* protocol channels frequently generate messages that are not surfaced to any higher channel in the channel stack. For example, consider the channel stack shown in Figure 6-3.

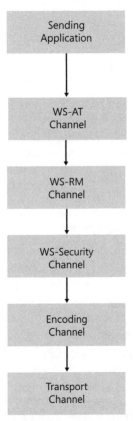

Figure 6-3   Channel stack with a WS-ReliableMessaging protocol channel

When the sending application passes a *Message* to the channel stack, the channel stack will ultimately encode the *Message* and send the bytes over the wire. Because there is a WS-RM channel in the channel stack, however, more than one *Message* is encoded and sent over the wire. In effect, the WS-RM channel can generate its own *Message* objects and send them to the next channel in the channel stack. Because WS-RM requires reply messages, the channels below the WS-RM channel must also be able to accept WS-RM reply messages. The WS-RM reply messages are pulled up the channel stack until they reach the WS-RM channel. Upon receipt of a WS-RM reply message, the WS-RM channel can then take some action as prescribed by the WS-RM specification, and the WS-RM channel is not required to pass that information to channels higher in the channel stack. If the sending application is using a two-way contract, the WS-RM channel will eventually pass a *Message* on to higher channels in the channel stack. More than one protocol channel can exist in a channel stack. In Figure 6-3, four protocol channels are shown. Each of these protocol channels functions in a manner similar to the aforementioned WS-RM example.

Shaping Channels

Shaping channels allow a channel stack to change shape within the channel stack. In so doing, shaping channels create a means for leveraging existing building blocks in new ways. For example, MSMQ is a means to send one-way messages to another application, and WCF supports the use of MSMQ in this manner. A custom shaping channel allows a WCF application to use MSMQ for duplex communication. Because duplex communication is at the atomic level a matter of sending and receiving messages concurrently, an MSMQ duplex shaping channel would need to wrap an MSMQ receiving channel and an MSMQ sending channel, as shown in Figure 6-4.

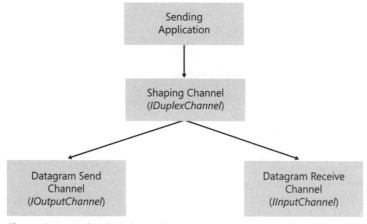

Figure 6-4   A shaping channel

Figure 6-4 shows that the shaping channel wraps an *IInputChannel* and an *IOutputChannel* to provide an *IDuplexChannel* shape to channels above it (hence the name). In practice, a shaping channel is not a trivial channel to write, as they can present interesting threading and synchronization concerns. As an example, consider the channel state machine transitions for a shaping channel. Since a shaping channel wraps other channels, all of the wrapped channels must transition through the channel state machine with the shaping channel. Because the channel above the shaping channel can invoke the *BeginOpen* and *BeginClose* methods on the shaping channel, the shaping channel must return an *IAsyncResult* that represents the *IAsyncResult* objects returned from the *BeginOpen* and *BeginClose* methods on the subordinate channels. For more information on this topic in particular, I recommend downloading and reviewing the PowerThreading library available at *http://wintellect.com*, as well as reviewing the threading chapter in Jeffrey Richter's *CLR via C#*.

Creating a Custom Channel

Now that you've seen the types used in the channel layer, let's build our own custom channel. The purpose of this channel is to print text in a console window. In the end, the channel that we build will be very useful in demonstrating the lifetime of a channel, as well as when an application invokes different channel members. Because our custom channel is going to print text to the console, it is necessary that our channel delegate all its method calls to the next channel in the stack. We'll call this channel the *DelegatorChannel*. Before we get started, it's important to note that you won't see all the code required to get our sample running until partway through Chapter 8, "Bindings." This is simply a byproduct of the way channels are created at run time.

One of the first considerations when building a custom channel is the shape or shapes the channel will support. The *DelegatorChannel* must work with all channel shapes (*IInputChannel*, *IOutputChannel*, *IDuplexChannel*, *IReplyChannel*, *IRequestChannel*, and all of the sessionful variants). As a result, we will build not one channel but rather several channels, and these channels will have a specific hierarchy.

Creating the Base Type

Because all of our channels will use the channel state machine and require a reference to the next channel in the channel stack, it makes sense to generalize those tasks into a base type. All of the types derived from our base type are different channel shapes, so it makes sense to make our base type generic. Because of these requirements, I call this base type *DelegatorChannelBase<TShape>*, where *TShape* must be a reference type and implement *IChannel*. (Remember that all channel shape interfaces implement *IChannel*.) *DelegatorChannelBase<TShape>* subclasses *ChannelBase* because this provides the common state machine and the means to propagate time-outs from the *Binding*. The initial definition for the *DelegatorChannelBase<TShape>* type is shown here:

```
internal class DelegatorChannelBase<TShape> : ChannelBase
  where TShape : class, IChannel {
  // implementation not shown yet
}
```

Adding the Constructor

A *DelegatorChannelBase<TShape>* object must never be placed at the bottom of a channel stack. In other words, a *DelegatorChannelBase<TShape>* object must have a reference to the next channel in the channel stack. By convention, we will pass this reference to the constructor. The type of this reference is the shape of the next channel in the channel stack, and because the generic parameter represents the channel shape, we will use the generic parameter as the type of this constructor parameter. The *DelegatorChannelBase<TShape>* constructor also requires a reference to the factory that creates the channel. As you've seen, one reason for this reference is to assist in the propagation of the time-outs from the binding all the way to the channel. Another reason for this reference is so that the channel can notify the factory when it is closed. You'll learn more about this topic in Chapter 7. The constructor of our base type is shown here:

```
internal class DelegatorChannelBase<TShape> : ChannelBase
    where TShape : class, IChannel {

  private TShape _innerChannel; // reference the next channel in the stack
  private String _source; // part of the String to print to the console

  protected DelegatorChannelBase(ChannelManagerBase channelManagerBase,
                              TShape innerChannel,
                              String source) : base(channelManagerBase){
    if(innerChannel == null) {
      throw new ArgumentNullException("DelegatorChannelBase requires a non-null channel.",
"innerChannel");
    }
    // set part of the String to print to console
    _source = String.Format("{0} CHANNEL STATE CHANGE: DelegatorChannelBase", source);
    // set the reference to the next channel
    _innerChannel = innerChannel;
  }
  // other implementation not shown yet
}
```

Notice the addition of the *_innerChannel* and *_source* member variables. As their comments indicate, these member variables are for storing the reference to the next channel in the stack and for holding the part of the *String* that we are going to print to the console. The first parameter in the constructor is of type *ChannelManagerBase*. The reference to the *ChannelManagerBase* is stored by the *ChannelBase* type through the *ChannelBase* constructor.

Adding the Channel State Machine

Because the *DelegatorChannelBase<TShape>* subclasses the *ChannelBase* abstract type and the *ChannelBase* abstract type subclasses the *CommunicationObject* abstract type but does not implement the abstract members defined in the *CommunicationObject*, the *DelegatorChannel-Base<TShape>* type must implement the abstract members defined in *CommunicationObject*. Since all of the state transitions in the *DelegatorChannelBase<TShape>* type must propagate to the other channels in the channel stack, our state transition methods delegate the call to the *_innerChannel* member variable, as shown here:

```
internal class DelegatorChannelBase<TShape> : ChannelBase
  where TShape : class, IChannel {

  private TShape _innerChannel; // reference to the next channel
  private String _source; // part of the String to output
```

```csharp
    // provide the _innerChannel to derived types
    protected TShape InnerChannel {
        get { return _innerChannel; }
    }

protected DelegatorChannelBase(ChannelManagerBase channelManagerBase,
                                TShape innerChannel,
                                String source) : base(channelManagerBase){
    if(innerChannel == null) {
      throw new ArgumentNullException("DelegatorChannelBase requires a non-null channel.",
"innerChannel");
    }
    // set part of the String to print to console
    _source = String.Format("{0} CHANNEL STATE CHANGE: DelegatorChannelBase", source);
    // set the reference to the next channel
    _innerChannel = innerChannel;
}
// IChannel implementation
public override T GetProperty<T>() {
    return this._innerChannel.GetProperty<T>();
}

#region CommunicationObject members
protected override void OnAbort() {
    PrintHelper.Print(_source, "OnAbort");
    this._innerChannel.Abort();
}

protected override IAsyncResult OnBeginClose(TimeSpan timeout,
                                             AsyncCallback callback,
                                             Object state) {
        // output that the method was called
        PrintHelper.Print( _source, "OnBeginClose");
        // delegate the call to the next channel
        return this._innerChannel.BeginClose(timeout, callback, state);
    }

protected override IAsyncResult OnBeginOpen(TimeSpan timeout,
                                            AsyncCallback callback,
                                            Object state) {
        // output that the method was called
        PrintHelper.Print(_source, "OnBeginOpen");
        // delegate the call to the next channel
        return this._innerChannel.BeginOpen(timeout, callback, state);
}

protected override void OnClose(TimeSpan timeout) {
    // output that the method was called
    PrintHelper.Print(_source, "OnClose");
    // delegate the call to the next channel
    this._innerChannel.Close(timeout);
}
```

```
protected override void OnEndClose(IAsyncResult result) {
  // output that the method was called
  PrintHelper.Print(_source, "OnEndClose");
  // delegate the call to the next channel
  this._innerChannel.EndClose(result);
}

protected override void OnEndOpen(IAsyncResult result) {
  // output that the method was called
  PrintHelper.Print(_source, "OnEndOpen");
  // delegate the call to the next channel
  this._innerChannel.EndOpen(result);
}

protected override void OnOpen(TimeSpan timeout) {
  // output that the method was called
  PrintHelper.Print(_source, "OnOpen");
  // delegate the call to the next channel
  this._innerChannel.Open(timeout);
}

#endregion
}
```

Each of the state transition methods (*OnAbort*, *OnBeginClose*, *OnBeginOpen*, *OnClose*, *OnEndClose*, *OnEndOpen*, and *OnOpen*) invokes the corresponding public state transition method on the next channel in the channel stack. Each state transition method also calls the static *Print* method on the *PrintHelper* type. The *PrintHelper* type does little more than print the *String* passed to it to the console.

Creating the Datagram Channels

Now that we have defined the base type for all of our channels, let's define the channels required for datagram message exchange. Since a datagram sending channel must implement the *IInputChannel* interface and the receiving channel must implement the *IOutputChannel* interface, we simply need to derive two types from *DelegatorChannelBase<TShape>* and implement the interfaces. Because the datagram interfaces are used by the duplex interfaces as well as the datagram and duplex sessionful interfaces, we will make our datagram channels generic.

> **Note**   We will start with the receiver, and then continue by defining the sender. For brevity, I will not show all of the members required in these derived types but rather show the pattern required in a full implementation.

The Datagram Receiving Channel

The datagram receiving channel subclasses the *DelegatorChannelBase<TShape>* type and implements the *IInputChannel* interface. Like *DelegatorChannelBase<TShape>*, our datagram receiving channel will also be generic, thereby allowing the channel to be reused by a duplex channel, as well as by the datagram and duplex variants. Because of these requirements, the name of our datagram receiving channel is *DelegatorInputChannel<TShape>*, as shown here:

```
internal class DelegatorInputChannel<TShape> :
  DelegatorChannelBase<TShape>, IInputChannel
  where TShape:class, IInputChannel {
  // implementation not shown
}
```

The *DelegatorInputChannel<TShape>* constructor must call the constructor on its base type, set the value of the output *String*, and call the *PrintHelper.Print* method, as shown here:

```
internal class DelegatorInputChannel<TShape> :
  DelegatorChannelBase<TShape>, IInputChannel
  where TShape:class, IInputChannel {

    private String _source; // store the String to output

  internal DelegatorInputChannel(ChannelManagerBase channelManagerBase,
                                 TShape innerChannel,
                                 String source) : base(channelManagerBase,
                                                       innerChannel,
                                                       source) {
    // assign the name and generic parameter to the String
    _source = String.Format("{0} CHANNEL: DelegatorInputChannel<{1}>",
                            source,
                            typeof(TShape).Name);
    // output that the method was called
    PrintHelper.Print(_source, "ctor");
    }
  // other implementation not shown
}
```

Next we need to implement the *IInputChannel* interface. For brevity, I will show only three of the members here:

```
public IAsyncResult BeginReceive(TimeSpan timeout,
                                 AsyncCallback callback,
                                 Object state) {
  // output that the method was called
  PrintHelper.Print(_source, "BeginReceive");
  // delegate the call to the next channel
  return this.InnerChannel.BeginReceive(timeout, callback, state);
}

public IAsyncResult BeginReceive(AsyncCallback callback, Object state) {
  // output that the method was called
  PrintHelper.Print(_source, "BeginReceive");
  // delegate the call to the next channel
  return this.InnerChannel.BeginReceive(callback, state);
}
```

```
public IAsyncResult BeginTryReceive(TimeSpan timeout,
                                    AsyncCallback callback,
                                    Object state) {
  // output that the method was called
  PrintHelper.Print(_source, "BeginTryReceive");
  // delegate the call to the next channel
  return this.InnerChannel.BeginTryReceive(timeout, callback, state);
}
```

The *DelegatorInputChannel<TShape>* type definition is complete only after the other members are added (*BeginWaitForMessage*, *EndReceive*, *EndTryReceive*, *EndWaitForMessage*, *LocalAddress*, *Receive*, *TryReceive*, and *WaitForMessage*).

The Datagram Sending Channel

The datagram sending channel is very similar to the datagram receiving channel, except that it implements the *IOutputChannel* interface. To avoid repetition, I will show the type definition here and leave it to the reader to draw the parallels with the *DelegatorInputChannel<TShape>* type definition:

```
internal class DelegatorOutputChannel<TShape> :
  DelegatorChannelBase<TShape>, IOutputChannel where
  TShape: class, IOutputChannel {

  private String _source; // store the String to output

  internal DelegatorOutputChannel(ChannelManagerBase channelManagerBase,
                                  TShape innerChannel,
                                  String source) : base(channelManagerBase,
                                                        innerChannel,
                                                        source) {
    _source = String.Format("{0} CHANNEL: DelegatorOutputChannel<{1}>", source,
typeof(TShape).Name);
    // output that the method was called
    PrintHelper.Print(_source, "ctor");
  }

  #region IOutputChannel Members
  public IAsyncResult BeginSend(Message message,
                                TimeSpan timeout,
                                AsyncCallback callback,
                                Object state) {
    // output that the method was called
    PrintHelper.Print(_source, "BeginSend");
    // delegate the call to the next channel
    return this.InnerChannel.BeginSend(message, timeout, callback, state);
  }

  public IAsyncResult BeginSend(Message message, AsyncCallback callback, object state) {
    // output that the method was called
    PrintHelper.Print(_source, "BeginSend");
    // delegate the call to the next channel
    return this.InnerChannel.BeginSend(message, callback, state);
  }
```

```
  public void EndSend(IAsyncResult result) {
    // output that the method was called
    PrintHelper.Print(_source, "EndSend");
    // delegate the call to the next channel
    this.InnerChannel.EndSend(result);
  }

  public EndpointAddress RemoteAddress {
    get {
      // output that the method was called
      PrintHelper.Print(_source, "RemoteAddress");
      // delegate the call to the next channel
      return this.InnerChannel.RemoteAddress; }
    }

  public void Send(Message message, TimeSpan timeout) {
    // output that the method was called
    PrintHelper.Print(_source, "Send");
    // delegate the call to the next channel
    this.InnerChannel.Send(message, timeout);
    }

  public void Send(Message message) {
    // output that the method was called
    PrintHelper.Print(_source, "Send");
    // delegate the call to the next channel
    this.InnerChannel.Send(message);
  }

  public Uri Via {
    get {
      // output that the method was called
      PrintHelper.Print(_source, "Via");
      // delegate the call to the next channel
      return this.InnerChannel.Via;
    }
  }
  #endregion
}
```

The Duplex Channel

Recalling our examination of channel shapes, remember that the *IDuplexChannel* interface is really the union of the *IInputChannel* and *IOutputChannel* interfaces. Because we already have type definitions that implement the *IInputChannel* and *IOutputChannel* interfaces, we can reuse one of them as the base type for our duplex channel. The *IInputChannel* interface has more members than the *IOutputChannel*, so (for no other reason) the *DelegatorInputChannel<TShape>* type will serve as the base type for our duplex channel.

Because our duplex channel implements the *IDuplexChannel* interface, let's call our duplex channel the *DelegatorDuplexChannel* and choose *IDuplexChannel* as the generic parameter in the base type, as shown here:

```
internal class DelegatorDuplexChannel :
  DelegatorInputChannel<IDuplexChannel>, IDuplexChannel {
  // implementation not shown yet
}
```

Because the *DelegatorDuplexChannel* is very similar to the *DelegatorInputChannel<TShape>* type definition, I will show only part of the type definition here:

```
internal class DelegatorDuplexChannel :
  DelegatorInputChannel<IDuplexChannel>, IDuplexChannel {

  private String _source; // store the String to output

  internal DelegatorDuplexChannel(ChannelManagerBase channelManagerBase,
                    // use IDuplexSession as the 2nd parameter
                    IDuplexChannel innerChannel,
                    String source) : base(channelManagerBase,
                                          innerChannel,
                                          source) {
    _source = String.Format("{0} CHANNEL: DelegatorDuplexChannel", source);
    PrintHelper.Print(_source, "ctor");
  }

  #region IOutputChannel Members

  public IAsyncResult BeginSend(Message message,
                    TimeSpan timeout,
                    AsyncCallback callback,
                    Object state) {
    PrintHelper.Print(_source, "BeginSend");
    return this.InnerChannel.BeginSend(message, timeout, callback, state);
  }
  // other IOutputChannel Members omitted for brevity

  #endregion
}
```

The Duplex Session Channel

From an object model perspective, sessionful channel shapes differ only slightly from the nonsessionful ones. For example, the *IDuplexSessionChannel* is really the union of the *IDuplexChannel* and the *ISessionChannel<IDuplexSession>* interfaces. Because we have already defined the *DelegatorDuplexChannel* type (which implements the *IDuplexChannel* interface), creating a sessionful variant is simply a matter of subclassing the *DelegatorDuplexChannel* and implementing the *IDuplexSessionChannel* interface, as shown here:

```
internal sealed class DelegatorDuplexSessionChannel :
  DelegatorDuplexChannel, IDuplexSessionChannel {

  private IDuplexSessionChannel _innerSessionChannel; // reference the next
                                                      // sessionful channel
  private String _source;   // store the String to output

  internal DelegatorDuplexSessionChannel(ChannelManagerBase
    channelManagerBase, IDuplexSessionChannel innerChannel, String source)
    : base(channelManagerBase, innerChannel, source) {

    _source = String.Format("{0} CHANNEL: DelegatorDuplexSessionChannel",
      source);
    PrintHelper.Print(_source, "ctor");
    // assign the reference to the next sessionful channel
    this._innerSessionChannel = innerChannel;
  }

  // IDuplexSessionChannel member that is not defined in IDuplexChannel
  public IDuplexSession Session {
    get {
      PrintHelper.Print(_source, "Session");
      return this._innerSessionChannel.Session; }
    }
}
```

Because the *DelegatorDuplexChannel* has a member variable of type *IDuplexChannel*, we need to store an additional reference to the same object via a local variable of type *IDuplexSessionChannel*. Doing so allows us to easily add the *Session* property to our type definition.

> **Note**   Given the patterns shown in the *DelegatorChannelBase<TShape>*, *DelegatorInputChannel<TShape>*, *DelegatorOutputChannel<TShape>*, *DelegatorDuplexChannel*, and *DelegatorDuplexSessionChannel*, it should be fairly easy for the reader to add channel implementations for *IInputSessionChannel*, *IOutputSessionChannel*, *IRequestChannel*, *IReplyChannel*, *IRequestSessionChannel*, and *IReplySessionChannel*. In the next two chapters, we will build the other types necessary to add these channels to a WCF application.

Summary

Because channels perform the real work of message, they are an essential part of all WCF applications, even though they are not readily visible to the application developer. In this chapter, we saw the channel state machine, the key types in the channel API, and an example of a custom channel. In Chapters 7 and 8, you'll learn how to plug our custom channel into a WCF application.

Chapter 7
Channel Managers

User code never directly instantiates a channel; that job is reserved for special factory types. Although these factory objects are not channels, they are considered part of the channel layer. In Chapter 6, "Channels," I borrowed *Design Pattern* terminology (by Erich Gamma et al, Addison-Wesley, 1995) and called these special types *channel factories*. In the Microsoft Windows Communication Foundation (WCF) type system, channel factories have specific names, and the names of these types differ on the sender and the receiver. On the receiver, these types are called *channel listeners*. On the sender, these types are called *channel factories*. Channel listeners and channel factories, although they share some common characteristics and purposes, have different object and behavioral models. When grouped together, channel listeners and channel factories are called *channel managers*. This chapter describes the internals of both types of channel managers: channel listeners and channel factories. In this chapter, you'll learn about the basics of these types and their object models, and then we'll look at examples illustrating how to build custom channel managers. Because a *Binding* creates a channel factory and a channel listener, the code sample will not run on its own until the end of the next chapter.

Because a channel is the physical means by which a WCF application implements some messaging functionality, channel factories and channel listeners are the means by which a WCF application creates that messaging functionality. Just as there is no one-size-fits-all channel definition, there is no one-size-fits-all channel factory or channel listener. Just as channels can be grouped according to their general functionality (for example, WS-ReliableMessaging, TCP/IP transport, and so on), channel managers can also be grouped according to the functionality of the channels they create. For example, the WS-ReliableMessaging channels are created by WS-ReliableMessaging channel managers, and those same channel managers would not also create transport channels.

This is not to say, however, that a channel manager can create only one type of channel. Quite the contrary, channel managers can and often do create several different kinds of channels, but these channels reside in a given functional group. Typically, the types of channels created by a given channel manager differ only in shape. In some cases, a channel manager can even create exactly the same type and shape of channel (for example, duplex channels).

Channel managers share many characteristics with channels. Because channels are frequently arranged in a stack at run time, channel managers are also frequently arranged in a stack. In one sense, the arrangement of channel managers within the stack dictates the arrangement of the channels in the channel stack. Channel managers implement the *ICommunicationObject* interface and share the same state machine described in Chapter 6. Furthermore, they also implement a query mechanism similar to the one available in channels.

The Concept of a Channel Manager

Channel managers share a common abstract base type: *System.ServiceModel.Channels. ChannelManagerBase*. The name of this type does not reflect its purpose. From the name, one might assume that the *ChannelManagerBase* type is a means to keep track of the channels that a channel factory or channel listener creates. In early incarnations of WCF (at that time, called Indigo), this was indeed the case. This early design tightly coupled the lifetime and state of a channel to the lifetime and state of the object that created it. For example, when a channel manager closed, it would then close all of the channels it created.

This model is workable on the sender, but less than ideal on the receiver, since a receiver can have only one channel listener stack per Uniform Resource Identifier (URI). Receivers frequently need to create new channel listener stacks and shut down the state of the existing listener stacks. Because closing a receiving channel can trigger substantial work (for example, WS-RM messages, committing or aborting transactions, and so on), shutting down the channel listener that created it can take a long time. If there is no coupling between a channel listener and the channels it creates, it is possible to shut down the current listener, let the existing work complete, and start a new channel listener to process new messages. This model is the one adopted by the team in the first version product, primarily because it enables better throughput on receiving applications.

In essence, the early concept of a channel manager is still valid on the sender. Instead of doing channel management work in the *ChannelManagerBase* type, however, channel factories manage the channels they create further down in their type hierarchy. As a result of these changes, the *ChannelManagerBase* type is simply a means to force channel factories and channel listeners to implement the state machine, implement the query mechanism, and pass timeouts from a *Binding* to the channels they create.

The Receiver: Channel Listeners

As their name implies, channel listeners do more than simply create channels; they listen for incoming connections. This model is borrowed from the Berkeley Sockets application programming interface (API). In Microsoft Windows programming, this model is visible in the Windows Sockets (Winsock) API. In Microsoft .NET Framework programming, this model is visible in the *System.Net.Sockets* namespace. In this model, a *TcpListener* or *Socket* binds to an address and then passively listens for incoming connections. When a connection becomes available (for example, a client connects to the listener), a method that begins with the word *Accept* returns an instance of a connected *Socket* or *TcpClient*, and the application can use that object to receive data.

In WCF, a channel listener performs the same sort of work. Channel listeners bind to a URI, begin passively waiting for incoming connections, and when a connection becomes available, a method that begins with the word *Accept* returns an instance of a channel. The application then uses the returned channel to receive a *Message*. Although all channel listeners define *Accept* methods, transport channel listeners are the only types of listeners that actually listen for incoming connections. As an example, think of a stack of channel listeners. Like a channel stack, a channel listener stack is ordered in such a way that the transport channel listener is at the bottom of the channel listener stack. The transport channel listener is the only channel listener that binds to an address and begins listening for connections. Channel listeners higher in the channel listener stack simply delegate their *Accept* method calls to the transport channel listener, as illustrated in Figure 7-1.

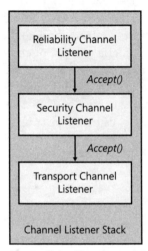

Figure 7-1   The channel listener stack

Not all transport channel listeners behave the same way. Their differences are, in large measure, due to the intrinsic differences between transports. For example, transport channel listeners for connection-oriented transports (for example, TCP/IP and named pipes) return a channel when that listener receives an incoming connection. Transport channel listeners for disconnected transports (for example, MSMQ) return a channel immediately because there is no incoming connection to wait for.

The *IChannelListener* Interface

All channel listeners implement the *System.ServiceModel.Channels.IChannelListener* interface. This interface is the type that forces all channels to implement the channel layer state machine and some basic channel listener members. The *IChannelListener* interface is shown here:

```
public interface IChannelListener : ICommunicationObject {
    IAsyncResult BeginWaitForChannel(TimeSpan timeout,
                                     AsyncCallback callback,
                                     Object state);
    Boolean EndWaitForChannel(IAsyncResult result);
    Boolean WaitForChannel(TimeSpan timeout);

    T GetProperty<T>() where T: class;
    // the listening address
    Uri Uri { get; }
}
```

The *WaitForChannel* method (and the asynchronous variant) is intended to return a *Boolean* indicating whether a channel is available. The *Uri* property is a way to access the listening address. The *GetProperty<T>* method is identical in structure and intended use to the one implemented in the *IChannel* interface. The *IChannelListener* interface does not implement the *IChannel* interface, because the *IChannel* interface is a means to identify a channel in the API. For example, many generic parameters are constrained to class and *IChannel*. The intention is to constrain that parameter to a channel that implements a particular shape. If *IChannelListener* implemented the *IChannel* interface, a channel listener type could be used in places otherwise reserved for a channel. However, channel listeners exist in a stack, and that stack must allow queries.

The *IChannelListener<TChannel>* Interface

All channel listeners also implement the *IChannelListener<TChannel>* interface. It is in this interface that we first see the *Accept* paradigm borrowed from the Berkeley Sockets API, shown here:

```
public interface IChannelListener<TChannel> : IChannelListener,
                                              where TChannel: class,
                                                             IChannel {
    TChannel AcceptChannel();
    TChannel AcceptChannel(TimeSpan timeout);
    IAsyncResult BeginAcceptChannel(AsyncCallback callback, Object state);
    IAsyncResult BeginAcceptChannel(TimeSpan timeout,
                                    AsyncCallback callback,
                                    Object state);
    TChannel EndAcceptChannel(IAsyncResult result);
}
```

Notice that the interface definition constrains the *TChannel* generic parameter to a concrete type that implements the *IChannel* interface. In the WCF API, channels that implement a particular shape meet this criterion. Taken as a whole, this means that a channel listener must reference a particular channel shape. This is subtly but distinctly different from the way channels use channel shapes. Channels implement a channel shape; channel listeners reference a channel shape and use that reference to build a channel that implements that shape.

When closed, a type implementing the *IChannelListener<TChannel>* interface returns instances of a channel that implements that shape via the *AcceptChannel* methods (and the asynchronous variants). As with several other members in the channel layer, there is an overloaded *AcceptChannel* method that accepts a *TimeSpan* parameter. Because receiving applications often need to listen passively for an indefinite length of time, the value of this argument is often *TimeSpan.MaxValue*.

The *ChannelListenerBase* Type

All channel listeners derive from the *System.ServiceModel.Channels.ChannelListenerBase* abstract type. The type definition for the *ChannelListenerBase* type is shown here:

```
public abstract class ChannelListenerBase : ChannelManagerBase,
                                            IChannelListener,
                                            ICommunicationObject {
  protected ChannelListenerBase();
  protected ChannelListenerBase(IDefaultCommunicationTimeouts timeouts);

  // IChannelListener implementation
  public IAsyncResult BeginWaitForChannel(TimeSpan timeout,
                                          AsyncCallback callback,
                                          Object state);
  public bool EndWaitForChannel(IAsyncResult result);
  public bool WaitForChannel(TimeSpan timeout);

  // Extensibility points for IChannelListener members
  protected abstract IAsyncResult OnBeginWaitForChannel(TimeSpan timeout,
    AsyncCallback callback, Object state);
  protected abstract bool OnEndWaitForChannel(IAsyncResult result);
  protected abstract bool OnWaitForChannel(TimeSpan timeout);
    public abstract Uri Uri { get; }

  // Query mechanism
  public virtual T GetProperty<T>() where T: class;

  // CommunicationObject timeouts
  protected override TimeSpan DefaultCloseTimeout { get; }
  protected override TimeSpan DefaultOpenTimeout { get; }

  // ChannelManagerBase timeouts
  protected override TimeSpan DefaultReceiveTimeout { get; }
  protected override TimeSpan DefaultSendTimeout { get; }
}
```

The constructor that accepts a *TimeSpan* is fairly interesting. As a result of the type hierarchy of the *ChannelListenerBase* type, it defines four protected *TimeSpan* properties. The WCF type system defaults each of these time-outs to one minute. If that is not acceptable for a channel listener (and the subsequent channels), you can pass an *IDefaultCommunicationTimeouts* to the constructor of the *ChannelListenerBase*. In the constructor, the time-outs from this type are assigned to the fields that back the *TimeSpan* properties. As you'll see in Chapter 8, "Bindings," a *Binding* implements the *IDefaultCommunicationTimeouts* interface, and this is indeed the means by which time-outs are moved from user code down to the channel layer.

The *ChannelListenerBase<TChannel>* Type

Channel listeners subclass the *System.ServiceModel.Channels.ChannelListenerBase<TChannel>* abstract type. This type derives from the *ChannelListenerBase* type and implements the *IChannelListener<TChannel>* type, as shown here:

```
public abstract class ChannelListenerBase<TChannel> : ChannelListenerBase,
    IChannelListener<TChannel>, where TChannel: class, IChannel {

  protected ChannelListenerBase();
  protected ChannelListenerBase(IDefaultCommunicationTimeouts timeouts);

  // IChannelListener<TChannel> implementation
  public IAsyncResult BeginAcceptChannel(AsyncCallback callback,
                                         Object state);
  public IAsyncResult BeginAcceptChannel(TimeSpan timeout,
    AsyncCallback callback, Object state);
  public TChannel EndAcceptChannel(IAsyncResult result);
  public TChannel AcceptChannel();
  public TChannel AcceptChannel(TimeSpan timeout);

  // extensibility points for IChannelListener<TChannel>
  protected abstract TChannel OnAcceptChannel(TimeSpan timeout);
  protected abstract IAsyncResult OnBeginAcceptChannel(TimeSpan timeout,
    AsyncCallback callback, Object state);
  protected abstract TChannel OnEndAcceptChannel(IAsyncResult result);
}
```

Building a Custom Channel Listener

Now that you've seen the types used in channel listeners, let's create our own. In the previous chapter, you learned how to build several different *DelegatorChannel* channels. In this section, you'll see how to build a channel listener that creates these channels on a receiving application. As mentioned at the outset of this chapter, this sample will not work on its own until the conclusion of Chapter 8.

When building a channel listener, one has to consider the shape of the channel that the channel listener is going to build. Because our *DelegatorChannel* example can be of any shape, our channel listener must be able to create all known *DelegatorChannel* channels. In

Chapter 6, we used generic parameters as a means to provide this type of flexibility, and we will do so again in this example.

Let's start with what we know. We know that the easiest way to create a channel listener is to derive a type from *ChannelListenerBase<TChannel>*. We also know that we need to make our channel listener generic, and this will allow our channel listener to work with the different possible channel shapes. With this in mind, our channel listener definition looks like the following:

```
internal sealed class DelegatorChannelListener<TShape> :
  ChannelListenerBase<TShape> where TShape : class, IChannel {
  // implementation omitted for clarity
}
```

Notice the access modifier of the *DelegatorChannelListener<TShape>* type. Like the channel definitions shown in Chapter 6, this channel listener does not need to be accessible to outside callers. We will provide that accessibility in Chapter 8, through the *Binding* and *BindingElement* objects. Now that we have the name and base type of our channel listener, let's add the implementation. The following is a full implementation of the *DelegatorChannelListener<TShape>* type:

```
internal sealed class DelegatorChannelListener<TShape> :
    ChannelListenerBase<TShape> where TShape : class, IChannel {
  // field referencing the next channel listener
  IChannelListener<TShape> _innerListener;

  // String to output to console
  String _consolePrefix = "LISTENER: DelegatorChannelListener";

  // builds the next channel listener, then assigns it to
  // the _innerListener field
  public DelegatorChannelListener(BindingContext context) {
    PrintHelper.Print(_consolePrefix, "ctor");
    this._innerListener = context.BuildInnerChannelListener<TShape>();
  }

  // Creates a DelegatorChannel of the correct shape and returns it
  private TShape WrapChannel(TShape innerChannel) {

    if(innerChannel == null) {
      throw new ArgumentNullException("innerChannel cannot be null", "innerChannel");
    }
    if(typeof(TShape) == typeof(IInputChannel)) {
      return (TShape)(Object)new DelegatorInputChannel<IInputChannel>(this,
(IInputChannel)innerChannel, "RECEIVE");
    }
    if(typeof(TShape) == typeof(IReplyChannel)) {
      return (TShape)(object)new DelegatorReplyChannel(this, (IReplyChannel)innerChannel,
"RECEIVE");
    }
    if(typeof(TShape) == typeof(IDuplexChannel)) {
      return (TShape)(object)new DelegatorDuplexChannel(this, (IDuplexChannel)innerChannel,
```

```
"RECEIVE");
    }
    if(typeof(TShape) == typeof(IInputSessionChannel)) {
       return (TShape)(object)new DelegatorInputSessionChannel(this,
(IInputSessionChannel)innerChannel, "RECEIVE");
    }
    if(typeof(TShape) == typeof(IReplySessionChannel)) {
       return (TShape)(object)new DelegatorReplySessionChannel(this,
(IReplySessionChannel)innerChannel, "RECEIVE");
    }
    if(typeof(TShape) == typeof(IDuplexSessionChannel)) {
       return (TShape)(object)new DelegatorDuplexSessionChannel(this,
(IDuplexSessionChannel)innerChannel, "RECEIVE");
    }

    // cannot wrap this channel
    throw new ArgumentException(String.Format("invalid channel shape passed:{0}",
innerChannel.GetType()));
  }

    // IChannelListener<TChannel> members
  protected override IAsyncResult OnBeginAcceptChannel(TimeSpan timeout, AsyncCallback
callback, object state) {
    PrintHelper.Print(_consolePrefix, "OnBeginAcceptChannel");
    return this._innerListener.BeginAcceptChannel(timeout, callback, state);
  }

  protected override TShape OnEndAcceptChannel(IAsyncResult result) {
    // create and return the channel
    PrintHelper.Print(_consolePrefix, "OnEndAcceptChannel");
    TShape innerChannel = _innerListener.EndAcceptChannel(result);
    // when closing, _inner.EndAcceptChannel returns null, nothing to wrap
    if (innerChannel != null) {
      return WrapChannel(innerChannel);
    }
    return null;
  }

    protected override TShape OnAcceptChannel(TimeSpan timeout){
    // delegate to next channel, wrap it, and return it
    PrintHelper.Print(_consolePrefix, "OnAcceptChannel");
    TShape innerChannel = _innerListener.AcceptChannel(timeout);
    // when closing, _inner.AcceptChannel returns null, nothing to wrap
    if (innerChannel != null) {
      return WrapChannel(innerChannel);
    }
    return null;
  }

  // IChannelListener members
  protected override IAsyncResult OnBeginWaitForChannel(TimeSpan timeout, AsyncCallback
callback, object state) {
    PrintHelper.Print(_consolePrefix, "OnBeginWaitForChannel");
    return this._innerListener.BeginWaitForChannel(timeout, callback, state);
  }
```

```
protected override bool OnEndWaitForChannel(IAsyncResult result) {
  PrintHelper.Print(_consolePrefix, "OnEndWaitForChannel");
  return this._innerListener.EndWaitForChannel(result);
}


protected override bool OnWaitForChannel(TimeSpan timeout) {
  PrintHelper.Print(_consolePrefix, "OnWaitForChannel");
  return this._innerListener.WaitForChannel(timeout);
}


public override Uri Uri {
  get {
    PrintHelper.Print(_consolePrefix, "Uri");
    return this._innerListener.Uri;
  }
}
public override T GetProperty<T>() {
  PrintHelper.Print(_consolePrefix, "GetProperty<" + typeof(T) + ">");
  return this._innerListener.GetProperty<T>();
}


// CommunicationObject members
protected override void OnAbort() {
  PrintHelper.Print(_consolePrefix, "OnAbort");
  this._innerListener.Abort();
}


protected override IAsyncResult OnBeginClose(TimeSpan timeout, AsyncCallback callback,
object state) {
  PrintHelper.Print(_consolePrefix, "OnBeginClose");
  return this._innerListener.BeginClose(timeout, callback, state);
}


protected override IAsyncResult OnBeginOpen(TimeSpan timeout, AsyncCallback callback,
object state) {
  PrintHelper.Print(_consolePrefix, "OnBeginOpen");
  return this._innerListener.BeginOpen(timeout, callback, state);
}


protected override void OnClose(TimeSpan timeout) {
  PrintHelper.Print(_consolePrefix, "OnClose");
  this._innerListener.Close(timeout);
}


protected override void OnEndClose(IAsyncResult result) {
  PrintHelper.Print(_consolePrefix, "OnEndClose");
  this._innerListener.EndClose(result);
}


protected override void OnEndOpen(IAsyncResult result) {
  PrintHelper.Print(_consolePrefix, "OnEndOpen");
  this._innerListener.EndOpen(result);
}
```

```
protected override void OnOpen(TimeSpan timeout) {
    PrintHelper.Print(_consolePrefix, "OnOpen");
    this._innerListener.Open(timeout);
}
}
```

A few parts of this type require some explanation. Let's start with the constructor. Like the *DelegatorChannel* definitions in the previous chapter, *DelegatorChannelListener<TShape>* objects exist in a stack with other channel listeners. There are several ways to build a channel listener stack, but in the end, the result must be a stack of channel listeners with the transport channel listener at the bottom of the stack. The *DelegatorChannelListener<TShape>* type defines a member variable of type *IChannelListener<TShape>* and assigns that member variable in the constructor via a constructor parameter. As you'll see in Chapter 8, the *BindingContext* object used at run time by a *Binding* is the primary way to build the channel listener stack. Another viable approach is to make the constructor parameter of type *IChannelListener<TShape>*. This offloads the responsibility of using the *BindingContext* to the caller. In my view, the difference between these two approaches is not substantive.

Most of the methods in the *DelegatorChannelListener<TShape>* are conceptually similar to the *DelegatorChannel* channels in that they simply delegate to the next channel listener in the channel listener stack. One interesting method in the *DelegatorChannelListener<TShape>* type is the *WrapChannel* private method. As indicated in the comments, the purpose of this method is to return an instance of a *DelegatorChannel* that has the same shape as the *TShape* generic parameter. The *innerChannel* parameter is passed to the constructor of the *DelegatorChannel* so that the channel stack can be built properly. The *OnAcceptChannel* and *OnEndAcceptChannel* methods are the only methods that call the *WrapChannel* method. Before these methods can call the *WrapChannel* method, however, they must call the appropriate method on the *_innerListener* member variable (*AcceptChannel* and *EndAcceptChannel*, respectively) and then pass the channel listener to the *WrapChannel* method.

When the channel listener stack is closing, the *DelegatorChannelListener<TShape>* type delegates the closing calls (for example, *Close*, *OnClose*, *Abort*, *OnAbort*) to the next channel listener in the channel listener stack. If the *BeginAcceptChannel* or *AcceptChannel* method was called prior to the closing method call, the delegated calls will return *null*. In this case, it is important that the *OnEndAcceptChannel* or *AcceptChannel* method return *null* also.

The Sender: Channel Factories

Channel factories are the means by which the sender creates channels. They share many similarities with channel listeners, but by virtue of the fact that they reside on the sender, they do not have responsibility for listening for incoming connections. Rather than passively waiting for an incoming connection and then creating a channel in response to that connection, they simply create a channel on demand via a *CreateChannel* method. Like channel listeners, channel factories are grouped according to the functionality of the channel they create.

In practice, this means that each transport channel will have a channel factory associated with it, as will the different WS-* protocol channels. As with channel listeners, user code does not directly instantiate a channel factory; that job is reserved for a *Binding* (as you'll see in Chapter 8). Like channel listeners, channel factories subclass the *ChannelManagerBase* type. The rest of their type hierarchy, however, is different. In this section, we will investigate the different types in the channel factory hierarchy and then continue our *DelegatorChannel* example by creating a custom channel factory.

The *IChannelFactory* Interface

All channel factories implement the *IChannelFactory* interface. This interface implements the *ICommunicationObject* interface and thus serves as a way to enforce the state machine you should now be familiar with. The *IChannelFactory* interface also forces types that implement it to expose a query mechanism similar to the one in channels and channel listeners, as shown here:

```
public interface IChannelFactory : ICommunicationObject {
    T GetProperty<T>() where T: class;
}
```

The *IChannelFactory<TChannel>* Interface

All channel factories implement the *IChannelFactory<TChannel>* interface as well. The *IChannelFactory<TChannel>* interface implements the *IChannelFactory* interface, so it is more commonly used than the *IChannelFactory* interface. The *IChannelFactory<TChannel>* interface defines two members that return a channel, as shown here:

```
public interface IChannelFactory<TChannel> : IChannelFactory {
    TChannel CreateChannel(EndpointAddress to);
    TChannel CreateChannel(EndpointAddress to, Uri via);
}
```

Notice the *CreateChannel* method with two parameters. The parameters are of type *EndpointAddress* and *Uri*. At run time, the *to* parameter is used as the *EndpointAddress* serialized into the *Message*, and the *via* parameter is used as the address that the channel will try to reach. These values of the *via* argument can be different from the *Uri* in the *to* argument when you want to send the message to one address and have that messaging participant forward the message to another messaging participant (as shown in Chapter 2, "Service Orientation").

The *ChannelFactoryBase* Type

Channel factories indirectly subclass the *ChannelFactoryBase* abstract type. Conceptually, the purpose of this type is similar to the purpose of the *ChannelListenerBase* type used in channel listeners. In other words, the *ChannelListenerBase* type provides a means to customize the default time-outs for opening, closing, sending, and receiving messages. The *ChannelFactoryBase* object model is shown here:

```
public abstract class ChannelFactoryBase : ChannelManagerBase,
                                           IChannelFactory {
  protected ChannelFactoryBase();
  protected ChannelFactoryBase(IDefaultCommunicationTimeouts timeouts);

  // IChannelFactory implementation
  public virtual T GetProperty<T>() where T: class;

  // CommunicationObject implementation
  protected override void OnAbort();
  protected override IAsyncResult OnBeginClose(TimeSpan timeout,
                                               AsyncCallback callback,
                                               Object state);
  protected override void OnClose(TimeSpan timeout);
  protected override void OnEndClose(IAsyncResult result);
  protected override TimeSpan DefaultCloseTimeout { get; }
  protected override TimeSpan DefaultOpenTimeout { get; }

  // ChannelManagerBase implementation
  protected override TimeSpan DefaultReceiveTimeout { get; }
  protected override TimeSpan DefaultSendTimeout { get; }
}
```

The *ChannelFactoryBase<TChannel>* Type

The *ChannelFactoryBase<TChannel>* type subclasses the *ChannelFactoryBase* type and implements the *IChannelFactory<TChannel>* interface. It serves as a base type for channel factories. Furthermore, the implementation in this type maintains references to and exerts control over the state of the channels it creates. (Recall the "The Concept of a Channel Manager" section earlier in this chapter.) The *ChannelFactoryBase<TChannel>* object model is shown here:

```
public abstract class ChannelFactoryBase<TChannel> : ChannelFactoryBase,
    IChannelFactory<TChannel> {

  // calls the other constructor, passing null as argument
  protected ChannelFactoryBase();
  // creates an object that manages the channels
  protected ChannelFactoryBase(IDefaultCommunicationTimeouts timeouts);

  // IChannelFactory<TChannel> implementation
  public TChannel CreateChannel(EndpointAddress address);
  public TChannel CreateChannel(EndpointAddress address, Uri via);
  // Extensibility point for IChannelFactory<TChannel> implementation
  protected abstract TChannel OnCreateChannel(EndpointAddress address, Uri via);

  // CommunicationObject implementation: changes state
  // of the channels it has created
  protected override void OnAbort();
```

```
  protected override IAsyncResult OnBeginClose(TimeSpan timeout, AsyncCallback callback,
object state);
  protected override void OnClose(TimeSpan timeout);
  protected override void OnEndClose(IAsyncResult result);

  // helper method that checks the State to see if the
  // channel factory can create channels (CommunicationState.Opened)
  protected void ValidateCreateChannel();
}
```

The *ChannelFactoryBase<TChannel>* constructor instantiates an object that maintains a reference to each of the channels that the *ChannelFactoryBase<TChannel>* creates. When a *ChannelFactoryBase<TChannel>* object closes or aborts, the object that is referencing the created channels ensures that the channels proceed through their state machine along with the *ChannelFactoryBase<TChannel>* object. The code that ensures that these state changes occur is located in the *CommunicationObject* implementation in the *ChannelFactory-Base<TChannel>* type.

Another interesting facet of the *ChannelFactoryBase<TChannel>* type is the *ValidateCreateChannel* method. This method simply ensures that the *State* of the object is *CommunicationState.Opened*. If the state is not *CommunicationState.Opened*, the method throws an *InvalidOperationException*. Both of the *CreateChannel* methods use this method as a means to ensure that the channel factory is in the appropriate point in the state machine.

Building a Custom Channel Factory

Now that you've seen the types that play important roles in channel factories, let's create a channel factory that continues our *DelegatorChannel* example. Like the *DelegatorChannel-Listener<TShape>* example earlier in this chapter, our channel factory must be able to create *DelegatorChannel* channels of any shape. As a result, our channel factory needs to be generic, as shown here:

```
internal sealed class DelegatorChannelFactory<TShape> :
    ChannelFactoryBase<TShape> {

  // reference the next channel factory in the stack
  IChannelFactory<TShape> _innerFactory;

  // the String to print to the console
  String _consolePrefix = "FACTORY: DelegatorChannelFactory";

  // ctor that builds the next channel factory in the stack,
  // then assigns the _innerFactory member variable
  internal DelegatorChannelFactory(BindingContext context) {
    PrintHelper.Print(_consolePrefix, "ctor");
    this._innerFactory = context.BuildInnerChannelFactory<TShape>();
  }

  // instantiates and returns a DelegatorChannel that
  // references another channel
```

```
private TShape WrapChannel(TShape innerChannel) {

  if(innerChannel == null) {
    throw new ArgumentNullException("innerChannel cannot be null",
      "innerChannel");
  }

  if(typeof(TShape) == typeof(IOutputChannel)) {
    return (TShape)(Object) new DelegatorOutputChannel<IOutputChannel>
      (this, (IOutputChannel)innerChannel, "SEND");
  }

  if(typeof(TShape) == typeof(IRequestChannel)) {
    return (TShape)(Object) new DelegatorRequestChannel
      (this, (IRequestChannel)innerChannel, "SEND");
  }

  if(typeof(TShape) == typeof(IDuplexChannel)) {
    return (TShape)(Object) new DelegatorDuplexChannel
      (this, (IDuplexChannel)innerChannel, "SEND");
  }

  if(typeof(TShape) == typeof(IOutputSessionChannel)) {
    return (TShape)(Object) new DelegatorOutputSessionChannel
      (this, (IOutputSessionChannel)innerChannel, "SEND");
  }

  if(typeof(TShape) == typeof(IRequestSessionChannel)) {
    return (TShape)(Object) new DelegatorRequestSessionChannel
      (this, (IRequestSessionChannel)innerChannel, "SEND");
  }

  if(typeof(TShape) == typeof(IDuplexSessionChannel)) {
    return (TShape)(Object) new DelegatorDuplexSessionChannel
      (this, (IDuplexSessionChannel)innerChannel, "SEND");
  }

  // cannot wrap this channel
  throw new ArgumentException(String.Format("invalid channel shape
    passed:{0}", innerChannel.GetType()));
}

// uses the _innerFactory member variable to build a channel
// then wraps it and returns the wrapped channel
protected override TShape OnCreateChannel(EndpointAddress address,
  Uri via) {
  // create and return the channel
  PrintHelper.Print(_consolePrefix, "OnCreateChannel");
  TShape innerChannel = this._innerFactory.CreateChannel(address, via);
  return WrapChannel(innerChannel);
}

protected override IAsyncResult OnBeginOpen(TimeSpan timeout,
                                            AsyncCallback callback,
                                            Object state) {
```

```
    PrintHelper.Print(_consolePrefix, "OnBeginChannel");
    return this._innerFactory.BeginOpen(timeout, callback, state);
  }

  protected override void OnAbort() {
    base.OnAbort();
    PrintHelper.Print(_consolePrefix, "OnAbort");
  }

  protected override void OnClose(TimeSpan timeout) {
    base.OnClose(timeout);
    PrintHelper.Print(_consolePrefix, "OnClose");
  }

  protected override void OnEndOpen(IAsyncResult result) {
    PrintHelper.Print(_consolePrefix, "OnEndOpen");
    this._innerFactory.EndOpen(result);
  }

  protected override void OnOpen(TimeSpan timeout) {
    PrintHelper.Print(_consolePrefix, "OnOpen");
    this._innerFactory.Open(timeout);
  }

  public override T GetProperty<T>() {
    PrintHelper.Print(_consolePrefix, "GetProperty<" + typeof(T).Name +
      ">");
    return this._innerFactory.GetProperty<T>();
  }
}
}
```

Conceptually, the *DelegatorChannelFactory<TShape>* type is very similar to the *DelegatorChannelListener<TShape>* type definition. It defines a private method named *WrapChannel* that wraps a channel in a *DelegatorChannel* of a specified shape and returns it. It also defines several methods that delegate state transitions to the *_innerFactory* member variable.

Summary

The WCF type system leverages channel listeners and channel factories to build channels. Channel listeners have the added responsibility of listening for the availability of a connection. The architectural model in channel listeners and channel factories is very similar to the one in the Berkeley Sockets API. Like channels, channel listeners and channel factories are stacked at run time, and each channel listener or channel factory in the stack is responsible for creating one channel in the channel stack. Like channels, a transport channel factory or channel listener must reside at the bottom of the stack. Channel listeners and channel factories are never directly instantiated by user code; that job is reserved for a *BindingElement*. *Binding* and *BindingElement* objects are the topic of the next chapter, and at the conclusion of that chapter, you'll see our *DelegatorChannel* channels, *DelegatorChannelListener<TShape>* and *DelegatorChannelFactory<TShape>*, in action.

Part III
WCF in the ServiceModel Layer

In this part:

Chapter 8
Bindings

A *binding* is a type that is the primary means by which a developer expresses intent for *how* a messaging application will interact with other messaging participants. Functionally, bindings create a stack of channel factory or channel listener objects. In *Design Pattern* terms, a binding is a factory. In terms of the service model layer and the channel layer, a binding is visible in the service model layer, and the objects it creates impact the channel layer. As you saw in Chapter 6, "Channels," and Chapter 7, "Channel Managers," the objects a binding directly (channel factories and channel listeners) and indirectly (channels) creates are the physical means by which a Microsoft Windows Communication Foundation (WCF) endpoint implements a set of messaging functionality (for example, transport, WS-* protocol, security, and transactional capability). With this in mind, one way to think of a binding is that it is a developer-facing type that encapsulates the run-time messaging functionality of an endpoint.

By default, WCF supports a wide variety of transports, message encodings, WS-* protocols, security options, and transactional capabilities. At first, the possible combinations of these capabilities might seem a bit overwhelming. For the most part, it is safe to assume that some combinations are going to have more relevance to real-world messaging requirements than others. To this end, the WCF team selected several broadly appealing messaging capabilities and exposed them in a set of bindings that are available in the WCF application programming interface (API). Among these default bindings are the *BasicHttpBinding*, *WsHttpBinding*, *NetMsmqBinding*, *NetPeerTcpBinding*, and *NetTcpBinding*. In general, the names of these bindings map fairly well to the functionality that they can create. For example, the *BasicHttpBinding* creates channel factory stacks and channel listener stacks for sending and receiving basic text-encoded messages over the HTTP transport. The *BasicHttpBinding* creates a messaging infrastructure that is WS-I Basic 1.1 compliant. The *NetMsmqBinding*, on the other hand, creates channel factory stacks and channel listener stacks for sending and receiving binary-encoded messages over MSMQ.

Like other parts of the WCF type system, bindings are extensible. This is very useful when an application needs capabilities that are not available in this out-of-the box set of bindings. As you saw in Chapters 6 and 7, the first steps in creating custom functionality in the channel layer (for example, new transport or protocol) are to create a custom channel, a custom channel factory, and a custom channel listener. When these types are in place, a custom *Binding* rounds out the custom types needed so that you can actually use the channels, channel factory, and channel listener. A custom *Binding* can consist of parts of existing bindings or be composed of entirely new functionality. In this chapter, we will build a custom binding that inserts a *DelegatorChannelListener* and *DelegatorChannelFactory* into their respective stacks, thereby finishing off the *DelegatorChannel* example started in Chapter 6 and continued in Chapter 7.

The Binding Object Model

All bindings derive from the *System.ServiceModel.Channels.Binding* abstract type, and as a result, all bindings share common characteristics. Unlike channel factories, channel listeners, and channels, the *Binding* type does not have a very complex type hierarchy. In fact, the *Binding* type derives directly from *Object* and implements only the *IDefaultCommunicationTimeouts* interface. As you saw in Chapter 7, channel factories and channel listeners use this interface for time-outs and they pass these time-outs to the channels they create. The origin of this handoff of time-out values starts with the *Binding* type. In addition to the members defined in the *IDefaultCommunicationTimeouts* interface, the *Binding* type also defines several factory methods and properties that relate to creating channel factories and channel listeners. The *Binding* type is shown here:

```
public abstract class Binding : IDefaultCommunicationTimeouts {
    // constructors
    protected Binding();
    protected Binding(String name, String ns);

    // test Methods for Channel Factories
    public virtual Boolean CanBuildChannelFactory<TChannel>(
      BindingParameterCollection parameters);
    public Boolean CanBuildChannelFactory<TChannel>(
      params Object[] parameters);

    // test Methods for Channel Listeners
    public virtual Boolean CanBuildChannelListener<TChannel>(
      BindingParameterCollection parameters) where TChannel: class, IChannel;
    public Boolean CanBuildChannelListener<TChannel>(
      params Object[] parameters) where TChannel: class, IChannel;

    // channel Factory Factory Methods
    public IChannelFactory<TChannel> BuildChannelFactory<TChannel>(
      params Object[] parameters);
    public virtual IChannelFactory<TChannel> BuildChannelFactory<TChannel>(
      BindingParameterCollection parameters);
```

```
    // channel Listener Factory Methods
    public virtual IChannelListener<TChannel> BuildChannelListener<TChannel>(
      BindingParameterCollection parameters) where TChannel: class, IChannel;
    public virtual IChannelListener<TChannel> BuildChannelListener<TChannel>(
      params Object[] parameters) where TChannel: class, IChannel;
    public virtual IChannelListener<TChannel> BuildChannelListener<TChannel>(
        Uri listenUriBaseAddress, params Object[] parameters)
        where TChannel: class, IChannel;
    public virtual IChannelListener<TChannel> BuildChannelListener<TChannel>(
        Uri listenUriBaseAddress, BindingParameterCollection parameters)
        where TChannel: class, IChannel;
    public virtual IChannelListener<TChannel> BuildChannelListener<TChannel>(
        Uri listenUriBaseAddress, String listenUriRelativeAddress,
      BindingParameterCollection parameters) where TChannel: class, IChannel;
    public virtual IChannelListener<TChannel> BuildChannelListener<TChannel>(
        Uri listenUriBaseAddress, String listenUriRelativeAddress,
      params Object[] parameters) where TChannel: class, IChannel;
    public virtual IChannelListener<TChannel> BuildChannelListener<TChannel>(
        Uri listenUriBaseAddress, String listenUriRelativeAddress,
        ListenUriMode listenUriMode, BindingParameterCollection parameters)
        where TChannel: class, IChannel;
    public virtual IChannelListener<TChannel> BuildChannelListener<TChannel>(
        Uri listenUriBaseAddress, String listenUriRelativeAddress,
        ListenUriMode listenUriMode, params Object[] parameters)
        where TChannel: class, IChannel;

    // timeouts
    public TimeSpan CloseTimeout { get; set; }
    public TimeSpan OpenTimeout { get; set; }
    public TimeSpan ReceiveTimeout { get; set; }
    public TimeSpan SendTimeout { get; set; }

    // factory Method for BindingElementCollection
    public abstract BindingElementCollection
  CreateBindingElements();

    // query mechanism
    public T GetProperty<T>(BindingParameterCollection parameters)
      where T: class;

    // the MessageVersion supported
    public MessageVersion MessageVersion { get; }

    // the Name and Namespace of the Binding
    public String Name { get; set; }
    public String Namespace { get; set; }

    // the URI Scheme
    public abstract String Scheme { get; }
}
```

Binding Constructors

The constructors provided by the *Binding* type are fairly straightforward, but the constructor that accepts two *String* parameters requires some explanation. These two parameters (*name* and *ns*) represent the XML name and namespace of the *Binding*. These values are distinctly different from the name of the *Binding*. They are important when an application needs to represent the capabilities of a *Binding* in an XML-based metadata format such as Web Services Description Language (WSDL). Because applications frequently need endpoint-specific information in WSDL and bindings are a key ingredient in the construction of an endpoint, this is a handy feature to have. Remember that the *Binding* type is abstract, so types derived from it can also define their own constructors with different parameters. Indeed, all of the default WCF bindings define at least one constructor that is not defined in the *Binding* type.

Binding Test Methods

The *Binding* type also defines several methods that test whether the *Binding* can create a channel factory stack or channel listener stack associated with a particular channel shape. These methods are named *CanBuildChannelFactory<TChannel>* and *CanBuildChannelListener<TChannel>*, and they return a *Boolean*. The *TChannel* generic parameter can be any valid channel shape, and these methods will return *true* if the binding can create a channel factory stack or channel listener stack associated with that channel shape.

 Note   The test methods in the *Binding* type interact with the *BindingContext* type and the *BindingElement* type. We will revisit how these test methods work in sections "The *BindingElement* Type" and "The *BindingContext* Type" later in this chapter.

Binding Factory Methods

As mentioned at the beginning of this chapter, the primary purpose of a *Binding* is to create channel factories and channel listeners. Bindings do this via the *BuildChannelListener* and *BuildChannelFactory* methods. One of the *BuildChannelFactory* methods accepts zero or more objects, and the other accepts a parameter of type *BindingParameterCollection*. Because a *BindingParameterCollection* is simply a generic collection of objects keyed by type, the former calls the latter. A *BindingParameterCollection* is simply a way to store information required to build channel factories and channel listeners. We will revisit the *BindingParameterCollection* type in the section "The *BindingElement* Type" later in this chapter.

The *Binding* type defines eight *BuildChannelListener* methods. The *BuildChannelListener* methods need more overloads because listening for a message is inherently more complex than sending one. The important arguments in the *BuildChannelListener* overloads are the *BindingParameterCollection*, *listenUriBaseAddress*, *listenUriRelativeAddress*, and *listenUriMode*. The *BindingParameterCollection* argument serves the same relative purpose that it does in the

BuildChannelFactory methods—that is, it stores information that might be required during the creation of a channel listener stack.

Specifying the Listening Address

The listening arguments listed earlier provide flexibility in how the channel listener listens for incoming connections. The *listenUriBaseAddress* is of type *Uri*, and the *listenUriRelativeAddress* is a *String*. Together, they are combined to form the *Uri* to listen on. For example, if the *listen-UriBaseAddress* is *net.tcp://localhost:4000* and the *listenUriRelativeAddress* is *ISomeContract*, the *Uri* the channel listener uses is *net.tcp://localhost:4000/ISomeContract*. At first glance, this capability might seem like it is of little value. In practice, however, it is very useful in scenarios where several channel listener stacks use the same base address. For example, a set of order processing services can use the same base address, and each channel listener stack can append its own *String* to the base address to create its own *Uri*. If the base address changes, changing the base address will automatically update all of the channel listener stacks the next time the listeners are built.

The *listenUriMode* argument is of type *ListenUriMode*. *ListenUriMode* is an enumerated type that defines two values: *ListenUriMode.Explicit* and *ListenUriMode.Unique*. When the *listenUriMode* argument is *ListenUriMode.Explicit*, the channel listener stack will listen on the *Uri* specified by the *listenUriBaseAddress* and *listenUriRelativeAddress*. When the *listenUriMode* argument is *ListenUriMode.Unique*, however, the channel listener stack will listen on a unique address. The unique address chosen by the transport channel listener can ignore some of the values of the *listenUriBaseAddress* and *listenUriRelativeAddress*. The exact form that the *Uri* takes in this case depends on the transport used by the transport channel listener. When listening on a TCP address, the channel listeners use a free port. When listening on an HTTP or a named pipe address, however, the channel listeners append a globally unique identifier (GUID) to the end of the *Uri*. In effect, when this argument is *ListenUriMode.Unique*, the values of the *listenUriBaseAddress* and *listenUriRelativeAddress* might be only part of the actual *Uri* that the channel listener stack listens on. For the next example, assume that the channel listener stack uses TCP.

Table 8-1 *BuildChanneListener* **Arguments and Their Impact (TCP)**

Argument	Value
listenUriMode	*ListenUriMode.Unique*
listenUriBaseAddress	*net.tcp://localhost:4000*
listenUriRelativeAddress	*ISomeContract*

Given the property values and parameters shown in Table 8-1, the address that the channel listener stack actually listens on would be something like this:

```
net.tcp://localhost:56446/ISomeContract
```

Even though the *listenUriBaseAddress* value uses port 4000, the channel listener chose port 56446. In essence, part of the *listenUriBaseAddress* is ignored. For the next example, assume that the channel listener stack uses HTTP.

Table 8-2   *BuildChannelListener* Arguments and Their Impact (HTTP)

Argument	Value
listenUriMode	*ListenUriMode.Unique*
listenUriBaseAddress	*http://localhost:4000*
listenUriRelativeAddress	*ISomeContract*

Given the property values and parameters shown in Table 8-2, the address that the channel listener stack actually listens on would be something like this:

```
http://localhost:4000/ISomeContract/705ca260-57b6-4f8d-930f-f2c49527b7f0
```

In this case, the transport channel listener kept port 4000 and the *listenUriRelativeAddress* but appended a GUID to the end of the *listenUriRelativeAddress*.

> **Note**   At first glance, this might look like a great capability for scenarios where you want the application to use a port or an address that is not already in use. In some cases (like in duplex communication on a sender), this capability is indeed useful. For many messaging scenarios, however, this form of unique addressing has a drawback. Because the address is not known until run time, there must be some out-of-band mechanism for informing sending applications of the address of the receiving application. The actual address that the receiving application uses is not published in metadata, so dynamic metadata discovery is not possible by default. As a result of this usability hurdle, I do not recommend using *ListenUriMode.Unique* for anything other than callbacks in duplex communication.

The *GetProperty<T>* Method

Like channels, channel factories, and channel listeners, the *Binding* type has a query mechanism that follows the *GetProperty<T>* paradigm. And as in channel factories and channel listeners, this query mechanism is not part of the *IChannel* interface, but it is very similar in its purpose. It simply allows the caller to interrogate the *Binding* for capabilities. For example, if you are building a custom hosting infrastructure, you might not know all of the bindings that other developers will use in your hosting infrastructure. If, in this case, your company has a corporate policy regarding security, you can interrogate the bindings used for a specific security capability before building any messaging infrastructure. Like channel factories, channel listeners, and channels, *GetProperty<T>* returns *null* if the capability is not found.

The *MessageVersion* Property

As you saw in Chapter 5, "Messages," a *Message* must have a *MessageVersion* associated with it. A *MessageVersion* is often associated with a particular set of messaging capabilities. For example, a *Message* associated with *MessageVersion.None* cannot participate in a WS-ReliableMessage (WS-RM) exchange, because by definition, there are no WS-Addressing headers to support such an exchange. Because a *Binding* is the primary means by which developers can express their intent for the messaging capabilities of an application and the *MessageVersion* is closely tied to those messaging capabilities, the *Binding* type exposes a *MessageVersion* property. The value returned by this property represents the *MessageVersion* used by the channel factories and channel listeners (and the channels) that the *Binding* creates.

The Scheme Property

All bindings use a transport, and that transport must have a Uniform Resource Identifier (URI) scheme associated with it. As you saw in Chapter 2, "Service Orientation," a URI scheme is nothing more than a string that identifies the transport. Some schemes, like HTTP, are well known. Others, like *net.tcp* and *net.msmq*, are arbitrary—that is to say, they are not known outside the world of WCF. In fact, if you were to develop your own transport and build the WCF infrastructure to use that transport, you would have to decide on the scheme for your transport (think carrier pigeons or baby strollers).

The *CreateBindingElements* Method

This aptly named method returns a collection of *BindingElement* objects. Conceptually, bindings share the stack archetype that we see in channels, channel listeners, and channel factories. This archetype splits the total messaging functionality of an application into discrete entities and arranges those entities in an ordered stack. The collection returned by the *CreateBindingElements* method is a blueprint for creating channel factory and channel listener stacks. As such, each node in this collection represents some part of the total messaging functionality of an endpoint.

Although bindings do conceptually adhere to the stack archetype, they do not arrange discrete messaging capabilities into a stack, but rather into a collection. The difference between the two is subtle, but important nonetheless. With channel stacks, channel factory stacks, and channel listener stacks, only the topmost node in the stack is visible. Any code interacting with the stack does not know how many nodes are in the stack and cannot interact directly with nodes below the top node. By returning a collection of nodes, the *Binding* type allows calling code to see and interact with any node in the stack. For most developers, this is a much more familiar model than an opaque stack, and this makes it a much more suitable model for such an essential part of the developer-facing API.

All types in the collection returned from the *CreateBindingElements* method are derived from the *BindingElement* type, and the ways that this collection is used are closely related to the behavior of the *BindingElement* type. Because the topic of the next section of this chapter is the *BindingElement* type, the full purpose of the collection is described in that section. By examining the contents of the collection returned from the *CreateBindingElements* method of a *Binding*, we should be able to glean some of the messaging functionality that *Binding* represents. Consider the following code sample:

```
using System;
using System.ServiceModel;
using System.Reflection;
using System.Collections.Generic;

internal sealed class ShowBindingElements {

  static void Main() {
    // Create a list of some Bindings
    List<Binding> bindings = new List<Binding>();

    bindings.Add(new BasicHttpBinding());

    bindings.Add(new NetTcpBinding());
    // change the security arg for NetTcpBinding
    bindings.Add(new NetTcpBinding(SecurityMode.Message, true));

    bindings.Add(new WSHttpBinding());

    bindings.Add(new NetMsmqBinding());
    // change the security arg for NetMsmqBinding
    bindings.Add(new NetMsmqBinding(NetMsmqSecurityMode.Message));

    OutputBindingElements(bindings);

  }

  private static void OutputBindingElements(List<Binding> bindings){
    // iterate through all the Bindings
    foreach (Binding binding in bindings) {
      // show the Binding name
      Console.WriteLine("Showing Binding Elements for {0}",
                        binding.GetType().Name);
      // iterate through all the BindingElements in the collection
      foreach (BindingElement element in binding.CreateBindingElements()) {
        // show the name of the BindingElement
        Console.WriteLine("\t{0}", element.GetType().Name);
      }
    }
  }
}
```

The preceding application simply creates a list of *Binding* objects and then iterates through that list, calls *CreateBindingElements* on each *Binding*, iterates through the collection returned from the *CreateBindingElements* method, and outputs the name of each *BindingElement* to the console. The output of this program is the shown here:

```
Showing Binding Elements for BasicHttpBinding
        TextMessageEncodingBindingElement
        HttpTransportBindingElement
Showing Binding Elements for NetTcpBinding
        TransactionFlowBindingElement
        BinaryMessageEncodingBindingElement
        WindowsStreamSecurityBindingElement
        TcpTransportBindingElement
Showing Binding Elements for NetTcpBinding
        TransactionFlowBindingElement
        ReliableSessionBindingElement
        SymmetricSecurityBindingElement
        BinaryMessageEncodingBindingElement
        TcpTransportBindingElement
Showing Binding Elements for WSHttpBinding
        TransactionFlowBindingElement
        SymmetricSecurityBindingElement
        TextMessageEncodingBindingElement
        HttpTransportBindingElement
Showing Binding Elements for NetMsmqBinding
        BinaryMessageEncodingBindingElement
        MsmqTransportBindingElement
Showing Binding Elements for NetMsmqBinding
        SymmetricSecurityBindingElement
        BinaryMessageEncodingBindingElement
        MsmqTransportBindingElement
```

Notice that one *Binding* type can create different *BindingElement* collections. In the preceding example, two *NetTcpBinding* objects are in the *bindings* list in *Main*, and they output different *BindingElement* collections. The contributing factor is the constructor. The default constructor was called one time, and the constructor that accepts some security options and a *Boolean* was called the other time. In the default constructor case, the *BindingElement* collection contains four *BindingElement* objects. The other case yields a *BindingElement* collection that contains five *BindingElement* objects. The same principle applies to the *NetMsmqBinding*. The point here is that the nodes in the collection returned from the *CreateBindingElements* method are determined at run time, and the state of the *Binding* object contributes to which nodes are included in the collection.

There is one more item worth noting about the preceding example. The names of the *BindingElement* objects in the collection reveal their purpose, and as a result, we can use the contents of the collection to get a general idea of the messaging functionality that a *Binding* encompasses. Notice that the *BasicHttpBinding* object creates a *BindingElement* collection containing *BindingElement* objects: *TextMessageEncodingBindingElement* and *HttpTransportBindingElement*. The *BasicHttpBinding* object creates a messaging infrastructure for sending and receiving text-encoded messages over the HTTP transport. As another example, notice that the second *NetTcpBinding* object creates a *BindingElement* collection containing five *BindingElement* objects: *TransactionFlowBindingElement*, *ReliableSessionBindingElement*, *SymmetricSecurityBindingElement*, *BinaryMessageEncodingBindingElement*, and *TcpTransportBindingElement*. In this case, the state of each *BindingElement* is important. In general, however, we can see that this *Binding* creates messaging infrastructure that has some transactional capability, some WS-ReliableMessaging capability (ReliableSession is the term that WCF uses for WS-RM), and some security capability. Furthermore, we see that the messaging infrastructure uses the TCP transport and that all messages are binary encoded.

The *BindingElement* Type

All of the *BindingElement* objects shown in the preceding code example derive from the *System.ServiceModel.Channels.BindingElement* abstract type. A *BindingElement* is a factory object. More specifically, the *BindingElement* type defines methods that return a channel factory or a channel listener. A *BindingElement* object is seldom used in isolation. A *BindingElement* usually resides in a *BindingElement* collection, and the primary way to create a *BindingElement* is via the *Binding.CreateBindingElements* method. As with channel factories, channel listeners, and channels, there is no one-size-fits-all *BindingElement*. As you saw in the preceding code example, the WCF type system abounds with types derived from *BindingElement*, and each represents some discrete part of the messaging capability supported by WCF out of the box. Developers are free to build their own types derived from the *BindingElement* type, however. In keeping with the WCF programming model, custom *BindingElement*-derived types are necessary any time you build a custom channel, channel factory, or channel listener.

Like the *Binding* type, the *BindingElement* type hierarchy is very simple. It implements no interfaces and derives directly from *Object*. The *BindingElement* type is shown here:

```
public abstract class BindingElement {

  // default constructor
  protected BindingElement() {
    ...
  }
  // clones the BindingElement argument
  protected BindingElement(BindingElement elementToBeCloned) {
    ...
  }
  // Factory method for channel factories
  public virtual IChannelFactory<TChannel> BuildChannelFactory<TChannel>(
    BindingContext context) {
    ...
  }
```

```
// Factory method for channel listeners
public virtual IChannelListener<TChannel> BuildChannelListener<TChannel>(
  BindingContext context) where TChannel: class, IChannel {
  ...
}

// Test methods for channel factories and listeners
public virtual bool CanBuildChannelFactory<TChannel>(
  BindingContext context) {
  ...
}

public virtual bool CanBuildChannelListener<TChannel>(
  BindingContext context) where TChannel: class, IChannel {
  ...
}

// returns a cloned BindingElement
public abstract BindingElement Clone(){
  ...
}

// Query mechanism
public abstract T GetProperty<T>(BindingContext context) where T: class {
  ...
}

}
```

Binding Element Constructors and the *Clone* Method

As odd as this might sound, the constructors of the *BindingElement* type are closely tied to the *Clone* method. Let's look at the constructors first. Neither has any implementation; they simply return. The purpose of the constructor that has an argument of type *BindingElement* is to allow derived types to clone themselves. Derived types are likely to have some state associated with them, and their form of this constructor should retrieve the values for these fields and assign them to the new object. The *BindingElement* type also defines an abstract method named *Clone*. As its name implies, this method returns a new instance of a *BindingElement*. The state of the *BindingElement* returned from the *Clone* method must be exactly the same as the instance that the *Clone* method was called on. Because a *BindingElement*-derived type can itself be used as a base type for another *BindingElement*, the *Clone* method should call the protected constructor in that type. This approach also ensures that derived types will survive the

addition of a field to the *BindingElement* type in the future. The following code snippet shows
the proper use of the *BindingElement* constructor and the *Clone* method:

```
public class SomeBindingElement : BindingElement {
  private String someValue; // an example field

  public SomeBindingElement(){
    this.someValue = "SomeString";
  }

  protected SomeBindingElement (SomeBindingElement elementToBeCloned)
      : base(elementToBeCloned) {
    // set the new object's field to the value of the arg
    this.someValue = elementToBeCloned.someValue;
  }

  // clone method calls the protected ctor
  public override BindingElement Clone(){
    return new SomeBindingElement(this);
  }
  // other implementation omitted for clarity
}

public sealed class OtherBindingElement : SomeBindingElement {
  private String otherValue;

  public OtherBindingElement(){
    this.otherValue = "SomeString";
  }

  private OtherBindingElement(OtherBindingElement elementToBeCloned) :
      base(elementToBeCloned) {
    // set the new object's field to the value of the arg
    // base .ctor gets called also
    this.otherValue = elementToBeCloned.otherValue;
  }

  // clone method calls the protected ctor
  public override BindingElement Clone(){
    return new OtherBindingElement(this);
  }
  // other implementation omitted for clarity
}
```

The *Clone* method is vital when testing the capabilities of a *Binding*, as well as when building
the channel factory and channel listener stacks. Nodes in a *BindingElement* collection are consumed when testing the capabilities of a *Binding* as well as during the construction of channel
factory and channel listener stacks. The *BindingElement* collection consumed during these
procedures is not the same object returned from the *CreateBindingElements* method, but
rather a clone of that object. Since cloning a collection is a matter of cloning each item in the
collection, cloning a *BindingElement* collection is a matter of cloning each *BindingElement*.

You'll learn more about the *Clone* method on the *BindingElement* type in the section "The *BindingContext* Type" later in this chapter.

BindingElement Test Methods

The *BindingElement* type also defines two test methods named *CanBuildChannel-Factory<TChannel>* and *CanBuildChannelListener<TChannel>* that return a *Boolean* indicating whether it is possible to build a channel factory stack or channel listener stack associated with a *TChannel* channel shape. Remember that *BindingElement* objects seldom exist in isolation, but rather they exist as part of a *BindingElement* collection. This is important when considering whether a *BindingElement* can create a channel factory stack or channel listener stack associated with a channel shape. Consider the case of a *BindingElement* collection that consists of a *BinaryMessageEncodingBindingElement* and an *HttpTransportBindingElement*. In this case, the test methods on the *BinaryMessageEncodingBindingElement* should return *true* only when the *TChannel* generic parameter is a channel shape compatible with the request/reply Message Exchange Pattern (MEP). If, however, we consider the case of a *BindingElement* collection that consists of a *BinaryMessageEncodingBindingElement* and a *TcpTransportBindingElement*, the test methods on the *BinaryMessageEncodingBindingElement* will not return *true* when the *TChannel* generic parameter is compatible with the request/reply MEP. The contributing factor for the *BinaryMessageEncodingBindingElement* is the other *BindingElement* in the collection. To generalize a bit, the test methods on a *BindingElement* object depend on the *BindingElement* objects that reside lower in the *BindingElement* collection.

In channel stacks, channel factory stacks, and channel listener stacks, each node in the stack has a reference to the next node in the stack. With *BindingElement* collections, however, an individual *BindingElement* has no reference to other *BindingElement* objects in the *BindingElement* collection. This certainly presents a problem in the test methods, because an individual *BindingElement* object needs to test lower *BindingElement* objects before returning a value. The answer to this riddle lies in the argument to the test methods in the *BindingElement* type.

The test methods on the *BindingElement* type resemble the test methods defined in the *Binding* type. They are different, however, in their arguments. In the *Binding* type, the arguments to these methods are a *BindingParameterCollection* or a *param,* which is an array of type *Object.* On the *BindingElement* type, however, the test methods have an argument of type *BindingContext.* You'll learn about the *BindingContext* type in more detail in the section "The *BindingContext* Type" later in this chapter, but we must examine some aspects of the *BindingContext* type here to fully understand how these test methods on the *BindingElement* type work. A *BindingContext* object stores an expendable list of *BindingElement* objects (a cloned version of the one returned from *Binding.CreateBindingElements*), a *BindingParameterCollection*, and some properties related to the listening address. The important point here is that a *BindingContext* object contains a consumable list of *BindingElement* objects, and that consumable list serves as a way for *BindingElement* objects to interrogate *BindingElement* objects that reside lower in the list.

With this in mind, the implementation of a test method on a *BindingElement*-derived type could look like the following:

```
public override Boolean CanBuildChannelListener<TChannel>(
    BindingContext context) {
  if (context == null) {
    throw new ArgumentNullException("context");
  }
  // This BindingElement works only with the datagram MEP
  if (typeof(TChannel) == typeof(IInputChannel)) {
    // check if the other elements work with the datagram MEP
    return context.CanBuildInnerChannelListener<IInputChannel>();
  }

  // if not, return false
  return false;
}

public override Boolean CanBuildChannelFactory<TChannel>(
    BindingContext context) {
  if (context == null) {
    throw new ArgumentNullException("context");
  }
  // This BindingElement works only with the datagram MEP
  if (typeof(TChannel) == typeof(IOutputChannel)) {
    // check if the other elements work with the datagram MEP
    return context.CanBuildInnerChannelFactory<IOutputChannel>();
  }
  return false;
}
```

Notice that both test methods leverage instance methods on the *BindingContext* argument. As you'll see in the section "The *BindingContext* Type" later in this chapter, the *CanBuildInnerChannelFactory<TChannel>* and *CanBuildInnerChannelListener<TChannel>* methods on the *BindingContext* type walk the remaining *BindingElement* objects and invoke the test methods on those *BindingElement* objects.

BindingElement Query Mechanism

The query mechanism in the *BindingElement* type appears similar to the one you saw in channels, channel factories, and channel listeners. Structurally, querying a *BindingElement* object for capabilities is similar to the test methods shown in the preceding section, because a *BindingElement* that cannot directly return a value must be able to delegate the query to another *BindingElement*. As you saw in the preceding section, the test methods on a *BindingElement* rely on the *BindingContext* type to provide references to the other *BindingElement* objects in the *BindingElement* collection. In a similar fashion, the query mechanism in the *BindingElement* type relies on the *BindingContext* type to delegate queries to other *BindingElement* objects in the collection. The following is an implementation of the query mechanism in a *BindingElement*-derived type that shows how to delegate queries to the *BindingContext* argument:

```
public override T GetProperty<T>(BindingContext context) {

  if (context == null) {
    throw new ArgumentNullException("context");
  }
  // this BindingElement delegates all queries except for
  // SomeCapability queries to other BindingElements
  if (typeof(T) != typeof(SomeCapabilility)) {
    // delegate the query to other BindingElements
    // via the BindingContext
    return context.GetInnerProperty<T>();
  }
  // return the capability - in this case it
  // is a field in the BindingElement
  return (T) this.someCapability;
}
```

In this example, the *SomeCapability* type is obviously fictional, but it represents any capability query that a *BindingElement* can return. The *GetInnerProperty<T>* method on the context type finds the next *BindingElement* in the list and invokes the *GetProperty<T>* method on that *BindingElement*. It's important to note that the *BindingContext* argument should be used only if the capability is not known to the current *BindingElement* (as shown in this example).

BindingElement Factory Methods

The two most important methods defined in the *BindingElement* type are the *BuildChannelFactory<TChannel>* and *BuildChannelListener<TChannel>* methods. I assert that these methods are the most important methods in the *BindingElement* type because they are the factory methods that create a channel factory or a channel listener, respectively. The channels created by the returned channel factory or channel listener are compatible with the *TChannel* generic parameter. Both the *BuildChannelFactory<TChannel>* and *BuildChannelListener<TChannel>* methods have an argument of type *BindingContext*. Like the test methods and the query mechanism, the *BindingContext* argument in these factory methods allows an entire channel factory stack or channel listener stack to be built from a single call site. The implementation of these *BindingElement* methods is roughly as follows:

```
public virtual IChannelFactory<TChannel> BuildChannelFactory<TChannel>(
    BindingContext context) {
  if (context == null) {
    throw new ArgumentNullException("context");
  }
  // delegate the call to the context argument
  return context.BuildInnerChannelFactory<TChannel>();
}
```

```
public virtual IChannelListener<TChannel> BuildChannelListener<TChannel>(
    BindingContext context) where TChannel: class, IChannel {
  if (context == null) {
    throw new ArgumentNullException("context");
  }
  // delegate the call to the context argument
  return context.BuildInnerChannelListener<TChannel>();
}
```

In *BindingElement*-derived types, these factory methods also need to return the channel factory stack or channel listener stack that contains the channel factory or channel listener that the *BindingElement* is associated with. Recalling the *DelegatorChannelListener* and the *DelegatorChannelFactory* example types from Chapter 7, a *BindingElement* associated with these types could look like the following:

```
// the type should be public, since it is
// part of the developer-facing API
public sealed class DelegatorBindingElement : BindingElement {

  // The factory method for the channel factory stack
  public override IChannelFactory<TShape> BuildChannelFactory<TShape>(
      BindingContext context) {
    if (context == null) {
      throw new ArgumentNullException("context");
    }

    // call the test method to ensure that TShape will work
    if (!this.CanBuildChannelFactory<TShape>(context)) {
      throw new InvalidOperationException("Unsupported channel type");
    }
    // instantiate a new DelegatorChannelFactory,
    // passing the context as an argument
    DelegatorChannelFactory<TShape> factory = new
      DelegatorChannelFactory<TShape>(context);
    // cast to an IChannelFactory<TShape> and return
    return (IChannelFactory<TShape>)factory;
  }


  // the factory method for the channel listener stack
  public override IChannelListener<TShape> BuildChannelListener<TShape>(
      BindingContext context) {
    if (context == null) {
      throw new ArgumentNullException("context");
    }

    // call the test method to ensure that TShape will work
    if (!this.CanBuildChannelListener<TShape>(context)) {
      throw new InvalidOperationException("Unsupported channel type");
    }
```

```
    // instantiate a new DelegatorChannelListener,
    // passing the context as an argument
    DelegatorChannelListener<TShape> listener = new
      DelegatorChannelListener<TShape>(context);
    // cast to an IChannelListener<TShape> and return
    return (IChannelListener<TShape>)listener;
  }

  // other implementation omitted for clarity
}
```

As with the test methods and the query mechanism, the real work in the factory methods is done by the *BindingContext* argument. It is important to note that the constructors of the channel listener and channel factory both accept arguments of type *BindingContext*. Many channel listeners and channel factories also accept an argument that is of type *BindingElement*, or some type derived from *BindingElement*. This is a means by which the channel factory or channel listener can receive information from the *BindingElement*. Notice also that the factory methods in the preceding example cast the channel factory stack or channel listener stack to the interface before returning.

The *TransportBindingElement* Type

Virtually the only hard rule applied to a *Binding* is that one of the *BindingElement* objects returned from *CreateBindingElements* must have the capability to create a transport channel factory or transport channel listener. From a theoretical perspective, this seems completely reasonable, since a messaging endpoint is of little value unless it is going to use some form of transport. Out of the necessity of this requirement, the WCF type system defines an abstract type named *System.ServiceModel.Channels.TransportBindingElement*. The *TransportBinding-Element* type defines several members needed by transport channel factories and listeners only, but it derives from *BindingElement*.

Because the *BindingElement* collection is a blueprint for the channel listener and channel factory stacks, a *TransportBindingElement* must appear at the end of the collection returned from the *CreateBindingElements* method on the *Binding* type. Both the *Binding* type and the *BindingContext* type enforce this rule.

The *TransportBindingElement* is shown here:

```
public abstract class TransportBindingElement : BindingElement {

  protected TransportBindingElement();
  protected TransportBindingElement(TransportBindingElement
    elementToBeCloned);

  public override T GetProperty<T>(BindingContext context) where T: class;
```

```
// does the channel add WS-Addressing info to messages
public bool ManualAddressing { get; set; }
// the size of the buffer pool
public virtual long MaxBufferPoolSize { get; set; }
// the maximum received message size
public virtual long MaxReceivedMessageSize { get; set; }
// the URI scheme
public abstract string Scheme { get; }
}
```

The names of the *MaxBufferPoolSize* and *MaxReceivedMessageSize* properties describe their purpose. The *MaxBufferPoolSize* sets the maximum size of the entire buffer pool in bytes, which can consist of zero or more buffers, while the *MaxReceivedMessageSize* property sets the maximum size of a received message in bytes. The *ManualAddress* property, however, requires some explanation. By default, this property has a value of *false*. When this property is set to *false*, the channel stack can add addresses to a message before it is sent. The format of the address depends on the binding used. More specifically, it depends on the *MessageVersion* of the *Message* objects that the channel stack uses. When this property is set to *true*, the channel stack does not add any addresses, but instead assumes that the caller has placed the appropriate addresses in outgoing messages. This capability is quite useful in more advanced addressing scenarios intrinsic to applications that serve as a router or an intermediary between other messaging participants.

The *BindingContext* Type

The *Binding* and *BindingElement* objects delegate most of the work of building a channel factory stack and channel listener stack to the *System.ServiceModel.Channels.BindingContext* type. As mentioned earlier in this chapter, the *BindingContext* type provides contextual information to the *BindingElement* collection during the creation, testing, or querying of the channel factory stack or channel listener stack. Each *BindingElement* must know the next *BindingElement* in the collection so that a channel factory or channel listener can reference the next channel factory or channel listener in the stack. Furthermore, each *BindingElement* must have access to any additional information (security options, transactional options, and so on) required to build each channel factory or channel listener. To this end, the *BindingContext* type stores a collection of *BindingElement* objects, exposes methods that build the channel factory or channel listener stack in an orderly manner, and maintains a collection of additional information that a channel factory or channel listener can use during its instantiation. The *BindingContext* type is shown here:

```
public class BindingContext {

  // calls the other ctor, passing null for addresses
  public BindingContext(CustomBinding binding,
                        BindingParameterCollection parameters);

  public BindingContext(CustomBinding binding,
                        BindingParameterCollection parameters,
                        Uri listenUriBaseAddress,
                        String listenUriRelativeAddress,
                        ListenUriMode listenUriMode);

  // factory methods for building channel factory / listener stacks
  public IChannelFactory<TChannel> BuildInnerChannelFactory<TChannel>();
  public IChannelListener<TChannel> BuildInnerChannelListener<TChannel>()
    where TChannel: class, IChannel;

  // test methods
  public bool CanBuildInnerChannelFactory<TChannel>();
  public bool CanBuildInnerChannelListener<TChannel>()
    where TChannel: class, IChannel;

  // shallow copy of the BindingContext
  public BindingContext Clone();

  // Query mechanism
  public T GetInnerProperty<T>() where T: class;

  // removes the next BindingElement in the collection
  // (private method shown intentionally)
  private BindingElement RemoveNextElement();

  // the Binding
  public CustomBinding Binding { get; }

  // extra information used in factory / listener creation
  public BindingParameterCollection BindingParameters { get; }

  // listening base address (channel listener only)
  public Uri ListenUriBaseAddress { get; set; }

  // listening mode (channel listener only)
  public ListenUriMode ListenUriMode { get; set; }

  // relative address (channel listener only)
  public string ListenUriRelativeAddress { get; set; }

  // the remaining binding elements
  public BindingElementCollection RemainingBindingElements { get; }

}
```

Notice that the constructor has arguments of type *CustomBinding* and *BindingParameter-Collection*, as well as the listening arguments required to build a channel listener. The *CustomBinding* argument is a general way to reference a *Binding*, and the constructor uses this *Binding* to create a private collection of *BindingElement* objects. The *BindingElement* object collection is available via the *RemainingBindingElements* property. In essence, a *CustomBinding* object can take the shape of any other *Binding* derived type.

BindingContext Factory Methods

The size of the collection returned from this method monotonically decreases as the *BuildInnerChannelFactory<TChannel>* or *BuildInnerChannelListener<TChannel>* is invoked. The general implementation of the *BuildInnerChannelFactory<TChannel>* and *BuildInnerChannelListener<TChannel>* methods is shown here:

```
public IChannelFactory<TChannel> BuildInnerChannelFactory<TChannel>() {
  // removes the next BindingElement from the private list,
  // then calls BuildChannelFactory on the removed BindingElement
  // the "this" argument contains the new list of BindingElements
  return this.RemoveNextElement().BuildChannelFactory<TChannel>(this);
}
public IChannelListener<TChannel> BuildInnerChannelListener<TChannel>()
    where TChannel: class, IChannel {
  // removes the next BindingElement from the private list,
  // then calls BuildChannelListener on the removed BindingElement
  // the "this" argument contains the new list of BindingElements
  return this.RemoveNextElement().BuildChannelListener<TChannel>(this);
}
```

The *RemoveNextElement* private method removes and then returns the next *BindingElement* from the internal list of *BindingElement* objects. When *RemoveNextElement* returns, the *BuildChannelListener<TChannel>* or *BuildChannelFactory<TChannel>* method executes on the newly removed *BindingElement*. Notice that *this* is passed to the *BuildChannelListener <TChannel>* and *BuildChannelFactory<TChannel>* methods, and *this* contains the shorter list of *BindingElement* objects.

 Note The test methods on the *BindingContext* type operate much the same way—that is, they use an internal collection of *BindingElement* objects and consume nodes in that collection until there are no more to consume.

Using a Binding

Now that you've seen the types that make bindings work, let's use a *Binding* to send and receive a *Message*. Although most WCF applications start with an address, a binding, and a contract, we are going to start this example more simply. In essence, this example will use a *Binding* to send and receive a *Message* without the help of most of the ServiceModel layer commonly associated with basic samples. In our example, we are going to use the *BasicHttpBinding* to send a message to a receiver and await a reply.

The receiver is the first part of the application that we need to build. To start, let's instantiate a *BasicHttpBinding* object and assign values for the *IDefaultCommunicationTimeouts* properties. After the binding is built and the time-outs are set, we'll create a *Uri* object to represent the address that our receiver will listen on. So far, our example looks like this:

```
using System;
using System.Collections.Generic;
using System.Text;
using System.ServiceModel;
using System.ServiceModel.Channels;

internal sealed class App {
  static void Main(){
    // create a binding
    BasicHttpBinding binding = new BasicHttpBinding();
    // set timeouts to large numbers for test purposes
    binding.OpenTimeout = TimeSpan.FromDays(1);
    binding.ReceiveTimeout = TimeSpan.FromDays(2);
    binding.SendTimeout = TimeSpan.FromDays(3);
    binding.CloseTimeout = TimeSpan.FromDays(4);
    // create an address
    Uri address = new Uri("http://localhost:4000/MyListener");
    PrintHelper.Print("BUILDING THE RECEIVER");
  }
}
```

Next we need to use the *Binding* to create the channel listener stack. There are a few ways to do this. For the sake of simplicity, we will use the *BuildChannelListener<TChannel>* method on the *BasicHttpBinding* type. First, however, we must decide on the channel shape that our receiving channels will use. Because HTTP forces the use of the request/reply MEP, our choice is between *IReplyChannel* and *IReplySessionChannel*. As it turns out, the *BasicHttpBinding* creates messaging infrastructure that is not session capable, so that rules out *IReplySessionChannel*. After we have created the channel listener stack, we need to open the channel listener. With this in mind, our receiving application becomes the following:

```
using System;
using System.Collections.Generic;
using System.Text;
using System.ServiceModel;
using System.ServiceModel.Channels;
```

```
internal sealed class App {
  static void Main(){
    // create a binding
    BasicHttpBinding binding = new BasicHttpBinding();
    // set timeouts to large numbers for test purposes
    binding.OpenTimeout = TimeSpan.FromDays(1);
    binding.ReceiveTimeout = TimeSpan.FromDays(2);
    binding.SendTimeout = TimeSpan.FromDays(3);
    binding.CloseTimeout = TimeSpan.FromDays(4);
    // create an address
    Uri address = new Uri("http://localhost:4000/MyListener");
    PrintHelper.Print("BUILDING THE RECEIVER");

    // use the Binding to create a channel listener stack
    // pass the address and an empty BindingParameterCollection as args
    IChannelListener<IReplyChannel> listenerStack =
      binding.BuildChannelListener<IReplyChannel>(address,
        new BindingParameterCollection());
    // open the channel listener stack
    listenerStack.Open();
  }
}
```

Now that the state of the channel listener stack is *CommunicationState.Opened*, we need to use the channel listener stack to create a channel stack. As you saw in Chapter 7, the *AcceptChannel* method and its asynchronous variant return a channel stack. The *AcceptChannel* method on the channel listener stack created by the *BasicHttpBinding* does not wait for an incoming connection before returning. Instead, it simply returns a channel stack that might or might not have a message to receive. The channel listener stacks created by the *MsmqIntegrationBinding* and the *NetMsmqBinding* also behave this way. Connection-oriented channel listener stacks like the ones created by *NetTcpBinding* and *NetNamedPipeBinding* do not behave in this way. In cases where the *AcceptChannel* method blocks until a sending connection is made, it is a far better idea to use *BeginAcceptChannel* as opposed to *AcceptChannel*. Because this is a simple example and *AcceptChannel* does not wait for a sending connection, we will use the *AcceptChannel* method. After the *AcceptChannel* method returns, we will have a reference to the receiving channel stack. As with the channel listener stack, we will also have to open the receiving channel stack. With this in mind, our example becomes the following:

```
// other code omitted for clarity
// ...
// open the channel listener stack
listenerStack.Open();
// BasicHttp will return (no sessions)
// 2 day timeout from the Binding (ReceiveTimeout)
IReplyChannel receiveChannelStack = listenerStack.AcceptChannel();
// Open the channel stack (1 day timeout)
receiveChannelStack.Open();
```

Notice in the preceding code that we are not calling the *AcceptChannel* or *Open* methods that accept *TimeSpan* arguments. In the channel listener stack and the channel stack, the methods that do not have *TimeSpan* arguments call the methods that do have *TimeSpan* arguments. In the case of the *AcceptChannel* method, the value of the *DefaultReceivingTimeout* is used. In the case of the *Open* method, the value of the *DefaultOpenTimeout* is used. Both of the values for these time-outs propagate from the binding.

Now that the state of our receiving channel stack is *CommunicationState.Opened*, let's try to receive a *Message*. Because we are going to write our sending application in the same *Main* method as our receiving application, it is important for the message receive to happen asynchronously. To this end, we will call the *BeginReceiveRequest* method on the receiving channel stack. In the *AsyncCallback* delegate, we will need to call *EndReceiveRequest*, read the received *Message*, generate a *Reply*, and then close the *RequestContext* and channel stack. Our code now looks like the following:

```
// Open the channel stack (1 day timeout)
receiveChannels.Open();
// receive a request on another thread
receiveChannels.BeginReceiveRequest(new AsyncCallback(receiveRequest),
                               receiveChannels);
// end of the Main method
}

// the AsyncCallback for BeginReceiveRequest
private static void receiveRequest(IAsyncResult ar) {
  // get the channel stack
  IReplyChannel channels = (IReplyChannel) ar.AsyncState;
  // get the requestContext
  RequestContext context = channels.EndReceiveRequest(ar);
  // show the received message
  PrintHelper.Print(String.Format("Message received:\n{0}",
    context.RequestMessage.ToString()));
  // create a reply Message
  Message reply = Message.CreateMessage(MessageVersion.Soap11, "urn:SomeReplyAction",
"Message back back");
  // send the reply
  context.Reply(reply);
  // close the context
  context.Close();
  // close the channels
  channels.Close();
}
```

At this point, the receiving part of our application is complete. Now let's build the sending part of our application. The first thing we need to build is our channel factory stack. For that, we return to our *Binding* and call the *BuildChannelFactory<TChannel>* method. The channel factory stack returned from this method must then be opened. After opening the channel factory stack, we then create a sending channel stack by calling the *CreateChannel* method on the channel factory stack. After we have a reference to the sending channel stack, we must then open it. The following code sample has these steps in place:

```
receiveChannels.BeginReceiveRequest(new AsyncCallback(receiveRequest),
                                    receiveChannels);

// create the channel factory stack
IChannelFactory<IRequestChannel> channelFactoryStack =
    binding.BuildChannelFactory<IRequestChannel>(
      new BindingParameterCollection());

// open the channel factory stack
channelFactoryStack.Open();

// create the channel stack from the channel factory stack
// pass a new EndpointAddress to set the target of the Message
IRequestChannel sendChannels = channelFactoryStack.CreateChannel(
  new EndpointAddress(address));
// open the channel stack
sendChannels.Open();
// end of the Main method
```

Now that our sending channels are open, we are free to call their *Request* or *BeginRequest* method. These methods send a *Message* to the receiving application and wait for a reply. The *Request* method blocks until a reply is received, and the *BeginRequest* method is asynchronous. Because this is the final task of our application and we cannot accept any user input, we will use the *Request* method. With this in place, the entire final example application is shown here:

```
using System;
using System.Collections.Generic;
using System.Text;
using System.ServiceModel;
using System.ServiceModel.Channels;

internal sealed class App {
  static void Main(){
    // create a binding
    BasicHttpBinding binding = new BasicHttpBinding();
    // set timeouts to large numbers for test purposes
    binding.OpenTimeout = TimeSpan.FromDays(1);
    binding.ReceiveTimeout = TimeSpan.FromDays(2);
    binding.SendTimeout = TimeSpan.FromDays(3);
    binding.CloseTimeout = TimeSpan.FromDays(4);
    // create an address
    Uri address = new Uri("http://localhost:4000/MyListener");
    PrintHelper.Print("BUILDING THE RECEIVER");

    // use the Binding to create a channel listener stack
    // pass the address and an empty BindingParameterCollection as args
    IChannelListener<IReplyChannel> listenerStack =
      binding.BuildChannelListener<IReplyChannel>(address,
        new BindingParameterCollection());
```

```
  // open the channel listener stack
  listenerStack.Open();
  // BasicHttp will return (no sessions)
  // 2 day timeout from the Binding (ReceiveTimeout)
  IReplyChannel receiveChannels = listenerStack.AcceptChannel();
  // Open the channel stack (1 day timeout)
  receiveChannels.Open();

  // receive a request on another thread

  // send a message to the receiver
  receiveChannels.BeginReceiveRequest(new AsyncCallback(receiveRequest),
                                      receiveChannels);

  // create the channel factory stack
  IChannelFactory<IRequestChannel> channelFactoryStack =
    binding.BuildChannelFactory<IRequestChannel>(
      new BindingParameterCollection());

  // open the channel factory stack
  channelFactoryStack.Open();

  // create the channel stack from the channel factory stack
  // pass a new EndpointAddress to set the target of the Message
  IRequestChannel sendChannels = channelFactoryStack.CreateChannel(
    new EndpointAddress(address));
  // open the channel stack
  sendChannels.Open();

  // send a request message
  Message reply = sendChannels.Request(
    Message.CreateMessage(MessageVersion.Soap11, "urn:SomeAction",
      "Hi there"));
  // show the contents of the reply
  PrintHelper.Print(String.Format("Reply received:\n{0}",
    reply.ToString()));

  // cleanup
  sendChannels.Close();
  channelFactoryStack.Close();
  listenerStack.Close();
}

// the AsyncCallback for BeginReceiveRequest
private static void receiveRequest(IAsyncResult ar) {
  // get the channel stack
  IReplyChannel channels = (IReplyChannel) ar.AsyncState;
  // get the requestContext
  RequestContext context = channels.EndReceiveRequest(ar);
  // show the received message
  PrintHelper.Print(String.Format("Message received:\n{0}",
    context.RequestMessage.ToString()));
  // create a reply Message
  Message reply = Message.CreateMessage(MessageVersion.Soap11,
    "urn:SomeReplyAction", "Hi there back");
```

```
    // send the reply
    context.Reply(reply);
    // close the context
    context.Close();
    // close the channels
    channels.Close();
  }
}
```

The preceding example sends and receives one message. If two messages arrive, the receiving application will not be able to process both. In more-real-world receiving applications, the job of continuing to listen for incoming messages is the job of a set of ServiceModel-layer dispatchers. These dispatchers are covered in Chapter 10, "Dispatchers and Clients."

Note   I really enjoy (perhaps this is sad) working with low-level applications like the one we just looked at. I encourage the reader to change the *Binding* several times and recode the rest of the example. Doing so will, over time, give you a level of comfort with the WCF programming model.

Creating Custom Bindings

Now that you've seen the different types that are important in the *Binding* object model and learned how to use them to send and receive messages, let's build our own binding. To continue the arc of the previous two chapters, our custom *Binding* will create channel factory and channel listener stacks with *DelegatorChannelFactory* and *DelegatorChannelListener* objects at the top of their respective stacks. Remembering that a *Binding* is really composed of a collection of *BindingElement* objects, let's begin by creating the *BindingElement* that interacts directly with the *DelegatorChannelFactory* and *DelegatorChannelListener* types. The *DelegatorBindingElement* is shown here:

```
using System;
using System.Collections.Generic;
using System.Text;
using System.ServiceModel.Channels;

// since the DelegatorBindingElement is part of
// the developer-facing API, make this class public
public sealed class DelegatorBindingElement : BindingElement {

  public override bool CanBuildChannelFactory<TShape>(
      BindingContext context) {
    if(context == null) {
      throw new ArgumentNullException("context");
    }
    // this BindingElement can wrap any shape of channel,
    // so defer to the context
    return context.CanBuildInnerChannelFactory<TShape>();
```

```
    }

    public override bool CanBuildChannelListener<TShape>(
        BindingContext context) {
      if(context == null) {
        throw new ArgumentNullException("context");
      }
      // this BindingElement can wrap any shape of channel,
      // so defer to the context
      return context.CanBuildInnerChannelListener<TShape>();
    }

    public override IChannelFactory<TShape> BuildChannelFactory<TShape>(
        BindingContext context) {
      if (context == null) {
        throw new ArgumentNullException("context");
      }

      // ensure that TShape is compatible
      if(!this.CanBuildChannelFactory<TShape>(context)) {
        throw new InvalidOperationException("Unsupported channel type");
      }

      // create a new DelegatorChannelFactory, passing context as argument
      // a channel factory stack is actually returned
      DelegatorChannelFactory<TShape> factory =
        new DelegatorChannelFactory<TShape>(context);
      // cast to IChannelFactory<TShape> and return
      return (IChannelFactory<TShape>) factory;
    }

    public override IChannelListener<TShape> BuildChannelListener<TShape>(
        BindingContext context) {
      if (context == null) {
        throw new ArgumentNullException("context");
      }

      // ensure that TShape is compatible
      if(!this.CanBuildChannelListener<TShape>(context)) {
        throw new InvalidOperationException("Unsupported channel type");
      }

      // create a new DelegatorChannelListener, passing context as argument
      // a channel listener stack is actually returned
      DelegatorChannelListener<TShape> listener =
        new DelegatorChannelListener<TShape>(context);
      return (IChannelListener<TShape>) listener;
    }

    public override BindingElement Clone() {
      // since there are no fields, use the default ctor
      return new DelegatorBindingElement();
    }
```

```
public override T GetProperty<T>(BindingContext context) {
  // delegate the call to the context arg
  return context.GetInnerProperty<T>();
  }
}
```

Notice that the test methods and the query mechanism delegate to the *BindingContext*. Notice also that the factory methods instantiate either a *DelegatorChannelFactory<TShape>* or a *DelegatorChannelListener<TShape>* and pass the *BindingContext* as an argument to the constructor. It is important to pass the *BindingContext* to the constructor so that the channel factory or the channel listener can access the *Binding* property of the *BindingContext*, because this is the only way that the channel factory and channel listener can set the default time-outs that can be set in the *Binding*.

Now that the *DelegatorBindingElement* is in place, let's turn our attention to the *Binding* that will add a *DelegatorBindingElement* to a *BindingElement* collection. Certainly this is possible without creating a *Binding*-derived type. All we would have to do is instantiate a *CustomBinding* object and pass a collection of *BindingElement* objects to the constructor. However, this does not provide an easy-to-use and reusable type. To best provide reusable code, let's define a *Binding* that will create a collection of *BindingElement* objects that contains a *DelegatorBindingElement* at the head of the collection.

Remembering that a *Binding*-derived type must implement a *CreateBindingElements* method that returns a collection of *BindingElement* objects, it is important to consider how our *Binding* will create the collection of *BindingElement* objects. Because there are several bindings included in WCF, we can call the *CreateBindingElements* method on one of these existing bindings and insert our *DelegatorBindingElement* at the head of the collection. This approach ensures that the *BindingElement* objects in the collection are compatible with each other. With this in mind, which default *Binding* should we choose? My guess is as good as yours, and it might not be the same choice another person might make. Let's attempt to please everyone by allowing the caller to choose one among several of the default WCF bindings. To do this, we will need an enumerated type that represents the WCF bindings we will mimic:

```
public enum BindingMode {
    Tcp,            // NetTcpBinding
    TcpRM,          // NetTcpBinding w/WS-ReliableMessaging
    WSHttp,         // WsHttpBinding
    WSHttpRM,       // WsHttpBinding w/WS-ReliableMessaging
    BasicHttp,      // BasicHttpBinding
    PeerChannel,    // NetPeerTcpBinding
    MSMQ,           // NetMsmqBinding
    MSMQSession     // NetMsmqBinding w/ExactlyOnce = true
}
```

The constructor of our *Binding* will include a parameter of type *BindingMode*. Furthermore, callers might want to insert the *DelegatorBindingElement* in a place other than the head of the list. This can be helpful in cases where WS-ReliableMessaging is used. Placing the *DelegatorBindingElement* between the *TransportBindingElement* and the *ReliableSessionBindingElement* will show the messages generated by the WS-ReliableMessaging channels, and placing it after the *ReliableSessionBindingElement* will not show as many messages. For this, we will need an *Int32* parameter that represents the place in the *BindingElement* collection where we want to put the *DelegatorBindingElement*. With this in mind, our *DelegatorBinding* looks like the following:

```
using System;
using System.ServiceModel.Channels;
using System.ServiceModel;
using System.Text;

// since this is part of the developer-facing API,
// make it public
public sealed class DelegatorBinding : Binding {

  String _scheme; // the scheme of the Binding
  BindingElementCollection _elements; // the BindingElement collection

  // this ctor delegates to the other ctor
  public DelegatorBinding(BindingMode mode) : this(mode, 0) {

  }

  public DelegatorBinding(BindingMode bindingMode, Int32 elementPosition) {
    // check the BindingMode arg and create
    // a BindingElement collection from it
    switch (bindingMode) {
      case (BindingMode.BasicHttp):
        BasicHttpBinding httpBinding =
          new BasicHttpBinding(BasicHttpSecurityMode.None);
        _elements = httpBinding.CreateBindingElements();
        _scheme = "http";
        break;
      case (BindingMode.Tcp):
        _elements = new NetTcpBinding(SecurityMode.None,
                                  false).CreateBindingElements();
        _scheme = "net.tcp";

        // set manual addressing (optional)
        TransportBindingElement transport =
          _elements.Find<TransportBindingElement>();
        transport.ManualAddressing = false;
        break;
      case (BindingMode.TcpRM):
        _elements = new NetTcpBinding(SecurityMode.None,
                                  true).CreateBindingElements();
        _scheme = "net.tcp";
        break;
      case (BindingMode.WSHttp):
```

```
                    _elements = new WSHttpBinding(SecurityMode.None,
                                              false).CreateBindingElements();
                    _scheme = "http";
                    break;
                case (BindingMode.WSHttpRM):
                    _elements = new WSHttpBinding(SecurityMode.None,
                                              true).CreateBindingElements();
                    _scheme = "http";
                    break;
                case (BindingMode.MSMQ):
                    NetMsmqBinding msmqBinding =
                       new NetMsmqBinding(NetMsmqSecurityMode.None);
                    msmqBinding.ExactlyOnce = false;
                    _elements = msmqBinding.CreateBindingElements();
                    _scheme = "net.msmq";
                    break;
                case (BindingMode.MSMQSession):
                    NetMsmqBinding msmqTransactionalBinding =
                       new NetMsmqBinding(NetMsmqSecurityMode.None);
                    msmqTransactionalBinding.ExactlyOnce = true;
                    _elements = msmqTransactionalBinding.CreateBindingElements();
                    _scheme = "net.msmq";
                    break;
                default:
                    throw new ArgumentOutOfRangeException("bindingMode");
            }

            // add the DelegatorBindingElement in the specified position
            _elements.Insert(elementPosition, new DelegatorBindingElement());
        }

        // returns the BindingElement collection built in ctor
        public override BindingElementCollection CreateBindingElements() {
            return _elements;
        }

        public override String Scheme {
            get {
                return _scheme;
            }
        }
    }
}
```

In this example, the constructor builds the *BindingElement* collection. Other bindings defer the creation of the *BindingElement* collection until the *CreateBindingElements* method. Because the *DelegatorBinding* does not expose any settable properties or contain any other relevant state, I opted to build the *BindingElement* collection in the constructor.

With the *DelegatorBinding* in place, we can now write an application that uses it. Let's borrow from the preceding section, where we used the *BasicHttpBinding* to send and receive a *Message*. For this example, all we need to do is replace the binding instantiation as follows:

```
BasicHttpBinding binding = new BasicHttpBinding();
```

Change to the following:

```
DelegatorBinding binding = new DelegatorBinding(BindingMode.BasicHttp);
```

If we run that application, we get the following output:

1. BUILDING THE RECEIVER, Thread:1
2. LISTENER: DelegatorChannelListener.GetProperty<
    System.ServiceModel.Channels.ISecurityCapabilities>, Thread:1
3. LISTENER: DelegatorChannelListener.OnOpen, Thread:1
4. LISTENER: DelegatorChannelListener.OnAcceptChannel, Thread:1
5. RECEIVE CHANNEL: DelegatorReplyChannel.ctor, Thread:1
6. RECEIVE CHANNEL STATE CHANGE: DelegatorChannelBase.OnOpen, Thread:1
7. TRYING TO RECEIVE A MESSAGE, Thread:1
8. RECEIVE CHANNEL: DelegatorReplyChannel.BeginReceiveRequest, Thread:1
9. BUILDING THE SENDER, Thread:1
10. FACTORY: DelegatorChannelFactory.ctor, Thread:1
11. FACTORY: DelegatorChannelFactory.GetProperty<ISecurityCapabilities>,
    Thread:1
12. FACTORY: DelegatorChannelFactory.OnOpen, Thread:1
13. FACTORY: DelegatorChannelFactory.OnCreateChannel, Thread:1
14. SEND CHANNEL: DelegatorRequestChannel.ctor, Thread:1
15. SEND CHANNEL STATE CHANGE: DelegatorChannelBase.OnOpen, Thread:1
16. SEND CHANNEL: DelegatorRequestChannel.Request (BLOCKING), Thread:1
17. RECEIVE CHANNEL: DelegatorReplyChannel.EndReceiveRequest, Thread:4
18. Message received:
      <s:Envelope xmlns:s="http://schemas.xmlsoap.org/soap/envelope/">
        <s:Header>
          <To s:mustUnderstand="1"xmlns=
            "http://schemas.microsoft.com/ws/2005/05/addressing/none">
            http://localhost:4000/MyListener
          </To>
          <Action s:mustUnderstand="1" xmlns=
            "http://schemas.microsoft.com/ws/2005/05/addressing/none">
            urn:SomeAction
          </Action>
        </s:Header>
        <s:Body>
          <string xmlns=
            "http://schemas.microsoft.com/2003/10/Serialization/">
            Hi there
          </string>
        </s:Body>
      </s:Envelope>, Thread:4
19. Reply received:
      <s:Envelope xmlns:s="http://schemas.xmlsoap.org/soap/envelope/">
        <s:Header />
        <s:Body>
          <string xmlns=
            "http://schemas.microsoft.com/2003/10/Serialization/">
            Hi there back
          </string>
        </s:Body>
      </s:Envelope>, Thread:1
```
```

20. `RECEIVE CHANNEL STATE CHANGE: DelegatorChannelBase.OnClose, Thread:4`
21. `SEND CHANNEL STATE CHANGE: DelegatorChannelBase.OnClose, Thread:1`
22. `FACTORY: DelegatorChannelFactory.OnClose, Thread:1`
23. `LISTENER: DelegatorChannelListener.OnClose, Thread:1`

As shown here, the *DelegatorBinding* allows us to see when an application creates a channel, all of the methods called on a channel, and the state changes of the channel and channel factory or channel listener stack.

> **Note**   I have found the *DelegatorBinding* to be very helpful in seeing how changes that I make in my application impact the channel layer. I encourage the reader to experiment with the *DelegatorBinding* to see how the different bindings impact channel shape, as well as which channel methods are called.

Summary

As part of the ABCs of WCF, a *Binding* is a critical part of the developer-facing API. Fundamentally, a *Binding* is a factory object that creates channel factory stacks and channel listener stacks. As such, a *Binding* is a developer-facing type that allows the developer to influence the composition of the channel layer. A *Binding* creates a collection of *BindingElement* objects, and each *BindingElement* in the collection begins the actual work of building channel factory stacks and channel listener stacks. Unlike channel factory stacks, channel listener stacks, and channel stacks, a *BindingElement* in the *BindingElement* collection has no knowledge of the other *BindingElement* objects in the collection. As a result, building channel factory stacks and channel listener stacks in an orderly manner requires another type. The *BindingContext* type serves this purpose. In essence, when a *BindingElement* builds a channel factory stack or a channel listener stack, it delegates some of the responsibility to a *BindingContext* object. Because a *BindingContext* object maintains a consumable collection of *BindingElement* objects, a *BindingContext* object is able to build channel factory stacks and channel listener stacks in an orderly manner.

Chapter 9
Contracts

Microsoft Windows Communication Foundation (WCF) contracts map Microsoft .NET Framework types to messaging constructs. To illustrate, consider a service that requests, confirms, and cancels restaurant reservations. This service consists of one endpoint located at *http://contoso.com/reservations*. The endpoint exposes three operations: *RequestReservation*, *ChangeReservation*, and *CancelReservation*. The *RequestReservation* and *ChangeReservation* operations use the request/reply Message Exchange Pattern (MEP), and the *CancelReservation* operation uses the datagram MEP. Some message structures are shared between these operations, and others are not. Using only the types shown in the preceding four chapters, it is possible to build this kind of messaging application. If we choose this path, however, we have to interact with raw messages, channels, and channel listeners. While this might be a good academic exercise, it is by no means a chore that we can accomplish quickly, and it is likely to be fraught with errors. By using contracts (and the techniques covered in Chapter 10, "Dispatchers and Clients"), we can place the burden of the work on the WCF infrastructure and greatly reduce the amount of code that we must write. As a result of the boost in productivity, virtually all WCF applications will use contracts and the WCF serialization infrastructure. This chapter describes the different kinds of contracts and how they impact the shape of a messaging application.

Contracts Defined

A *contract* is an agreement between messaging participants. An agreement of this sort names, defines, and provides addresses for the operations that a Web service exposes. In doing so, it describes each operation in a service, the MEP of each operation, and the message structures supported by an operation. Over time, the industry has developed and refined vendor-agnostic grammars like Web Services Description Language (WSDL) and Extensible Schema Definition (XSD) to provide common ground for these agreements, and most modern Web service platforms are able to produce as well as understand WSDL and XSD documents. As a result, a contract in a messaging application is often assumed to be a set of WSDL and XSD documents. In WCF applications, a contract is not necessarily a set of WSDL and XSD documents, but rather a set of .NET type definitions. Once in place, these type definitions can then be turned into a set of WSDL and XSD documents as needed.

If one embraces the tenets of service orientation in the purest sense, a contract is the logical place to start designing a service. In the real world, businesses operate in much the same fashion. Trading partnerships between large organizations take their true shape in the legal contract between organizations. No two large companies would ever start trading goods without first having a legal framework in place that governs that trade. In this setting, a legal contract defines liability, terms of payment, jurisdictions, ownership, and so on. The legal contract must be understood by both parties. If one organization uses terms that are not known to the other organization, the contract must spell out those terms explicitly before the other organization signs the contract. In essence, a legal contract becomes a clearly defined playing field that removes assumptions about the responsibilities and behaviors of parties entering into the contract. Similarly, a Web service contract defines the responsibilities and behaviors of messaging participants, and it should be in place before message exchange begins. Because of the contract's critical role, it is often a good idea to start design and development efforts by working on the contract.

WCF contracts are .NET type definitions annotated with special attributes, and these annotated type definitions can be used to generate industry-standard WSDL and XSD documents. WCF contracts map types and members of those types to services, operations, messages, and message parts. There are three types of contracts in WCF: service contracts, data contracts, and message contracts. *Service contracts* map types to service definitions and type members to service operations. *Data contracts* and *message contracts* map types to service operation message definitions. A message contract offers more control over a message definition than a data contract does. A data contract maps the body of a message to type members, while a message contract maps the headers *and* the body of a message to type members.

WCF Contract Gross Anatomy

Service contracts, data contracts, and message contracts differ by the attributes used in the contract definition. The important attributes names are *ServiceContractAttribute*, *OperationContractAttribute*, *DataContractAttribute*, *DataMemberAttribute*, *MessageContract-Attribute*, *MessageHeaderAttribute*, and *MessageBodyMemberAttribute*. These attributes are part of the *System.ServiceModel* namespace, and the names of each attribute adequately describe the category of contract they can define.

Note   Remember that attribute annotations change the metadata of a type definition. By themselves, attribute annotations are completely inert. For attributes to have any value, another set of objects must interrogate this metadata via the reflection application programming interface (API) and use the presence of that metadata to drive behavior. The WCF infrastructure uses reflection to interrogate contract metadata and uses the contract metadata and other type information during the construction of an endpoint.

Service Contracts

Service contracts describe a service. This includes defining facets of the service, the operations of the service, the MEP of each operation, and the messages that each operation uses. The first step in creating a service contract is to establish the names of the operations and the MEPs that they use. In our restaurant example, the service contains three operations: *RequestReservation*, *ChangeReservation*, and *CancelReservation*. Let's assume that the *RequestReservation* and *ChangeReservation* operations use the request/reply MEP and that the *CancelReservation* operation uses the datagram MEP. Given the complexion of this service, our service contract becomes the following:

```
[ServiceContract]
public interface IRestaurantService {
    [OperationContract]
    Int32? RequestReservation(DateTime? resDateTime,
                              String restaurantName,
                              String partyName);
    [OperationContract]
    void ChangeReservation(Int32? reservationId, DateTime? resDateTime);
    [OperationContract(IsOneWay=true)]
    void CancelReservation(Int32? reservationId);
}
```

Note   I am taking a few liberties with the method parameters and return types in these interface methods. We will revisit the method signatures in the sections "Data Contracts" and "Message Contracts" later in this chapter.

At the surface, this type definition looks like any other .NET interface. In fact, the only differentiating factor between this interface and a normal .NET interface is the addition of the *ServiceContractAttribute* and the *OperationContractAttribute* definitions. The addition of the *ServiceContractAttribute* to the interface means that the WCF infrastructure can use the interface as a service contract. The addition of the *OperationContractAttribute* to each interface method means that each method is an operation in the service.

The *ServiceContractAttribute* and *OperationContractAttribute* types define several instance properties. When used in a service contract, these instance properties offer control over the contract. The *ServiceContractAttribute* is defined as the following:

```
[AttributeUsage(AttributeTargets.Interface | AttributeTargets.Class,
                Inherited=false, AllowMultiple=false)]
public sealed class ServiceContractAttribute : Attribute {
    public Type CallbackContract { get; set; }
    public String ConfigurationName { get; set; }
    public Boolean HasProtectionLevel { get; }
    public String Name { get; set; }
    public String Namespace { get; set; }
    public ProtectionLevel ProtectionLevel { get; set; }
    public SessionMode SessionMode { get; set; }
}
```

The *CallbackContract* property is for duplex contracts. The *ConfigurationName* property is the alias that can be used in a configuration file to reference the service. The aptly named *Name* and *Namespace* properties are the name and namespace of the service, and these values propagate to the XML name and namespace of the service, as well as the messages.

> **Note** Notice that the *ServiceContractAttribute* can be applied to an interface definition and a class definition. I greatly prefer the use of an interface for a service contract because an interface forces the separation of the contract from implementation.

The *ProtectionLevel* Property

The *ProtectionLevel* property indicates the level of message security that a binding must have when using the contract. This property is of type *System.Net.Security.ProtectionLevel*, and the three values of the enumeration are *None*, *Sign*, and *EncryptAndSign*. When the *ServiceContractAttribute.ProtectionLevel* property is set to *Sign*, all messages that the service sends and receives must be signed. When the property is set to *EncryptAndSign*, all of the messages that the service sends and receives must be encrypted and signed. When the property is *None*, the contract indicates that no message security is needed for the service.

> **Note** The *ProtectionLevel* property impacts only the security applied to the body of the message. It has no impact on the infrastructure headers present in a message. Examples of these infrastructure headers are WS-Addressing and WS-ReliableMessage headers.

Each binding has security capabilities, and the *ProtectionLevel* property in the *ServiceContractAttribute* can force the use of those security capabilities. This ability to set the minimum security requirements in a contract has immense practical application. It means that the contract developer can establish minimum message security requirements, and any endpoint that uses the contract must meet or exceed those minimum requirements. Without this level of control at the service contract level, it is possible that an application developer or application administrator could add an endpoint that has no message-based security on it, and this might not be something that the contract developer ever intended. Conceptually, control over security at the contract blurs the line between a binding and a contract, because a binding is the primary means by which developers express their intent for how a messaging application functions. The blurring of this line might seem like a design problem to the purist. In my opinion, the practical value of this capability is worth the blurring of the boundary.

The *SessionMode* Property

The *SessionMode* property indicates whether the channels used in the application must, can, or cannot use sessionful channel shapes. The *SessionMode* property is of type *System. ServiceModel.SessionMode*, and the three values of the enumeration are *Allowed*, *Required*, and *NotAllowed*. In Chapter 8, "Bindings," you saw how the *Binding* type can create channel managers and that a channel manager has the capability to create a channel that implements a particular channel shape. If the *SessionMode* property is set to *Required*, the *BuildChannelFactory* and *BuildChannelListener* methods on a binding are invoked with sessionful shapes. If the binding cannot support sessionful channel shapes, an exception is thrown at run time. The default value of the *SessionMode* property is *Allowed*. When the *SessionMode* property is set to the default value, there is no session-based restriction on the application.

Operations in a Service Contract

Service contracts include a description of the operations in the service. When describing an operation in a service contract, it is necessary to describe the MEP of the operation, the structure of the messages that the operation will receive, and the structure of the messages that the operation will return (if any). Because service contracts are annotated class or interface definitions, operations are annotated method definitions within a service contract. Let's take another look at the restaurant reservation service contract:

```
[ServiceContract]
public interface IRestaurantService {
    [OperationContract]
    Int32? RequestReservation(DateTime? resDateTime,
                              String restaurantName,
                              String partyName);
    [OperationContract]
    void ChangeReservation(Int32? reservationId, DateTime resDateTime);
    [OperationContract(IsOneWay=true)]
    void CancelReservation(Int32? reservationId);
}
```

The *OperationContractAttribute* annotation has several instance properties that control the MEP, security, sessionful capabilities, and message structure of the operation. The *OperationContractAttribute* is valid only on methods. The following is the public API of the *OperationContractAttribute*:

```
[AttributeUsage(AttributeTargets.Method)]
public sealed class OperationContractAttribute : Attribute {
  public Boolean AsyncPattern { get; set; }
  public Boolean HasProtectionLevel { get; }
  public ProtectionLevel ProtectionLevel { get; set; }
  public Boolean IsOneWay { get; set; }
  public Boolean IsInitiating { get; set; }
  public Boolean IsTerminating { get; set; }
  public String Name { get; set; }
  public String Action { get; set; }
  public String ReplyAction { get; set; }
}
```

The *AsyncPattern* Property

The *AsyncPattern* property indicates whether the operation is part of the Asynchronous Programming Model (APM) pattern. When this property is set to *true*, the attribute must be applied to the *Begin<methodname>* method in the Begin/End pair. The *End<methodname>* method does not need the *OperationContractAttribute* applied to it. If, for some reason, the *End<methodname>* method is not present, the contract will not be used. When the *AsyncPattern* property is set to *true*, the receiving infrastructure will asynchronously invoke the *Begin<methodname>* method. Receiving applications that perform I/O within their operations should set this property to *true* because it will make the receiving application more scalable. For more information on this topic, see Jeffrey Richter's *CLR via C#*. An operation should not, however, set this property to *true* if the operation is performing computationally bound tasks, because this will result in a suboptimal performance. The *AsyncPattern* property is completely transparent to sending applications.

The *ProtectionLevel* Property

The *ProtectionLevel* property on the *OperationContractAttribute* is very similar to the same property on the *ServiceContractAttribute*, but at a different scope. The *ProtectionLevel* property on the *ServiceContractAttribute* sets the minimum security for all operations in the service, and the *ProtectionLevel* property on the *OperationContractAttribute* sets the minimum security level for that operation. The *ProtectionLevel* property on the *OperationContractAttribute* can be less secure than the *ProtectionLevel* property on the *ServiceContractAttribute*.

The *IsOneWay* Property

By default, all operations are assumed to use the request/reply MEP. As you saw in Chapter 2, "Service Orientation," this is by far the most pervasive and familiar MEP. At first glance, it might appear that defining an operation with a *void* return type is enough to create a datagram operation. A *void* return type on a method means that the receiving application will generate a reply, and that reply will not contain any information in the body of the message. If you want to use the datagram MEP in an operation, the method must have a *void* return type and the *IsOneWay* property must be set to *true*. As I mentioned in Chapter 2, I am a big fan of the datagram MEP, and I encourage you to embrace this MEP because of the scalability and advanced messaging scenarios it allows.

However, error handling is markedly simpler with the request/reply MEP than it is with the datagram MEP, and this was a contributing factor in the team's decision to make request/reply the default MEP. When the receiver processes a request/reply message and an error occurs, the receiver can automatically send a fault back to the sender. This is particularly simple when the messaging participants are using the HTTP transport. In the case of a fault, the receiver sends the sender a fault via the transport back channel. In a contract, errors from a datagram MEP operation must be returned to the sender via the address specified in the WS-Addressing *FaultTo* header block.

For security reasons, this behavior is not enabled by default. Consider a message sender that sends a message to the receiver and specifies an address in the *FaultTo* header block. Using the WS-Addressing mindset, if this message creates a fault, the receiver will route the fault to the address specified in the *FaultTo* header block. A malicious sender could specify a third-party address in the *FaultTo* and then send a high volume of these messages to that address, thereby flooding the third-party address with network traffic, and the source of that network traffic would be the WS-Addressing–compliant service. This type of exploitation is a form of a smurfing attack, and the team did not want to allow this sort of behavior by default. I would not let this deter you from using the datagram MEP. Safely using the datagram MEP requires the receiver to interrogate the *FaultTo* address before sending a fault to that address. Given the nature of trading relationships in business, the domain names of the possible recipients of a fault might be known. In this case, you simply allow faults to propagate to those addresses, and you could even do similar work to validate the sender.

The *IsInitiating* and *IsTerminating* Properties

The *IsInitiating* and *IsTerminating* properties impact the sessionful behavior of an endpoint. If the *IsInitiating* property is set to *true*, the receipt of a message at that operation will start a new session on the receiver. If the *IsTerminating* property is set to *true*, the receipt of a message at that operation will terminate the existing session. An operation can have both the *IsInitiating* and the *IsTerminating* properties set to *true*. Setting either of these properties to *true* is possible only if the *SessionMode* property on the *ServiceContractAttribute* is set to *Required*.

These properties are most applicable in services where there is a natural start and end of the session. Consider a purchasing service that defines operations for creating a purchase order, adding items to the purchase order, and submitting a purchase order. The natural flow of these operations from creating a purchase order to submission lends itself to making the purchase order creation operation an initiating operation and the submission a terminating operation.

The impact of these properties depends on the type of session created via the binding. There are four kinds of sessions possible in WCF: security sessions, WS-ReliableMessaging sessions, MSMQ sessions, and socket-based sessions. The choice of binding determines the type of session the application uses at run time. Within one binding, it is possible to combine sessions. For example, the *NetTcpBinding* normally uses socket-based sessions. In the constructor of the *NetTcpBinding* type, however, you can add support for WS-ReliableMessaging sessions.

In security and WS-ReliableMessaging sessions, an initiating operation creates a context on the sender and the receiver. This context is the result of a message choreography between the sender and the receiver. With these types of sessions, the terminating operation invalidates the context, thereby requiring the sender and the receiver to establish a new context before future message exchanges can begin.

With socket-based communication, like the kind resulting from the *NetTcpBinding*, the sender and receiver must establish a socket connection before any communication can begin. When a service defines an operation that has the *IsInitiating* property set to *true*, the first message sent to the receiver must be to that operation; otherwise, an exception is thrown. After the sender sends a message to the initiating operation, the sender is free to send messages to other operations on the receiver. When the sender sends a message to an operation that has the *IsTerminating* property set to *true*, the socket is closed after the receiver receives the message.

MSMQ sessions are distinctly different from other sessions. Other types of sessions rely on some form of interactive communication between the sender and the receiver. With security and WS-ReliableMessaging sessions, this involves a message choreography. With socket-based sessions, the sender and the receiver must establish a socket connection. Neither of these types of sessions will work for MSMQ because MSMQ is a connectionless transport. Due to the nature of the transport, MSMQ sessions are the combination of several messages into one message. Like other sessions, operations in a service can have the *IsInitiating* and *IsTerminating* properties set. When an operation has the *IsInitiating* property set to *true*, the operation begins a new session. When the sender sends a message to an *IsInitiating* operation, a message is stored in memory rather than sent through the entire channel stack and out to the MSMQ transport. Subsequent message sends to other operations add messages to the existing message. When the sender sends a message to a terminating operation, the entire aggregated message is sent through the entire channel stack and to an MSMQ queue.

The *Name*, *Action*, and *ReplyAction* Properties

The *Name* property provides the capability to map the name of an operation to the name of an interface method. By default, this property is set to the name of the interface or class method that the annotation is associated with. The *Action* property sets the WS-Addressing action associated with received messages, and the *ReplyAction* property sets the WS-Addressing action associated with reply messages. If the *Action* property is set to *, that operation can be the target of messages with any WS-Addressing action header block. This setting can be useful in scenarios where an operation needs to receive many different kinds of messages, like a router.

Operation Method Arguments

The method definition of an operation in a service contract indicates the structure of the messages that the operation receives and sends as a reply. Examine the *RequestReservation* method from our service contract:

```
[OperationContract]
Int32? RequestReservation(DateTime? resDateTime,
                          String restaurantName,
                          String partyName);
```

The *resDateTime*, *restaurantName*, and *partyName* parameters are just normal interface method parameters. However, when they are part of an operation contract, they become the basic structure for a received message. At run time, the parameters in an operation contract are used to build a data contract dynamically, and that data contract is used as the template for the body of a message. The definition for the dynamic data contract is built during service initialization, and not each time it is needed. The same paradigm holds true for a method return type. In the preceding example, the return type *Int32?* is actually used as the basis for a dynamic data contract, and ultimately as a template for the reply message body.

Mapping a Service Contract to a Service Object

Received messages must be processed by a type that contains some business logic for the receiving application to have any value. If a service contract is the embodiment of an agreement between messaging participants, there must be a way for the receiving application to ensure that it complies with the service contract. If we choose to implement a service contract as an interface, we can rely on interface inheritance for enforcement. Here is an example of a type definition that meets the criterion of the service contract via interface inheritance:

```
internal sealed class RestaurantService : IRestaurantService {
  public Int32? RequestReservation(DateTime? resDateTime,
                                   String restaurantName,
                                   String partyName) {
    // do the work to request reservation
    // return a reservation ID
    return 5; // we can change the 5 later
  }

  public void ChangeReservation(Int32? reservationId,
                                DateTime? resDateTime) {
    // try to change a reservation to a new datetime
  }

  public void CancelReservation(Int32? reservationId) {
    // use the reservation ID to cancel that reservation
  }
}
```

The methods in the *RestaurantService* type are the implementation of the *IRestaurantService* interface. Because the *IRestaurantService* interface is the service contract, the *RestaurantService* type is an implementation of the service contract. At run time, the WCF infrastructure creates a *RestaurantService* object when it receives a message at an endpoint (assuming that the endpoint references the service contract), and the lifetime of that object is configurable. You'll learn more about how the WCF infrastructure creates one of these objects in the next chapter. For now, it is important to see that the WCF infrastructure builds an instance of the *RestaurantService* type and invokes one of its instance methods when a message is received. The method invoked on a *RestaurantService* object depends on the *Action* of the message. Because each operation will have a unique WS-Addressing *Action* header block, the WCF infrastructure can use the *Action* header block to route messages to the appropriate method. If the application is not using a binding that forces the addition of a WS-Addressing *Action* header block, routing can occur based on the body of the message, assuming that the body of the message is unique.

Data Contracts

Data contracts map .NET types to the body of a message and are a key component of message serialization and deserialization. A data contract can stand on its own, but it is often referred to by an operation in a service contract. Like service contracts, data contracts are annotated type definitions. The important attributes in a data contract are the *DataContractAttribute* and the *DataMemberAttribute*. As mentioned in the section "Operation Method Arguments" earlier in this chapter, the arguments in a service contract operation are used to create a data contract dynamically when an operation contract contains .NET primitives. The dynamic data contract that the WCF infrastructure creates at run time for the *RequestReservation* operation has a definition similar to the following:

```
[DataContract]
public sealed class RequestReservationParams {
    [DataMember(Name="resDateTime")]    private DateTime? _resDateTime;
    [DataMember(Name="restaurantName")] private String _restaurantName;
    [DataMember(Name="partyName")]      private String _partyName;

    public RequestReservationParams(DateTime? resDateTime, String restaurantName, String
partyName) {
        this._partyName = partyName;
        this._resDateTime = resDateTime;
        this._restaurantName = restaurantName;
    }

    public DateTime? ResDateTime {
        get { return _resDateTime; }
    }

    public String RestaurantName {
        get { return _restaurantName; }
    }

    public String PartyName {
        get { return _partyName; }
    }
}
```

I have taken some liberties with the name of the type, the constructor, and the properties. (The actual form of the type generated by the WCF infrastructure is not documented.) The important point is that the data contract contains members that can hold all of the state of the arguments in the *RequestReservation* operation. Notice also that the only items different from the data contract definition and a regular .NET class definition are the *DataContractAttribute* and *DataMemberAttribute* annotations. The presence of the *DataContractAttribute* indicates to the WCF serialization infrastructure that the type can be serialized, and the presence of the *DataMemberAttribute* on the stateful members of the type indicates which members should be serialized. Notice that the two *String* members and the *DateTime* member use the *private* access modifier. Object-oriented visibility has no impact on whether a member can be serialized by the default WCF serialization infrastructure.

Even though the WCF infrastructure creates a type like the *RequestReservationParams* type automatically, it is sometimes necessary to create an explicit data contract and to reference that data contract in an operation contract. Reasons for creating an explicit data contract include needing to reference several explicit data contracts from one data contract and encapsulating the state passed to an operation. I'll offer some guidance to help you choose in the section "My Philosophy on Contracts" later in this chapter. For now, I simply want to make the point that explicit data contracts are a viable option for defining a service contract. The service contract shown here illustrates how to use the *RequestReservationParams* type in a service contract:

```
[OperationContract]
    Int32? RequestReservation(RequestReservationParams resParams);
```

The *DataContractAttribute* Type

The *DataContractAttribute* can be applied to enumerated types, structures, and classes. The *Name* and *Namespace* properties are the only two instance properties defined on the *DataContractAttribute*. The *Name* property maps the name of the data contract to the name of the annotated type, and the *Namespace* property sets the XML namespace of the data contract, as shown here:

```
[DataContract(Name="ReservationInformation",
              Namespace="http://contoso.com/Restaurant")]
public sealed class RequestReservationParams {
  [DataMember(Name="resDateTime")]  private DateTime? _resDateTime;
  [DataMember(Name="restaurantName")] private String _restaurantName;
  [DataMember(Name="partyName")]    private String _partyName;
  // other implementation omitted for clarity
}
```

The *DataMemberAttribute* Type

The *DataMemberAttribute* can be applied to fields and properties. It defines several instance properties: *EmitDefaultValue*, *IsRequired*, *Name*, and *Order*. The *EmitDefaultValue* property indicates whether the default value should be emitted or extracted from the serialized data. For reference types, the default value is *null*, and for value types, the default value is *0*. The *IsRequired* property indicates whether the member must be present in the serialized data. The *Name* property maps the name of the type member to an element name in the serialized data. The *Order* property indicates the order of the members in the serialized data.

The *EmitDefaultValue* and *IsRequired* properties are important in situations where a field must have a value. If the field in the data contract does not need to be present in the serialized data, set the *IsRequired* property to *false*. With this setting, the absence of a value for a field does not create any data in the resultant serialized data. If the field is required and the default value has meaning (for example, it is *null* or *0*), two paths are possible. The first path is to manually set the field to its default value before serialization. The second option is to set the *EmitDefaultValue* property to *true*. When the *EmitDefaultValue* property is true, the serialized data will contain the default value, even though the field did not have a value in the data contract. If a field in a data contract is a nullable type, the default value is *null*.

Message Contracts

The last type of WCF contract is the message contract. A message contract offers more control over the content of the serialized data than a data contract, because a message contract defines message headers and the message body. In addition, message contracts also provide the means to express the security requirements of a member during serialization. The paradigm for creating a message contract is similar to the paradigm for creating a data contract in that a message contract is an annotated type definition and a service contract references a message contract in an operation.

 Note   All message contracts must implement a public parameterless constructor.

The attributes used in a message contract are the *MessageContractAttribute*, the *MessageHeaderAttribute*, and the *MessageBodyMemberAttribute*. The following code snippet shows a message contract that encapsulates the parameters of the *ChangeReservation* operation:

```
[MessageContract(WrapperName = "ChangeReservationNewDateTime",
                 WrapperNamespace="http://contoso.com/Restaurant")]
public sealed class ChangeReservationNewDateTime {

  [MessageHeader(Name="reservationId", MustUnderstand = true)]
  private Int32? _reservationId;

  [MessageBodyMember(Name="newDateTime")]
  private DateTime? _newDateTime;

  public ChangeReservationNewDateTime() {  }

  public ChangeReservationNewDateTime(Int32? reservationId,
                                      DateTime? newDateTime) {
    this._newDateTime = newDateTime.Value;
    this._reservationId = reservationId;
  }
```

```
public Int32? ReservationId {
  get { return _reservationId; }
}

public DateTime? NewDateTime {
  get { return _newDateTime; }
}
}
```

Notice that the _reservationId field is annotated with the *MessageHeaderAttribute*. As its name implies, a field annotated with the *MessageHeaderAttribute* will be serialized as a message header. The primary reason for adding a field as a message header is to make it available to messaging infrastructures. I show the *reservationId* field as a header for illustrative purposes only. In real life, values that messaging routers or other intermediaries act on are good candidates for message headers. If the illustrated restaurant reservation system used the *reservationId* field to route the reservation to a restaurant for confirmation of the change, then and only then would the *reservationId* field make sense as a header.

> **Note**   Adding a message header to a message contract should be done with caution, because message headers are applicable only in message formats that allow headers. Some message formats like Plain Old XML (POX) do not allow message headers, so forcing a field to be a message header throws an *InvalidOperationException*.

The *MessageHeaderAttribute* defines several instance properties that map to standard SOAP header attributes: *Actor*, *MustUnderstand*, and *Relay*. Setting these properties changes the serialized data as well as how the message contract is used after a receiving application receives a message.

The *MessageBodyMemberAttribute* annotation indicates the fields placed in the body of a message. One message can include multiple body members, and the *MessageBodyMember-Attribute* defines an *Order* property that specifies the order of the body members.

The *MessageContractAttribute*, *MessageHeaderAttribute*, and *MessageBodyMemberAttribute* types define a *ProtectionLevel* property. This property indicates the minimum security that must be applied to that member; the paradigm for this property follows the *ProtectionLevel* property on the *OperationContractAttribute*. In effect, this property provides granular control over the minimum security level for the entire contract, a header, or a member in the body.

Operation Compatibility

The operations in a service contract define the structure for the messages sent to the operation and the messages that the operation sends as a reply. WCF categorizes these messages into two broad categories: typed and untyped. *Typed messages* are message contracts and the *System.ServiceModel.Channels.Message* type. *Untyped messages* are data contracts and serializable types. Typed messages cannot be commingled with untyped messages. The following are examples of viable operations in a service:

```
[ServiceContract]
public interface ISomeService {

  // BEGIN TYPED MESSAGES
  [OperationContract]
  void SomeOperation(Message input);

  [OperationContract]
  Message SomeOperation2(Message input);

  [OperationContract]
  Message SomeOperation3(SomeMessageContract input);

  [OperationContract]
  void SomeOperation4(SomeMessageContract input);
  // END TYPED MESSAGES

  // BEGIN UNTYPED MESSAGES
  [OperationContract]
  void SomeOperation5(Int32? input);

  [OperationContract]
  Int32? SomeOperation6(Int32? input, String otherInput);

  [OperationContract]
  Int32? SomeOperation7(SomeDataContract input);

  [OperationContract]
  Int32? SomeOperation8(SomeDataContract input, Int32? input2);
  // END UNTYPED MESSAGES
}
```

Pay close attention to the last operation in the preceding code snippet. An operation's parameter can be the combination of a data contract and another serializable type. The WCF infrastructure treats typed and untyped messages differently. Typed messages can include header definitions, whereas untyped messages cannot. If an operation uses typed messages, there would be ambiguity about where other parameters should go. Rather than make an arbitrary decision, the team opted to keep a clean separation between typed and untyped messages.

My Philosophy on Contracts

WCF is fundamentally a platform that can handle a wide variety of messaging functionality. I view WCF as a progression from distributed object platforms, and I believe that forcing yesterday's paradigms of distributed computing will not work in the long run in WCF. Over time, I have seen a few observations about distributed computing hold true, and these observations have shaped my view on how to approach WCF contracts:

- Complex object-oriented type hierarchies are hard to manage in the long term, especially in distributed computing.

- What seems simple today becomes complex tomorrow, and what seems complex today becomes unmanageable tomorrow.

- Any single-vendor environment becomes a multiple-vendor environment over time.

As a result of these observations, I offer the following recommendations about contracts.

Avoid Defining Methods in Data Contracts and Message Contracts

Data contracts and message contracts are fundamentally state containers. As they are serialized and sent over the proverbial wire, method implementations are not sent with them. In my view, this simple fact is enough to bolster the case for dumbing down the definition of a data or message contract to simply stateful members. Any implementation that I add to a data or message contract is for the purpose of simplifying the instantiation of a contract or extracting state from the object.

Obviously, data and message contracts reside in more complex type hierarchies either at the sender or the receiver. Adding implementation to these contracts rather than to other parts of your type hierarchies means that the line between a contract and an implementation is blurred. Blurring this line can lead to major versioning problems and should be avoided.

In my view, a better approach is to build factories that can build a stateful data contract or message contract on demand. These factory types should also include a facility to parse an object and do meaningful work based on the state of that object. This sort of design ensures that the objects that are serialized and sent over the wire adhere to the contract they must uphold.

Seal Contracts

I like sealed classes, and I think contracts should be sealed. Sealed classes simplify testing and make the behavior of classes more predictable, and invoking methods on sealed classes is more efficient than on unsealed classes. In fact, I think that the Microsoft Visual C# team should have made classes sealed by default and offered up an unsealed keyword instead. If a class is sealed today and it needs to be unsealed tomorrow, the change is not a breaking one. In type hierarchies (other than contracts), inheritance can come in quite handy. Among other things, it paves the way for virtual methods, and this gives our type hierarchies tremendous flexibility and extensibility. With contracts, however, I do not think inheritance makes sense.

If you buy off on the idea that contracts should not contain implementation, the only viable reason to need inheritance is to serialize members in a base class. It is important to keep in mind that a contract maps .NET constructs to messaging constructs. In essence, a contract maps a vendor-specific type system that has full object-oriented support to what should be a vendor-agnostic type system with questionable object-oriented support. While XSD has some low fidelity means to express inheritance, what about messaging structures that are not XML based? How can you express inheritance in messaging structures like JSON (JavaScript Object Notation)? You simply can't do this with any reliability. If this is true, there is no way to reliably express the complexities of a contract type hierarchy in a truly vendor-agnostic way.

In some organizations, there might be a view that their applications need to work only with other WCF applications. In these scenarios, a contract type hierarchy might make sense, but I urge caution. Businesses change, businesses buy other businesses, and trading alliances that seem impossible today have a way of becoming reality tomorrow. While there is never any guarantee that an application can deal with tomorrow's changes, making contract types sealed does offer much more protection against the inevitable changes of tomorrow than does a complex contract type hierarchy.

Use Nullable Types

If a WCF application needs to interoperate, contract members that are value types should be nullable value types. In my view, all WCF applications should be designed to interoperate because of the possibilities that offers for the future. The prototypical example is the *DateTime* type. In Java, the *Date* type is a reference type. In the .NET Framework, it is a value type. If such a date representation is used as a field in a contract, the Java application can send a value of *null* for it. Since a *null* value for a *DateTime* has no meaning in the .NET Framework, an exception will be thrown. If the *DateTime* is set to a nullable *DateTime*, the WCF application can deal with a null *DateTime* field.

From Contract Definition to Contract Object

As you've seen, a WCF contract is nothing more than an annotated type definition. On its own, an annotated type definition does nothing, because the annotations are nothing more than metadata changes. Since the attribute annotation in a contract changes the metadata of a contract definition and reflection is a way to read metadata at run time, turning a WCF contract into something meaningful demands the use of reflection. To this end, the WCF infrastructure defines several types that use reflection to read the metadata of a contract and use that metadata as a blueprint for building endpoints. These types are called *descriptions*. Just as there are several types of WCF contracts, there are several types of descriptions:

- *System.ServiceModel.Description.ContractDescription*
- *System.ServiceModel.Description.OperationDescription*
- *System.ServiceModel.Description.MessageDescription*

A *ContractDescription* describes all of the operations in a service, the *OperationDescription* details one operation, and a *MessageDescription* describes information about a message used in an operation. All of these description types are related to service contracts because a service contract defines the operations in a service, the MEPs of those operations, and the messages that those operations send and receive.

The *ContractDescription* type wraps an *OperationDescription* collection and a *MessageDescription* collection. Each *OperationDescription* maps to an operation in the service contract. Each *OperationDescription* has at least one *MessageDescription* associated with it. If the *OperationDescription* uses the datagram MEP, that *OperationDescription* contains one *MessageDescription*. All other MEPs have two *MessageDescription* objects per *OperationDescription* object. The *ContractDescription* type also defines members that correspond to other parts of the *ServiceContractAttribute* annotation on the service contract. For example, the *ServiceContractAttribute* defines a *Namespace* instance property. The *ContractDescription* type's *Namespace* property is set to the same value when the *ContractDescription* is created.

> **Note**   The *IContractBehavior* collection in the *ContractDescription* type does not come from a service contract.

The *ContractDescription* type defines a factory method named *GetContract* that accepts a type as an argument. The type used for this argument must be a service contract. Once the *ContractDescription* object is built, it provides a means to access *OperationDescription* and *MessageDescription* objects. In normal cases, user code never directly instantiates a *ContractDescription* object. That job is reserved for other parts of the WCF infrastructure; I show it in this section for completeness. The following example shows how to create a *ContractDescription* object and illustrates how to access an *OperationDescription* and a *MessageDescription* object via the *ContractDescription* object:

```
// using directives omitted for clarity

// service contract referenced in the Main method
[ServiceContract(Namespace = "http://contoso.com/Restaurant")]
public interface IRestaurantService3 {
  [OperationContract]
  Int32? RequestReservation(RequestReservationParams resParams,Int32? someNumber);
  [OperationContract]
```

```
    void ChangeReservation(ChangeReservationNewDateTime newDateTime);
    [OperationContract(IsOneWay = true)]
    void CancelReservation(Int32? reservationId);
}

class App {
  static void Main() {
    ContractDescription cDescription =
      ContractDescription.GetContract(typeof(IRestaurantService3));

    foreach(OperationDescription opDesc in cDescription.Operations) {
      Console.WriteLine("\nOperation Name: {0}", opDesc.Name);

      foreach (MessageDescription msgDesc in opDesc.Messages) {
        Console.WriteLine("  Message Direction: {0}", msgDesc.Direction);
        Console.WriteLine("  Message Action: {0}", msgDesc.Action);
        Console.WriteLine("  Message Type: {0}",
          msgDesc.MessageType != null ? msgDesc.MessageType.ToString() :
            "Untyped");
      }
    }
  }
}
```

When this code runs, it produces the following output (some parts of the Message Action are omitted for clarity):

```
Operation Name: RequestReservation
  Message Direction: Input
  Message Action: http://contoso.com/.../RequestReservation
  Message Type: Untyped
  Message Direction: Output
  Message Action: http://contoso.com/.../RequestReservationResponse
  Message Type: Untyped

Operation Name: ChangeReservation
  Message Direction: Input
  Message Action: http://contoso.com/.../ChangeReservation
  Message Type: ChangeReservationNewDateTime
  Message Direction: Output
  Message Action: http://contoso.com/.../ChangeReservationResponse
  Message Type: Untyped

Operation Name: CancelReservation
  Message Direction: Input
  Message Action: http://contoso.com/.../CancelReservation
  Message Type: Untyped
```

Once built, a *ContractDescription* object contains all the information needed to build the rest of the infrastructure needed to send and receive messages. On the sender, the *ContractDescription* is an integral part of the *ClientRuntime*, and on the receiver, the *ContractDescription* is an integral part of the *DispatchRuntime*. At a higher level, a *ContractDescription* is the *C* part of the ABCs of WCF.

Summary

Contracts describe the operations in a service, the message exchange patterns in each operation, and the structure of each message in each operation. Contracts are categorized as Service Contracts, Data Contracts, and Message Contracts. Service Contracts describe the operations in a service. Data Contracts and Message Contracts describe the structure of each message in an operation. Data Contracts describe the body of a message, and Message Contracts describe the body and header blocks of a message. Service Contracts, Data Contracts, and Message Contracts are annotated type definitions. These annotated type definitions do nothing by themselves. Other parts of WCF's ServiceModel layer use these annotated type definitions to build description objects. Each category of contract has a corresponding description type, and the description objects built from these description types serve as a blueprint for critical parts of the messaging infrastructure. In the next chapter, we will see how this occurs.

Chapter 10
Dispatchers and Clients

In Chapters 5 through 7, we've looked at the *Message* type and how Microsoft Windows Communication Foundation (WCF) sends and receives *Message* objects. In Chapter 8, "Bindings," you saw how a binding, a channel manager, and a channel stack work together to send and receive messages (*Message* objects). Channel managers, channels, and to some extent the *Message* type and bindings are part of the channel layer. By using the channel layer exclusively, it is possible to create a fully functional messaging application, but doing so is tedious, error prone, and time consuming. WCF makes developers' lives easier via the *ServiceModel* layer. The *ServiceModel* layer manages the creation and lifetime of channel layer objects. Its tasks also include pumping *Message* objects into and out of the channel layer, serializing and deserializing *Message* contents into meaningful objects, dispatching those objects to objects that contain business logic, and managing the lifetime of the objects that contain business logic. (See Chapter 4, "WCF 101," for more information about the boundary between the channel layer and the *ServiceModel* layer.) Chapter 9, "Contracts," addresses a few of these tasks by describing the roles that contracts play in abstracting the structure of the messaging application and the messages that the application interacts with. In essence, contracts serve as a blueprint to the *ServiceModel* layer during the creation of the messaging application.

This chapter discusses the parts of the *ServiceModel* layer responsible for the lifetime of channel layer constructs, how *Message* objects and parts of *Message* objects are dispatched to objects containing business logic, and the management of the lifetime of the objects that contain business logic. There is no single *ServiceModel* type responsible for these tasks; instead, the WCF type system broadly categorizes these *ServiceModel* types on the sender and the receiver. On the sender, this category of types is known as the *client*, but it is also known as the *proxy*. Pre-beta versions and several beta versions of WCF used *proxy*, and the name was changed in later versions to *client*. Even though I am not a fan of this naming convention because of its close association with client/server architectures, I will refer to this category of types on the sender as the client. On the receiver, this category of types is known as the *dispatcher*. Like other parts of the WCF infrastructure, there is a symmetry between the *ServiceModel* infrastructures on the sender and the receiver, so the client and the dispatcher have much in common. It is not a perfect symmetry, however, because the tasks of the client and the dispatcher are so different.

The client and the dispatcher have numerous extensibility points that allow for a seemingly countless number of different run-time characteristics. Many of these extensibility points are called *behaviors*. WCF provides an abundance of behaviors, and developers can quickly choose from these behaviors cafeteria-style. With an appropriately fatalistic view of functionality, WCF also allows developers to create custom behaviors and insert them into the client or dispatcher at run time.

Much has been written elsewhere about the default and custom WCF behaviors (check the Windows SDK code samples). In this chapter, we'll focus on how the client and the dispatcher manage the lifetime of the channel layer, how messages and message contents are routed, and how user code is invoked. For completeness, I will also discuss behavior anatomy, but that is not the primary focus of this chapter. In my experience, once you understand the major parts of the client and the dispatcher, understanding behaviors is a relatively simple affair. On the other hand, trying to understand behaviors before understanding the client and the dispatcher is often a confusing and frustrating task. Thus, this chapter begins with a description of the roles the client and the dispatcher play in the lifetime of a messaging application and then moves into the anatomy of the dispatcher, the *ServiceHost* type, and the client.

Questions to Ask Yourself

The normal programming model in WCF relies on addresses, bindings, and contracts. Nowhere in that programming model is there mention of channels or channel managers. As you've seen in previous chapters, channels and channel managers do real messaging work, but working directly with these types is prohibitive in most environments. Instead of being part of the normal programming model, channels and channel managers are a vital part of the flexibility needed for current and future messaging requirements. This includes the transports, protocols, and message encodings required in an application, as well as the ones that will undoubtedly arise in the future. The *ServiceModel* layer serves to manage the lifetime of these channel layer constructs, provide higher-level functionality not suited to the channel layer (like service instancing and message filtering), and expose to the developer an easy-to-use developer application programming interface (API).

Before we delve into the anatomy of the client and the dispatcher, let's spend some time examining the issues that we would need to take into account if we rely only on the channel layer. Consider the following application, which sends itself a message using the messaging infrastructure created by the *BasicHttpBinding*:

```
using System;
using System.Collections.Generic;
using System.Text;
using System.ServiceModel;
using System.ServiceModel.Channels;

internal sealed class App {

  static void Main() {

    // create a binding
    BasicHttpBinding binding = new BasicHttpBinding();

    // create an address
    Uri address = new Uri("http://localhost:4000/MyListener");

    // build the ChannelListener stack
    IChannelListener<IReplyChannel> listenerStack =
      binding.BuildChannelListener<IReplyChannel>(address,
        new BindingParameterCollection());

    // Open the listener stack
    listenerStack.Open();

    // Create the Channel stack
    IReplyChannel receiveChannels = listenerStack.AcceptChannel();

    // Open the channel stack
    receiveChannels.Open();

    // Try to Receive a Message, need to do async
    receiveChannels.BeginReceiveRequest(
      new AsyncCallback(receiveRequest), receiveChannels);

    // build the channel factory stack
    IChannelFactory<IRequestChannel> channelFactoryStack =
      binding.BuildChannelFactory<IRequestChannel>(
        new BindingParameterCollection());

    // open the channel factory stack
    channelFactoryStack.Open();

    // create the channel stack from the channel factory stack
    IRequestChannel sendChannels =
      channelFactoryStack.CreateChannel(new EndpointAddress(address));

    // open the channel stack
    sendChannels.Open();

    // send a message to the receiver
    Message reply =
```

```
                sendChannels.Request(Message.CreateMessage(MessageVersion.Soap11,
                                                "urn:SomeAction",
                                                "Hi there"));

        // show the contents of the reply
        Console.WriteLine("\nReply Received:\n{0}", reply.ToString());

        // cleanup
        sendChannels.Close();
        channelFactoryStack.Close();
        listenerStack.Close();
    }

    // invoked when a message is received
    private static void receiveRequest(IAsyncResult ar) {
        // get the channel stack
        IReplyChannel channels = (IReplyChannel)ar.AsyncState;

        // get the requestContext
        RequestContext context = channels.EndReceiveRequest(ar);

        // show the received message
        Console.WriteLine("\nRequest Received:\n{0}",
                        context.RequestMessage.ToString());

        // create a reply
        Message reply = Message.CreateMessage(MessageVersion.Soap11,
                                        "urn:SomeReplyAction",
                                        "Hi there back");

        // send the reply
        context.Reply(reply);

        // close the context
        context.Close();

        // close the channels
        channels.Close();
    }
}
```

Most of these lines of code are devoted to creating and managing the lifetime of the channel managers and channels required to send and receive a message. Even with all of this code, this application is limited in its functionality. For example, we can send and receive only one message; adding support for additional transports, protocols, and encodings requires much more code; the sender and receiver have no way to expose a contract via Web Services Description Language (WSDL) and Extensible Schema Definition (XSD); and so on. Adding this sort of functionality manually is a daunting task. Among their other roles, the dispatcher and the client automate this work, thereby allowing us to focus on the functionality of our application rather than the infrastructure.

The Dispatcher

The dispatcher is a collection of types in the *ServiceModel* layer in a receiving application. The most important type in the dispatcher is the *System.ServiceModel.Dispatcher. ChannelDispatcher* type. The *ChannelDispatcher* type references the other dispatcher types, and the *ChannelDispatcher* delegates quite a bit of its work to these other types. Following are some of the tasks performed by the *ChannelDispatcher* and the types referenced by the *ChannelDispatcher*:

- Creating a channel listener from a binding
- Managing how channels are received from the channel listener
- Managing the listening loop
- Managing the lifetime of the channel listener and the resultant channel stacks
- Limiting the pace at which messages are received from the channel stack (also called *throttling*)
- Managing the the creation, lifetime, and number of service objects
- Routing received messages to the intended service object instance
- Deserializing meaningful objects from received messages
- Using these deserialized objects to invoke a method on a service object
- Serializing the return values of service object methods into reply messages
- Routing reply messages to the appropriate channel stack and sending them back to the sender via that channel stack
- Handling errors in the preceding tasks
- Managing the execution of default and custom behaviors in the preceding tasks

Figure 10-1 summarizes the roles of a *ChannelDispatcher*.

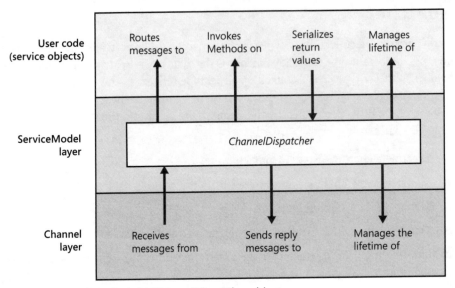

Figure 10-1 The roles of a *ChannelDispatcher* object

ChannelDispatcher Anatomy

The *ChannelDispatcher* defines over 30 members. Some of these members allow the *ChannelDispatcher* to do work on its own, and other members allow the *ChannelDispatcher* to delegate work to other dispatcher types. In general, a receiving application has a *ChannelDispatcher* for each address it is listening on. Because channel listeners listen for incoming messages, every *ChannelDispatcher* has a reference to a channel listener, and that channel listener listens on a Uniform Resource Identifier (URI) unique to that receiving application. Because a receiving application can listen on multiple URIs, a receiving application can have multiple *ChannelDispatcher* objects. Likewise, a single channel listener may have multiple channel dispatchers. At run time, a *ChannelDispatcher* must be attached to a *ServiceHost* object, so a *ChannelDispatcher* object never exists in isolation, and several of the members on the *ChannelDispatcher* type reference either a *ServiceHost* or a *ServiceHostBase* type. You'll learn more about the *ServiceHost* type in the section "The ServiceHost Type" later in this chapter. Figure 10-2 shows the general composition of the *ChannelDispatcher* type.

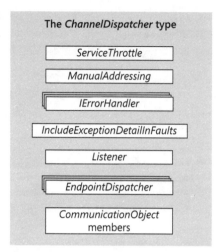

Figure 10-2   *ChannelDispatcher* anatomy.

CommunicationObject Members

Because the *ChannelDispatcher* must manage the creation and the life cycle of channel managers and channel stacks, the *ChannelDispatcher* derives from *CommunicationObject*. As a result, several of the *ChannelDispatcher* members are *CommunicationObject* implementations. When one of these *CommunicationObject* members is invoked, the *ChannelDispatcher* drives the other *CommunicationObject* members that it references through the *CommunicationObject* state machine. For more information about the channel state machine, see Chapter 6, "Channels."

The *ServiceThrottle* Property

The *ChannelDispatcher* type exposes a property named *ServiceThrottle* that is of type *System.ServiceModel.Dispatcher.ServiceThrottle*. The public API of the *ServiceThrottle* is very simple. It has three read/write properties: *MaxConcurrentCalls*, *MaxConcurrentInstances*, and *MaxConcurrentSessions*. There are no public constructors in the *ServiceThrottle* type. The *ServiceHostBase* type is the only type that instantiates a *ServiceThrottle* object. (More on this in the section "The ServiceHost Type," later in this chapter.) The *ServiceThrottle* type limits the usage of the entire *ServiceHost* instance, rather than on one *ChannelDispatcher*. The *ChanneDispatcher* uses this type to limit the usage of the receiving application. Because there can be more than one *ChannelDispatcher* in a receiving application, the *ServiceThrottle* type tracks the usage of all *ChannelDispatcher* objects.

The *ManualAddressing* Property

By default, the *ServiceModel* layer and the channel layer control the application of WS-Addressing headers to outgoing messages. In the normal case, the transport channel adds these headers. Some *BindingElement*-derived types expose a property named

ManualAddressing (for example, *HttpTransportBindingElement*). When this property is set to *true*, the channel layer will not add WS-Addressing headers (for example, *To*, *ReplyTo*, *RelatesTo*, and so on) to outgoing messages. If you must have these headers, it's up to you to add them to outgoing messages manually.

Remember that a *ChannelDispatcher* object also contains a reference to a channel listener and that a binding creates a channel listener. In other words, part of the creation of a *ChannelDispatcher* demands the existence of a binding, and that binding can have a *TransportBindingElement* whose *ManualAddressing* property is set to *true*. The value of the *ManualAddressing* property on that *TransportBindingElement* object determines the value of the *ManualAddressing* property on a *ChannelDispatcher* object.

The *ChannelDispatcher* can also override the value of the *ManualAddressing* property on a *TransportBindingElement*. The only reason I see for doing this is to force a receiving application to either use or not use *ManualAddressing*. To override the value passed from a *TransportBindingElement*, you have to manually change the *ManualAddressing* property on the *ChannelDispatcher*. The one catch is that the *ChannelDispatcher* must be in the *Created* state. Once the *ChannelDispatcher* opens, these parts of the *ChannelDispatcher* become immutable.

Remember that a *ServiceHost* object references at least one *ChannelDispatcher* object. That *ServiceHost* object is responsible for driving the state changes of the *ChannelDispatcher* objects it references, and the *ServiceHost* does not, by default, expose *ChannelDispatcher* objects when they are in the *Created* state. To access the *ChannelDispatcher* collection before each *ChannelDispatcher* transitions to the *Opened* state, you can subclass the *ServiceHost type* or you can create a custom behavior.

Note   In my view, a better approach is to interrogate the *ManualAddressing* property of the *BindingElement* at run time and throw an exception if the value is not set to your liking. I'll demonstrate how to do this in the section "The *ServiceHost* Type" later in this chapter.

The *ErrorHandlers* Collection

ChannelDispatcher objects swallow exceptions. Because the *ChannelDispatcher* is near the top of the stack in a receiving application, it is able to swallow exceptions from channel listeners, channels, service objects, and behaviors. This is good news if you want your application to stay "up" no matter what. In my view, this approach is like propping up a fighter with a harness in a boxing ring. With the extra help of the harness, the fighter is sure to never lose his or her footing. With this sort of rig, I might even be able to make it to the end of a round with a heavyweight champion (more than likely not, though). Sometimes, however, it is entirely appropriate to lose your footing in a boxing ring. Staying upright when you should be lying on the mat is dangerous.

I believe that if an application throws an exception and that exception is not handled, the application should crash. I don't view this sort of behavior as a bug, but rather as some circumstance that the developers and architects did not envision, and the application can account for that circumstance in a patch or future release. If as a boxer I keep getting knocked out, either I should reevaluate my career or I should train differently. All too often, developers catch and swallow all exceptions "to keep the application from crashing" when they should really be writing better code. In my view, catching and swallowing exceptions is untenable because it casts too wide a net around what the application can recover from. At a minimum, exceptions that are swallowed should be logged to the Windows Event Log by default. Luckily, we are not stuck with this behavior, because a *ChannelDispatcher* object can define its own error handling characteristics via the *ErrorHandlers* collection. All objects in this collection implement the *IErrorHandler* interface. The *IErrorHandler* interface defines *HandleError* and *ProvideFault* methods. The *ProvideFault* method is used to specify the fault sent to the other messaging participant. The *HandleError* method is where you can specify what you want to happen (for example, *Environment.FailFast*) as a result of an exception thrown elsewhere in the application. If *HandleError* returns *true*, the other *IErrorHandler.HandleError* methods are not called.

The *Endpoints* Property

The *ChannelDispatcher* exposes a collection of *EndpointDispatcher* objects via a property named *Endpoints*. Once a *ChannelDispatcher* pulls a *Message* from the channel, it then forwards the *Message* to an *EndpointDispatcher*. An *EndpointDispatcher* is responsible for matching a received *Message* to an instance of a service object and invoking a method on that service object. It is also responsible for deserializing the contents of the *Message* into arguments to that method and serializing the return value into a reply *Message*.

EndpointDispatcher Anatomy

The *EndpointDispatcher* has a relatively simple anatomy composed of two major components: filters and the *DispatchRuntime* type. The *EndpointDispatcher* type defines an *AddressFilter* property and a *ContractFilter* property. These properties work together to ensure that a received message is dispatched to the correct method on a service object. The *DispatchRuntime* property returns an object of type *DispatchRuntime*, and it is responsible for selecting the method to invoke on the service object, serialization and deserialization of parameters to that method, and managing the lifetime of that object. Figure 10-3 shows the anatomy of *EndpointDispatcher*.

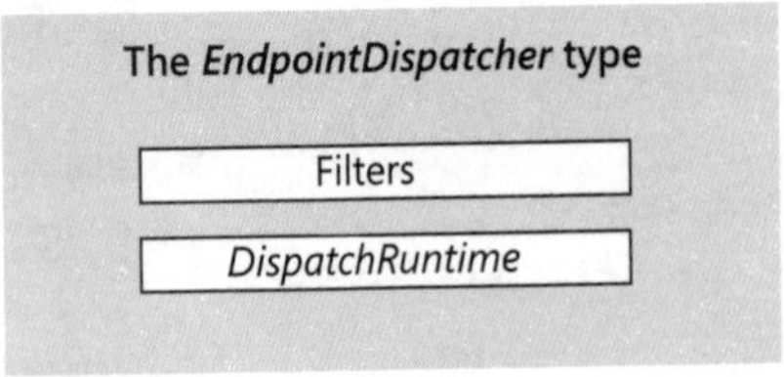

Figure 10-3   *EndpointDispatcher* anatomy

Filters

The *AddressFilter* and *ContractFilter* properties available on the *EndpointDispatcher* type derive from the *System.ServiceModel.Dispatcher.MessageFilter* abstract type. The *MessageFilter* type defines two *Match* methods and a *CreateFilterTable* method. The *Match* methods accept either a *Message* or a *MessageBuffer* as an argument and return a Boolean indicating whether the contents of the *Message* or *MessageBuffer* match predefined criteria.

The WCF type system provides six *MessageFilter*-derived types that match on different criteria: *ActionMessageFilter*, *EndpointAddressMessageFilter*, *MatchAllMessageFilter*, *MatchNoneMessageFilter*, *PrefixEndpointAddressMessageFilter*, and *XPathMessageFilter*. As its name implies, the *ActionMessageFilter* matches based on the *Action* header block of a *Message*. The *EndpointAddressMessageFilter* matches based on the *To* header block in a *Message*. The *MatchAllMessageFilter* matches all *Message* objects, and the *MatchNoneMessageFilter* matches no *Message* objects. The *PrefixEndpointAddressMessageFilter* is similar to the *EndpointAddressMessageFilter*, but the URI used in the comparison is used as a prefix for the match (similar to wildcards). This means that the *To* header block of a *Message* can be more specific than the URI used in the *PrefixEndpointAddressMessageFilter* and the filter will still match the *Message*. The *XPathMessageFilter* matches any part of the *Message* based an an XML Path Language (XPath) expression.

The *DispatchRuntime* Type

Once a *ChannelDispatcher* uses the filters to match a *Message* to an *EndpointDispatcher*, it forwards the *Message* to the *DispatchRuntime* in that *EndpointDispatcher*. The *DispatchRuntime* then manages the lifetime of the service object that will ultimately be the target of the *Message*, passes the *Message* through a list of *MessageInspector* instances, selects the method on the service object to dispatch the *Message* to, and then dispatches the *Message* to a method on the service object. Like the *ChannelDispatcher* and the *EndpointDispatcher*, the *DispatchRuntime* delegates quite a bit of work to other types. The types related to the instancing work are *IInstanceProvider*, *IInstanceContextProvider*, and *InstanceContext*. The types that inspect *Message* objects implement the *IDispatchMessageInspector* interface. The type that selects the method on the service object implements the *IDispatchOperationSelector* interface. Last but certainly not least, the type responsible for dispatching the *Message* to a particular method on the service object is the *DispatchOperation* type. Figure 10-4 shows the anatomy of *DispatchRuntime*.

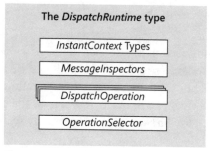

The *DispatchRuntime* type

| *InstantContext* Types |
| *MessageInspectors* |
| *DispatchOperation* |
| *OperationSelector* |

Figure 10-4   *DispatchRuntime* anatomy

The *InstanceContext* Related Types

The purpose of the *InstanceContext* related types is to manage the creation and lifetime of the service object. In general, service objects are wrapped by contextual information. This contextual information helps route a *Message* to the appropriate object, and this is particularly important with sessions. Each channel layer session might need to map to a unique instance of a service object, and the context around the service object provides the mechanism for this mapping. All of the *InstanceContext* related types are grouped via the interface that they implement.

Types that implement the *IInstanceProvider* interface are responsible for creating and returning an actual instance of the service object. Within the WCF type system, there are three not publicly visible *IInstanceProvider* types. One is for creating a COM+ service object (for COM+ interop), another is for creating a service object as a result of a duplex callback, and another is for the normal creation of a service object as a result of a received *Message*.

Types that implement the *IInstanceContextProvider* interface are responsible for creating and returning the contextual wrapper around the service object. WCF provides three types that implement the *IInstanceContextProvider* interface. The difference between these types is the way that they map received *Message* objects to instances of a service object. The first type maps each received *Message* to a new service object, the second maps received *Message* objects to service objects based on a session, and the third maps all received *Message* objects to a single service object.

The *InstanceContext* type is the wrapper around a service object. It derives from *CommunicationObject*, and as such uses the same state machine as the *CommunicationObject* type. Because a service object can be mapped to a particular set of channels based on the *IInstanceContextProvider*, the *InstanceContext* has references to receiving and sending channel stacks. Because the channel stacks use the *ICommunicationObject* state machine, the *InstanceContext* type must also implement the state machine.

The *MessageInspectors* Property

The *MessageInspectors* property on the *DispatchRuntime* type returns a collection of types that implement the *IDispatchMessageInspector* interface. This interface defines two methods: *AfterReceiveRequest* and *BeforeSendReply*. The *AfterReceiveRequest* method allows the type to inspect the message after the request is received but before it is sent to the operation, and the *BeforeSendReply* allows the type to inspect the reply message before it is sent to the channel layer. The objects in the collection returned from the *MessageInspectors* property see all of the *Message* objects for the service.

The *OperationSelector* Property

The *OperationSelector* property of the *DispatchRuntime* returns a type that implements the *IDispatchOperationSelector* interface. This interface defines one method named *SelectOperation* that accepts a *Message* as an argument and returns a *String*. The *String* returned from the *SelectOperation* method is used to look up the *DispatchOperation* in the *DispatchOperation* collection. The *String* returned from the default *IDispatchOperationSelector* is the value of the *Action* header block in the *Message*.

The *DispatchOperation* Collection

Once the *OperationSelector* property returns a *String*, that *String* is used to look up the *DispatchOperation* associated with that *String*. This is done via the *Operations* property on the *DispatchRuntime* type. The *Operations* property returns a dictionary of *DispatchOperation* objects, and the key in this dictionary is, by default, the value of the *Action* header block associated with that operation. The value of the key in the dictionary can come from the contract (*OperationContract.Action* property), but it can also be set manually in code. By default, the values of the *Action* property on the *OperationContract* annotation appear as keys in this dictionary.

The *DispatchOperation* Type

Once the node is found from the key, the value part of the dictionary is of type *DispatchOperation*. The *DispatchOperation* type deserializes method parameters from received *Message* objects, invokes a method on the service object, and serializes the return value from a service object method into a reply *Message*. The *DispatchOperation* deserializes received *Message* objects and serializes reply *Message* objects via the *Formatter* property. This property returns a type that implements the *IDispatchMessageFormatter* interface. The *IDispatchMessage-Formatter* interface defines two methods: *DeserializeRequest* and *SerializeReply*. The *DeserializeRequest* method accepts a *Message* argument and populates an array of objects. The *SerializeReply* method accepts arguments of type *MessageVersion*, *Object[]*, and *Object*, and it returns a *Message*. The *MessageVersion* argument is used during the construction of the *Message*, and the *Object* argument is used to serialize the body of the *Message*. The *Object[]* argument consists of the parameters that were originally passed to the service object method.

The *ServiceHost* Type

The *ChannelDispatcher*, *EndpointDispatcher*, *DispatchRuntime*, and *DispatchOperation* types are never used outside the context of a *ServiceHost* or a *ServiceHostBase* type. In fact, the *ChannelDispatcher* will throw an *InvalidOperationException* if you attempt to use it on its own. The *ServiceHost* type is at the very top of the call stack in a receiving application, and it encapsulates the complexity of the *ChannelDispatcher*, *EndpointDispatcher*, *DispatchRuntime*, and *DispatchOperation* types. The *ServiceHost* type defines an easy-to-use API that simplifies the addition of listening endpoints. At run time, the *ServiceHost* type ultimately creates the channel listeners, channel stacks, *ChannelDispatcher*, *EndpointDispatcher*, *DispatcherRuntime*, and *DispatchOperation*. In essence, the *ServiceHost* type leverages the types we have examined in this book to build a coherent receiving application, thereby shielding developers from the gory details of messaging. Much has been written about the *ServiceHost* type, so I will not repeat it here (see Windows SDK for examples).

The Client

The *ServiceModel* layer on the sender is simpler than the *ServiceModel* layer on the receiver as a result of the relative simplicity of sending a *Message* versus receiving and dispatching a *Message*. Even though the tasks are much simpler, the *ServiceModel* infrastructure on the sender has some symmetry with the *ServiceModel* infrastructure on the receiver. As mentioned earlier in this chapter, much of the *ServiceModel* layer infrastructure on the sender is called the *client*. Like the dispatcher, the client is not composed of one type, but rather is a mosaic of other types, and the subtasks required to send a *Message* are delegates to these types.

When describing the dispatcher, we start by describing how a *Message* is read from the channel stack and how the channel listener is managed. From the perspective of the receiving application, the receipt of a *Message* initiates work in the dispatcher. With the client, user code initiates action within the client. The client then uses a binding, an *EndpointAddress*, and contractual information to send a *Message*. As you now know about channels, there must be a channel stack in place before we send a *Message*. And the only way to create sending channels is via an *IChannelFactory*-derived type. The client infrastructure manages all of this. In a manner consistent with what you've learned so far, the client uses a binding to create a stack of channel factories and then uses that stack of channel factories to create a channel stack. Once the channel stack is in place, the client then creates a *Message* and sends it to the channel stack for delivery to another messaging participant.

The only twist in the sequence of events is how the client exposes types that are consistent with the contract of the service that it sends messages to. There are two types central in making the client infrastructure consistent with the service contract of the receiving application. They are the *System.ServiceModel.ChannelFactory<TChannel>* type and the *System.ServiceModel.ClientBase<TChannel>* type. Do not confuse the *ChannelFactory<TChannel>* type with the stack of channel factory objects that creates the channel stack. The *ChannelFactory<TChannel>* creates the client infrastructure required to send a message to another endpoint and can be created by user code. The channel factory objects on the other hand, build the channel stack and can be created only by a *Binding* or a *BindingElement*.

Let's look at how we can use the *ChannelFactory<TChannel>* type and then discuss how it works internally. The following code snippet shows how to use the *ChannelFactory<TChannel>* type:

```
using System;
using System.ServiceModel;
using System.ServiceModel.Channels;
using System.Runtime.Remoting;

internal sealed class Sender{

  static void Main() {
    // instantiate a binding
    BasicHttpBinding binding = new BasicHttpBinding();
    // create an EndpointAddress
    EndpointAddress address =
      new EndpointAddress("http://localhost:4000/IRestaurantService");

    // instantiate a ChannelFactory, passing binding and EndpointAddress
    ChannelFactory<IRestaurantService3> factory =
      new ChannelFactory<IRestaurantService3>(binding, address);

    // create the client infastructure
    IRestaurantService3 client = factory.CreateChannel();
    Boolean trans = RemotingServices.IsTransparentProxy(client);
    // prints "true"
    Console.WriteLine("IsTransparentProxy: {0}", trans);

    // invoke a method on the client, and retrieve the result
    Int32? result =
      client.RequestReservation(new RequestReservationParams(DateTime.Now,
                                              "Dusty's BBQ",
                                              "Justin"));

  }
}
```

As you can see from this example, the *ChannelFactory<TChannel>* type accepts a *Binding* and an *EndpointAddress* as arguments, and a service contract can be the *TChannel* generic parameter. When the *CreateChannel* method is called, the *ChannelFactory<TChannel>* type uses reflection to generate transparent proxy that is of type *TChannel*. Note that this method does not actually create any channels. When we call one of the methods on the transparent proxy, the binding is used to create the channel factory stack and the subsequent channel stack.

Summary

In this chapter, we see how the dispatcher and the client simplify the WCF development experience. The dispatcher's tasks include routing received messages to the appropriate service object instance, managing service object lifetime, throttling the usage of a *ServiceHost* instance, and handling errors. The client's tasks include using a binding and a contract to build the channel factory and channel stack to send a *Message* to a receiving application.

Index

Justin Smith

Justin Smith works as a Technical Evangelist at Microsoft. Prior to joining Microsoft, Justin worked as an author, trainer, and consultant at Wintellect. As anyone who has taken one of his courses or worked with him as a consultant can tell you, Justin has a talent for taking complex ideas and distilling them into manageable language.

Justin became interested in software development toward the end of his engineering courses at Georgia Tech. Bridging the gap between engineering and software development, Justin's first job out of Tech was as an implementation consultant with Parametric Technology Corporation (http://www.ptc.com). Justin later took a job with Engineering Animation Incorporated, where he developed custom UNIX and Windows CAD/CAM/CAE applications with C/C++ and Java. During his time in the CAD world, Justin built and integrated several applications (eVis, VisView, Pro/Intralink, and Pro/Engineer) that facilitated the design, testing, and manufacture of military and commercial aerospace components.

After EAI, Justin co-founded Lighthouse Business Solutions, a document management development and consulting firm. During his tenure at Lighthouse, Justin designed, built and integrated document management systems for more than 30 large corporations and distinguished himself as one of the premier document management experts in the country.

What do you think of this book?

We want to hear from you!

Do you have a few minutes to participate in a brief online survey?

Microsoft is interested in hearing your feedback so we can continually improve our books and learning resources for you.

To participate in our survey, please visit:

www.microsoft.com/learning/booksurvey/

...and enter this book's ISBN-10 number (appears above barcode on back cover*).
As a thank-you to survey participants in the United States and Canada, each month we'll randomly select five respondents to win one of five $100 gift certificates from a leading online merchant. At the conclusion of the survey, you can enter the drawing by providing your e-mail address, which will be used for prize notification only.

Thanks in advance for your input. Your opinion counts!

* Where to find the ISBN-10 on back cover

ISBN-13: 000-0-0000-0000-0
ISBN-10: 0-0000-00000

00000

Example only. Each book has unique ISBN.

Microsoft
Press

No purchase necessary. Void where prohibited. Open only to residents of the 50 United States (includes District of Columbia) and Canada (void in Quebec). For official rules and entry dates see:

www.microsoft.com/learning/booksurvey/